Introduction to Islamic
Banking and Finance

Introduction to Islamic Banking and Finance

Brian Kettell

A John Wiley and Sons, Ltd., Publication

This edition first published in 2011
© 2011 Brian Kettell

Registered office
John Wiley & Sons Ltd, The Atrium, Southern Gate, Chichester, West Sussex, PO19 8SQ, United Kingdom

For details of our global editorial offices, for customer services and for information about how to apply for permission to reuse the copyright material in this book please see our website at www.wiley.com.

ISBN 978-0-470-97804-7 (paperback)
ISBN 978-1-119-99060-4 (ebook)
ISBN 978-1-119-99061-1 (ebook)
ISBN 978-1-119-99127-4 (ebook)

A catalogue record for this book is available from the British Library.

Typeset in 10/12pt Times by Aptara Inc., New Delhi, India
Printed in Great Britain by CPI Antony Rowe, Chippenham, Wiltshire

To my wife Nadia, our son Alexei and daughter Anna.
Nadia keeps the whole fleet on an even keel with only the
occasional shipwreck.

Contents

Preface   **xiii**

About the Author   **xvii**

1   Muslim Beliefs   **1**
1.1   Five Pillars of Faith   1
     1.1.1   Profession of Faith   2
     1.1.2   Five Daily Prayers   2
     1.1.3   Almsgiving   3
     1.1.4   Fasting   3
     1.1.5   Pilgrimage to Mecca   3
1.2   Six Islamic Creeds   4
     1.2.1   Definition of *Iman*   4
     1.2.2   *Iman* as Basis of Righteous Deeds   5
1.3   Belief in Allah and His Attributes   5
1.4   Belief in Destiny   6
1.5   Belief in Angels   7
1.6   Belief in Apostles   7
1.7   Belief in the Revealed Books   8
1.8   Belief in the Hereafter   9

2   *Sharia'a* Law and *Sharia'a* Boards: Roles, Responsibility and Membership   **13**
2.1   Definition of the *Sharia'a*   13
2.2   Allah is the Law Giver   13
2.3   Objectives of the *Sharia'a*   14
     2.3.1   *Sharia'a*: The Framework of Islamic Banking   14
2.4   Sources of the *Sharia'a*   16
     2.4.1   *Qur'an*: The Primary Source of the *Sharia'a*   17
     2.4.2   *Sunnah*: The Second Primary Source of the *Sharia'a*   18
     2.4.3   *Ijma* (Consensus): The First Secondary Source of the *Sharia'a*   20
     2.4.4   *Qiyas* (Analogical Reasoning): The Second Secondary Source of the *Sharia'a*   20
     2.4.5   *Ijtihad*   21
     2.4.6   Compliance with the Scheme of *Sharia'a* Laws   22

2.5   *Sharia'a* Islamic Investment Principles   22
2.6   Conditions for Investment in Shares   23
2.7   *Sharia'a* Supervisory Board (SSB)   23
    2.7.1   Function and Responsibilities   24
    2.7.2   *Sharia'a* Boards: Roles and Scope of Responsibilities   24
    2.7.3   Dubai Islamic Bank (DIB)   26
2.8   *Sharia'a* Board Scholar Qualifications   27
    2.8.1   Dr Hussain Hamid Hassan   27
    2.8.2   Dr Ali AlQaradaghi   27
    2.8.3   Dr Mohamed Elgari   27
    2.8.4   Dr Mohd. Daud Bakar   28
    2.8.5   Sheikh Nizam M.S. Yaquby   28
    2.8.6   Sheikh Muhammed Taqi Usmani   28
    2.8.7   Sheikh Abdullah Bin Suleiman Al-Maniya   29
    2.8.8   Sheikh Dr Abdullah bin Abdulaziz Al Musleh   29
    2.8.9   Sheikh Dr Muhammad Al-Ali Al Qari bin Eid   29
2.9   State Bank of Pakistan (SBP): Proper Criteria for Appointment of *Sharia'a*
    Advisors   29
    2.9.1   Solvency and Financial Integrity   30
    2.9.2   Personal Integrity, Honesty and Reputation   30

3   Definition of Islamic Banking   **31**
3.1   Conventional Bankers and Islamic Banking   31
3.2   Six Key Islamic Banking Principles   33
    3.2.1   Predetermined Payments are Prohibited   33
    3.2.2   Profit and Loss Sharing   33
    3.2.3   Making Money Out of Money is Not Acceptable   34
    3.2.4   Uncertainty is Prohibited   35
    3.2.5   Only *Sharia'a*-Approved Contracts are Acceptable   35
    3.2.6   Sanctity of Contract   35
3.3   Definition of Asymmetric Information   36
    3.3.1   Adverse Selection   36
    3.3.2   Moral Hazard   36
3.4   Origins of Asymmetric Risk within Islamic Banking   37
3.5   *Riba* in the *Qur'an* and *Sunnah* or *Hadith*   37
    3.5.1   Textual Evidence for the Ban on Interest   38
    3.5.2   Islamic Rationale for Banning Interest (*Riba*)   39
3.6   Five Reasons for the Prohibition of *Riba*   39
    3.6.1   Interest is Unjust   40
    3.6.2   Interest Corrupts Society   41
    3.6.3   Interest Implies Unlawful Appropriation of Other People's
        Property   41
    3.6.4   Interest-Based Systems Result in Negative Growth   41
    3.6.5   Interest Demeans and Diminishes Human Personality   42

4   *Murabaha* as a Mode of Islamic Finance   **43**
4.1   *Murabaha* Transactions   43
    4.1.1   Definition of *Musawama*   44
    4.1.2   Some Terminological Issues   44

4.2   What Makes *Murabaha Sharia'a* Compliant?   45
4.3   Islam Treats Money and Commodities Differently   46
        4.3.1   Commodity Transactions with Credit can Involve an Excess   46
4.4   *Murabaha* and the *Sharia'a*   47
4.5   Practicalities of Implementing *Murabaha*   47
4.6   *Sharia'a* Rules Concerning *Murabaha*   48
4.7   Reasoning Behind *Sharia'a* Rules   49
        4.7.1   Important Exceptions to *Sharia'a* Rules   50
4.8   Practical Examples of the Application of *Murabaha*   50
        4.8.1   Mortgages   50
        4.8.2   Working Capital   50
        4.8.3   Syndicated Credits   50
        4.8.4   Financing of GSM Licences   51
        4.8.5   Letters of Credit   51
        4.8.6   Car and House Purchase   52
4.9   Key Issues Associated with *Murabaha*   52
        4.9.1   Use of an Interest Rate as a Benchmark   52
        4.9.2   *Gharar* Issues   54
        4.9.3   Collateral Provisions Against the *Murabaha* Payment   55
        4.9.4   Guaranteeing the *Murabaha*   55
        4.9.5   Penalty of Default   56
        4.9.6   No Roll-Over in *Murabaha*   57
        4.9.7   Rebate on Earlier Payment   57
        4.9.8   Subject Matter of *Murabaha*   57
        4.9.9   Rescheduling of the Payments in *Murabaha*   58
        4.9.10 Securitisation of *Murabaha*   58
4.10   Comparison of *Murabaha* with Interest-Based Finance   58
4.11   *Murabaha* Differences from the other Islamic Financing Techniques 58
        4.11.1 Islamically Permissible Deferred Sales Contracts   59
        4.11.2 Profit and Loss Share (PLS) Contracts   60
4.12   Summary   60
        Reference   61

5   *Mudaraba* **as a Mode of Islamic Finance**   63
5.1   Definition of *Mudaraba*   63
        5.1.1   Types of *Mudaraba*   64
        5.1.2   Two-tier *Mudaraba* and the Asset and Liability Structure of
                an Islamic Bank   64
        5.1.3   Sources of Finance for an Islamic Bank   66
        5.1.4   *Mudaraba* as Limited Recourse Debt Finance   67
5.2   What makes *Mudaraba Sharia'a* Compliant?   67
        5.2.1   Origin of the Term *Mudaraba*   67
5.3   Practicalities of Implementing *Mudaraba*   68
5.4   *Sharia'a* Rules Concerning *Mudaraba*   68
5.5   Practical Examples of *Mudaraba*   69
        5.5.1   Target Profit Rates and *Mudaraba*   71
5.6   Key Issues Associated with *Mudaraba*   72
5.7   Comparison of *Mudaraba* with the Conventional Banking Equivalent 72

5.8	*Mudaraba*: Differences from the other Islamic Financing Techniques	73
	5.8.1 Profit and Loss Share (PLS) Contracts	73
	5.8.2 Islamically Permissible Deferred Sales Contracts	74
5.9	Summary	75
	Reference	76

6 *Musharaka* as a Mode of Islamic Finance   **77**

6.1	Definition of *Musharaka*	77
6.2	What makes *Musharaka Sharia'a* Compliant?	78
6.3	Practicalities of Implementing *Musharaka*	79
6.4	*Sharia'a* Rules Concerning *Musharaka*	79
6.5	Practical Examples of *Musharaka*	80
	6.5.1 Application of Diminishing *Musharaka*	80
	6.5.2 Application of *Musharaka* in Domestic Trade	82
	6.5.3 Application of *Musharaka* for the Import of Goods	82
	6.5.4 Letters of Credit on a *Musharaka* Basis	82
	6.5.5 Application of *Musharaka* in Agriculture	83
	6.5.6 Securitisation of *Musharaka*: *Musharaka Sukuk*	83
6.6	Problems Associated with *Musharaka*	84
	6.6.1 Confidence of Depositors	84
	6.6.2 Dishonesty: Asymmetric Risk	84
	6.6.3 Secrecy of the Business	85
6.7	Comparison of *Musharaka* with the Conventional Banking Equivalent	85
	6.7.1 Profit and Loss Share (PLS) Contracts	85
	6.7.2 Islamically Permissible Deferred Sales Contracts	87
6.8	Summary	87
	Reference	88

7 *Ijara* as a Mode of Islamic Finance   **89**

7.1	Definition of *Ijara*	89
	7.1.1 Definition of Usufruct	90
	7.1.2 *Ijara* and *Ijara wa Iqtina*	90
	7.1.3 Definition of *Ijara wa Iqtina*	91
	7.1.4 Leasing as a Mode of Financing	91
7.2	What makes *Ijara Sharia'a* Compliant?	91
7.3	Practicalities of Implementing *Ijara*	91
7.4	*Sharia'a* Rules *Concerning Ijara*	92
7.5	Basic Rules of Islamic Leasing	93
	7.5.1 Benchmarking Against LIBOR is Permitted with *Ijara*	94
7.6	Practical Examples of *Ijara*	95
	7.6.1 Lease Purchase Transactions	96
7.7	Key Differences between an *Ijara* Contract and a Conventional Lease	97
	7.7.1 Rental Payments Based on Interest	97
	7.7.2 Penalty Interest with a Default	97
	7.7.3 Insurance and Maintenance Issues	97
	7.7.4 *Sharia'a* Board Issues	98
7.8	Comparison of *Ijara* with the Conventional Banking Equivalent	98

  7.9   *Ijara*: Differences from the other Islamic Financing Techniques   98
          7.9.1   Islamically Permissible Deferred Sales Contracts   99
          7.9.2   Profit and Loss Share (PLS) Contracts   100
  7.10 Summary   101
          Reference   101

8   *Istisna'a* as a Mode of Islamic Finance   103
  8.1   Definition of *Istisna'a*   103
          8.1.1   *Istisna'a* and Parallel *Istisna'a*   104
  8.2   What makes *Istisna'a Sharia'a* Compliant?   105
  8.3   Practicalities of Implementing *Istisna'a*   105
  8.4   *Sharia'a* Rules Concerning *Istisna'a*   106
  8.5   Practical Examples of *Istisna'a*   107
  8.6   Key Issues Associated with *Istisna'a*   108
          8.6.1   Guarantees   109
          8.6.2   Other Issues Relating to *Istisna'a*   110
  8.7   Comparison of *Istisna'a* with the Conventional Banking Equivalent   111
  8.8   *Istisna'a*: Differences from the other Islamic Financing Techniques   111
          8.8.1   Islamically Permissible Deferred Sales Contracts   112
          8.8.2   Profit and Loss Share (PLS) Contracts   113
          8.8.3   Differences Between *Istisna'a* and *Salam*   113
          8.8.4   Differences between *Istisna'a* and *Ijara*   114
  8.9   Summary   114
          Reference   115

9   *Salam* as a Mode of Islamic Finance   117
  9.1   Definition of *Salam*   117
  9.2   What makes *Salam Sharia'a* Compliant?   118
  9.3   Practicalities of Implementing *Salam*   118
  9.4   *Sharia'a* Rules Concerning *Salam*   119
  9.5   *Sharia'a* Rules Concerning Parallel *Salam*   120
  9.6   Practical Examples of *Salam*   121
  9.7   Benefits of the *Salam* Contract   121
  9.8   Problems Associated with *Salam*   121
  9.9   Comparison of *Salam* with the Conventional Banking Equivalent   122
  9.10 *Salam*: Differences from the other Islamic Financing Techniques   122
          9.10.1   Islamically Permissible Deferred Sales Contracts   123
          9.10.2   Profit and Loss Share (PLS) Contracts   123
          9.10.3   Differences between *Salam* and *Istisna'a*   124
  9.11 Summary   124
          Reference   126

10   *Takaful*: Islamic Insurance   127
  10.1 Case for Islamic Insurance   127
  10.2 Islamic Issues with Conventional Insurance   127
          10.2.1   Issues in Conventional Insurance   127
  10.3 Definition and Concept of *Takaful*   128

          10.3.1   How *Tabarru'* Eliminates the Problems of Conventional
                   Insurance   128
          10.3.2   Derivation of the Term *Takaful*   128
   10.4   Islamic Origins of *Takaful*   129
   10.5   Where Insurance Fits within Islam   129
   10.6   Definition of the Parties to a *Takaful*   129
   10.7   *Takaful* in Practice   130
   10.8   *Takaful* and Conventional Insurance   130
   10.9   Alternative Models of *Takaful*   130
          10.9.1   *Ta'awun* Model   130
          10.9.2   Nonprofit Model   131
          10.9.3   *Mudaraba* Model   132
          10.9.4   *Wakala* Model   132
          10.9.5   Applying the Relevant Model   132
   10.10 *Sharia'a* Law as Applied by *Takaful* Operators   132
          10.10.1   Principles of Contract   132
          10.10.2   Principles of Liability   133
          10.10.3   Principle of Utmost Good Faith   133
          10.10.4   Principles of *Mirath* and *Wasiyah*   134
          10.10.5   Principles of *Wakala* (Agency)   134
          10.10.6   Principles of *Dhaman* (Guarantee)   134
          10.10.7   Principles of *Mudaraba* and *Musharaka*   134
          10.10.8   Principles of Rights and Obligations   134
          10.10.9   Principles of Humanitarian Law   135
          10.10.10 Principles of Mutual Cooperation   135
   10.11 *Takaful* Operators   135
   10.12 Definition of Re*Takaful* (Reinsurance)   136
   10.13 Re*takaful*   136
   10.14 Role of the *Sharia'a* Board in *Takaful*   137
          10.14.1   Legal Basis for Assigning the *Sharia'a* Board   138
          10.14.2   Nature of the *Sharia'a* Board's Decisions   138
          10.14.3   *Sharia'a* Board's General Duties   138
          10.14.4   *Sharia'a* Board's Detailed Duties   138

Appendix 1. Comparative Features of Islamic Financing Techniques   **141**
   A.1   Nature of the Financing   141
   A.2   Role of the Finance Provider in the Management/Use of Funds   141
   A.3   Risk Bearing by the Finance Provider   142
   A.4   Uncertainty of the Rate of Return on Capital for the Finance Provider 142
   A.5   Cost of Capital for the Finance User   144
   A.6   Relationship Between the Cost of Capital and the Rate of Return on
         Capital   144

Appendix 2. Top 500 Islamic Institutions 1–73   **145**

Glossary   **151**

Bibliography   **157**

Index   **165**

Preface

When asked what Islamic banking is, a conventional banker is likely to mumble something about religion. He may then say, 'Well they cannot charge interest but they use something else which is the same thing'. This 'something else', incidentally, is never defined. The banker may then move on to describe Islamic banking as being about smoke and mirrors. To conclude he will then profoundly announce that, with a few tweaks, it is what he does every day anyway. And that is the end of it.

If pushed to actually describe an Islamic financial instrument or, even worse, to define some Islamic terminology such as *Murabaha* or *Mudaraba*, then the banker's eyes will start to gloss over.

Frankly this stereotyped image is all too prevalent within the banking world. In an endeavour to both enlighten conventional bankers and broaden the understanding of Islamic banking principles, this book highlights the key characteristics of Islamic banking that differentiate it from conventional banking.

As the reader will learn, Islamic banking is not about smoke and mirrors. It is in fact about banking based on Islamically-ethical principles which are, in many ways, very different indeed from conventional banking principles. So what exactly is Islamic banking all about?

The first modern experiment with Islamic banking was undertaken in Egypt without projecting an Islamic image for fear of being seen as a manifestation of Islamic fundamentalism that was anathema to the political regime. The pioneering effort, led by Ahmad Elnaggar, took the form of a savings bank based on profit-sharing in the Egyptian town of Mit Ghamr in 1963. This experiment lasted until 1967.

Islamic banking is a banking system that is consistent with the *Sharia'a* (Islamic law) and, as such, an important part of the system is the prohibition on collecting *riba* (interest or usury). The *Sharia'a* also prohibits trading in financial risk because this is seen as a form of gambling, something forbidden in Islam. Another prohibition under the *Sharia'a* is that Muslims cannot invest in businesses that are considered *haram* (forbidden or sinful) such as those that sell alcohol, pork, engage in gambling or produce un-Islamic media.

The central religious precept driving the Islamic finance industry is the idea that *riba* is *haram*. At first glance, this appears to rule out most aspects of modern finance. But although the *Qur'an* bans the creation of money, by money, it does allow money to be used for trading tangible assets and businesses – which can then generate a profit.

Consequently Islamic financial products are designed to create trading or business arrangements that pay profits to investors (or lenders) from business transactions backed by tangible assets, ideally sharing risk and rewards.

Ironically, some of these structures and techniques echo those that flourished in Christendom in Europe between the 12th and 15th centuries. In AD 325, the Christian Council of Nicea banned the practice of usury among the clergy and in AD 1140 this principle was extended to church members.

When trade expanded in Europe from the 12th century onwards, however, merchants at trade fairs became adept at constructing financial transactions that avoided religious censure. Loans were sometimes considered to be rent charges, or interest payments were classified as *damnum emergens* (opportunity loss) or *lucrum cessens* (forgone income), which were permitted by the Church. Another popular scheme was the *contractus trinius*, a three-way partnership scheme. (Meanwhile, Jews were permitted to continue money-lending because Christians presumed that they were already excommunicated.) These practices eventually died out in the 16th century, when the Church loosened its ban on usury payments.

The structure of an Islamic bank is radically different from its conventional, Western, counterpart. A conventional bank is primarily a borrower of funds on the one hand and a lender on the other. An Islamic bank is rather a partner with its depositors, as well as with entrepreneurs, sharing profit or loss on both sides of the balance sheet.

Another distinction is that a conventional bank would not stop charging interest even if the deployment of its capital fails to bear profit for the entrepreneur, whereas an Islamic bank cannot claim profit if the outcome is a genuine loss.

Islamic banks have been operating in places such as Bahrain, Saudi Arabia, Malaysia and Dubai for some time. Conventional bankers have traditionally viewed the sector as a small, exotic niche, focused on household investors. But in the past ten years something extraordinary has occurred behind the scenes.

Many Western investment banks have increasingly started working with Muslim clerics to create a new range of financial products designed for devout Muslims. The new Islamic banking products range from simple savings schemes or mortgages, to the type of complex capital market products that large corporations and governments use to raise billions of dollars. Some devout Muslims view this trend with dismay, claiming it perverts the true spirit of their religion. However, many more welcome it.

Estimates of the size of the Islamic finance industry currently vary wildly from US$800 billion to US$950 billion. However, everyone agrees that the business is expanding rapidly. This is particularly true given the oil wealth of the Gulf states, which have fuelled demand for such financial services. Yet another factor contributing to this increased demand is the growing Muslim population in Europe and the United States.

The increased demand for Muslim financial institutions in the West has also prompted Western firms to begin providing these services. HSBC, Lloyds Bank, Deutsche Bank and Citigroup are among the most notable examples of Western firms adapting to tap these new funds. Appendix 2 lists out details of some 500 Islamic financial institutions.

Companion texts are also available from the publishers: *The Islamic Banking and Finance Workbook* and *Case Studies in Islamic Banking and Finance*.

Note on the text

Over the years, problems of transliteration have resulted in a variety of acceptable English spellings for Arabic terminology. For example, the Islamic holy scriptures can be spelt in English as *Koran*, *Qoran*, *Quran* and *Qur'an*. This book applies one convention consistently and so readers should have no problems following the text, but this issue is something to bear in mind when searching for information on the Internet.

About the Author

Brian Kettell has a wealth of practical experience in the area of Islamic banking and finance. He worked for several years as an Advisor for the Central Bank of Bahrain where he had numerous Islamic banking responsibilities.

Subsequently, Brian taught courses on Islamic banking and finance at a range of financial institutions including the World Bank, National Commercial Bank (Saudi Arabia), Global Investment House (Kuwait), Noor Islamic Bank (UAE), the UK Treasury, the Central Bank of Iran, the Central Bank of Syria, the Chartered Institute for Securities and Investment, the Institute for Financial Services and Scotland Yard.

Brian's vast academic expertise in Islamic finance is highlighted by his role as former Joint Editor of the *Islamic Finance Qualification Handbook* and his past teaching work at a number of top universities worldwide including the London School of Economics, the City University of Hong Kong, the American University of the Middle East in Kuwait and London Metropolitan University Business School.

Brian's impressive list of publications include over 100 articles in journals, business magazines and the financial press including *Islamic Business and Finance*, *Islamic Banking and Finance*, the *Central Banking Journal*, *Euromoney*, the *Securities Journal* and the *International Currency Review*. He has also published 16 books on Islamic banking and financial markets.

1

Muslim Beliefs

Islam is the name of the religion transmitted by the Prophet Mohammed as revealed to him by God (Allah). Central to Islamic beliefs is The *Qur'an*, which can be defined as 'the book containing the speech of God revealed to the Prophet Mohammed in Arabic and transmitted to us by continuous testimony'. The *Qur'an* is deemed to be a proof of the prophecy of Mohammed, is the most authoritative guide for Muslims and is the first source of the *Sharia'a*. The *Ulema* (religious scholars) are unanimous on this point, and some even say that it is the only source and that all other sources are explanatory of the *Qur'an*. The salient attributes of the *Qur'an*, which are indicated in this definition, can be summarised in five points:

- It was revealed exclusively to the Prophet Mohammed.
- It was put into writing.
- It is all *mutawatir* (universally accurately reported).
- It is the inimitable speech of God.
- It is recited in *salah* (ritual prayer).

1.1 FIVE PILLARS OF FAITH

The structure of Islam is founded on pillars. Just as the strength and stability of any structure depends on the supporting pillars, the strength and stability of Islam depends on its pillars. Muslims are duty-bound to acquaint themselves with the nature of Islam's pillars.

During the 10 years between his arrival in Medina and his death in AD 632, Mohammed laid the foundation for the ideal Islamic state. A core of committed Muslims was established, and a community life was ordered according to the requirements of the new religion. In addition to general moral injunctions, the requirements of the religion came to include a number of institutions that continue to characterise Islamic religious practice today.

Foremost among these institutions are the five pillars of Islam. These are the essential religious duties required of every mentally able, adult Muslim. The five pillars are each described in some part of the *Qur'an* and were already being practised during Mohammed's lifetime. They are:

- the profession of faith (*Shahada*);
- daily prayer (*Salat*);
- almsgiving (*zakat*);
- fasting (*sawm*);
- pilgrimage (*hajj*).

Although some of these practices had precedents in Jewish, Christian and other Middle Eastern religious traditions, taken together they distinguish Islamic religious practices from those of other religions. The five pillars are thus the most central rituals of Islam and constitute the core practices of the Islamic faith.

1.1.1 Profession of Faith

The absolute focus of Islamic piety is *Allah*, the supreme, all knowing, all-powerful, God. The Arabic word *Allah* means 'the God', and this God is understood to be the God who brought the world into being and sustains it to its end. By obeying God's commands, human beings express their recognition of and gratitude for the wisdom of creation, and live in harmony with the universe.

The profession of faith, or witness to faith (*Shahada*), is therefore the prerequisite for membership in the Muslim community. On several occasions during a typical day, and in the saying of daily prayers, a Muslim repeats the profession 'I bear witness that there is no God but Allah and that Mohammed is his prophet'. There are no formal restrictions on when and where these words can be repeated.

To become a member of the Muslim community, a person has to profess and act upon this belief in the Oneness of God (*Tawhid*) and the prophethood of Mohammed. To be a true profession of faith, which represents a relationship between the speaker and God, the verbal utterance must express genuine knowledge of its meaning as well as sincere belief. A person's deeds can be subjected to scrutiny by other Muslims, but a person's utterance of the profession of faith is sufficient evidence of membership of the Muslim community.

1.1.2 Five Daily Prayers

The second pillar of Islam is the religious duty to perform five prescribed daily prayers (*Salat*). All adult Muslims are obliged to perform five prayers, preceded by ritual cleansing or purification of the body at different intervals of the day. The *Qur'anic* references also mention the acts of standing, bowing and prostrating during prayers and facing a set direction, known as *qibla*. Muslims were first required to face Jerusalem during prayer, but already during Mohammed's lifetime they were commanded to face the *Kaaba*, an ancient shrine in the city of Mecca.

The most detailed descriptions of the rituals for prayer derive from the example set by the prophet Mohammed and are preserved in later Islamic traditions (*Ahadith*). Some details of these rituals vary. However all Muslims agree that there are five required daily prayers to be performed at certain times of day:

- dawn (*fajr* or *subh*);
- noon (*zuhr*);
- mid-afternoon (*asr*);
- sunset (*maghrib*);
- evening (*isha*).

The dawn, noon and sunset prayers do not start exactly at dawn, noon and sunset; instead, they begin just after, to distinguish the Islamic ritual from earlier pagan practices of worshipping the sun when it rises or sets.

A prayer is made up of a sequence of units called bowings (*rak'as*). During each of these units, the worshipper stands, bows, kneels and prostrates while reciting verses from the *Qur'an*.

Wherever Muslims live in substantial numbers throughout the world, the call to prayer (*adhan*) is repeated five times a day by a *muezzin* (crier) from a mosque, the Muslim place of worship.

The Friday noon prayer is led by an *imam*, who is a prayer leader in the *Sunni* division of Islam. This prayer differs from the usual noon prayers of the other days of the week. As a required part of the ritual at this congregational meeting, two sermons precede the prayer. On other days, Muslims can pray anywhere they wish, either individually or in groups. They must, however, observe the rituals of praying at certain times of day, facing in the direction of Mecca, observing the proper order of prayers and preparing for prayer through symbolic purification.

1.1.3 Almsgiving

The third pillar of Islam is almsgiving (*zakat*). A religious obligation, *zakat* is considered an expression of devotion to Allah. It represents the attempt to provide for the poorer sectors of society, and it offers a means for Muslims to purify their wealth and attain salvation. The *Qur'an*, together with other Islamic traditions, strongly encourages charity and constantly reminds Muslims of their moral obligation to the poor, orphans and widows. However it distinguishes between general, voluntary charity (*sadaqah*) and *zakat*, the latter being an obligatory charge on the money or produce of Muslims.

1.1.4 Fasting

The fourth pillar of Islam is fasting (*sawm*). Clear *Qur'anic* references to fasting account for the early introduction of this ritual practice. The *Qur'an* prescribes fasting during the month of Ramadan, the ninth month of the 12-month Islamic lunar year. The month of Ramadan is sacred because the first revelation of the *Qur'an* is said to have occurred during this month. By tradition the month starts with the sighting of the new moon by at least two Muslims. For the entire month, Muslims must fast from daybreak to sunset and refrain from eating, drinking and sexual intercourse. Menstruating women, travellers and sick people are exempted from fasting, but have to make up the days they miss at a later date.

According to various traditional interpretations, the fast introduces physical and spiritual discipline, serves to remind the rich of the misfortunes of the poor and fosters, through this rigorous act of worship, a sense of solidarity and mutual care among Muslims of all social backgrounds.

1.1.5 Pilgrimage to Mecca

The fifth pillar requires that Muslims who have the physical and financial ability should perform the pilgrimage, or *hajj*, to Mecca at least once in a lifetime. Arabs before the rise of Islam practised the pilgrimage and the ritual continues from the early days of Islam.

The *hajj* is distinct from other pilgrimages. It must take place during the 12th lunar month of the year, known as *Dhu al-Hijja*, and it involves a set and detailed sequence of rituals that are practised over the span of several days. All pilgrimage rituals take place in the city of Mecca and its surroundings, and the primary focus of these rituals is a cubical structure called the *Kaaba*.

According to Islamic tradition (*Hadith*), the *Kaaba*, also referred to as the House of God, was built at God's command by the prophet Ibrahim (Abraham of the Hebrew and Christian

Bibles) and his son Ismail (Ishmael). The *Qur'an* provides detailed descriptions of various parts of the ritual, and it portrays many of these rituals as re-enactments of the activities that Ibrahim and Ismail undertook in the course of building the *Kaaba*. Set into one corner of the *Kaaba* is the sacred Black Stone, which according to one Islamic tradition (*Hadith*) was given to Ibrahim by the angel Gabriel.

Once pilgrims arrive in Mecca, ritual purification is performed. Many men shave their heads, and men and women put on seamless white sheets. This simple and common dress symbolises the equality of all Muslims before God, a status further reinforced by the prohibition of jewellery, perfumes and sexual intercourse. After this ritual purification, Muslims circle the *Kaaba* seven times, run between al-Safa and al-Marwa, two hills overlooking the *Kaaba*, seven times, and perform several prayers and invocations.

After these opening rituals, the *hajj* proper commences on the seventh day and continues for the next three days. Again, it starts with the performance of ritual purification followed by a prayer at the *Kaaba* mosque. The pilgrims then assemble at Mina, a hill outside Mecca, where they spend the night. The next morning they go to the nearby plain of Arafat, where they stand from noon to sunset and perform a series of prayers and rituals. The pilgrims then head to Muzdalifa, a location halfway between Arafat and Mina, to spend the night. The next morning, the pilgrims head back to Mina, on the way stopping at stone pillars symbolising Satan, at which they throw seven pebbles.

The final ritual is the slaughter of an animal (sheep, goat, cow or camel). This is a symbolic re-enactment of God's command to Ibrahim to sacrifice his son Ismail, which Ibrahim and Ismail duly accepted and were about to execute when God allowed Ibrahim to slaughter a ram in place of his son. (In the Hebrew and Christian Bibles, Abraham is called to sacrifice his son Isaac rather than Ishmael.)

Most of the meat of the slaughtered animals is to be distributed to poor Muslims. The ritual sacrifice ends the *hajj* and starts the festival of the sacrifice, *'id al-adha*. The festivals of breaking fast (*'id al-fitr*) at the end of Ramadan and *'id al-adha* are the two major Islamic festivals celebrated by Muslims all over the world.

During the pilgrimage most Muslims visit Medina, where the tomb of the Prophet is located, before returning to their homes. If the pilgrimage rituals are performed at any time of the year other than the designated time for *hajj*, the ritual is called *umra*. Although *umra* is considered a virtuous act, it does not absolve the person from the obligation of *hajj*.

1.2 SIX ISLAMIC CREEDS

The *Shahada* is the Muslim declaration of belief in the oneness of Allah and acceptance of Mohammed as God's prophet. The declaration reads: 'There is no God but Allah; Mohammed is the messenger of Allah'. The complete *Shahada* cannot be found in the *Qur'an* but comes from the *Ahadith*. The application of these principles is known, to Muslims, as *Iman*.

1.2.1 Definition of *Iman*

Iman (faith) is to proclaim the *Kalimah* and affirm its truth. By proclaiming the *Kalimah*, Muslims express their beliefs in the following Articles of Faith:

- existence and Attributes of Allah;
- destiny (*Qada'ar*);

- angels;
- prophets;
- revealed Books;
- The Hereafter.

Belief in these six Articles together forms the Creed of Islam. Belief in any one of these implies belief in the others as well, and rejection of one implies rejection of all.

1.2.2 *Iman* as Basis of Righteous Deeds

Iman is the basis of acts of worship and righteous deeds in Islam. Without the firm foundation of *Iman*, Muslims believe that no act of worship and no deed, however sincerely and devotedly performed, will be acceptable to Allah.

1.3 BELIEF IN ALLAH AND HIS ATTRIBUTES

The Islamic reasoning behind the first Article of Faith is as follows:

1. The unimaginably vast universe around us, which contains millions of stars and planets and galactic systems, cannot have come about by mere chance, by material and physical accident or by a chain of accidents, but has been created by Allah in accordance with His will and design.
2. Allah is the creator of each and every thing in the universe. Nothing has come into being of its own accord; and everything depends on Allah for its existence and survival.
3. Allah is eternal: He is ever-living and will never cease to be.
4. Allah is one: everything depends on Him, but He depends on none. He is All-powerful, and none has the power to change or evade His will or verdict. He has neither parents, nor offspring, nor clan.
5. Allah is unique both in His essence and attributes. He exists by Himself and is Self-sufficient, and does not stand in need of anybody else's aid to establish His rights and powers.
6. Nothing is beyond Him: nothing conceivable is beyond His control and power. He is above every conceivable defect, weakness or fault.
7. Allah is the real sovereign of the whole universe: He is the source of all sovereignty: everything is functioning according to His will.
8. Allah is the real source and centre of all power: no power exists besides His.
9. Allah is omnipresent: He watches over everything: nothing is hidden from Him either in the depths of the earth or in the limitless vastnesses of the heavens. He is the knower of the unseen and is fully aware of man's intentions, thoughts, feelings, even hidden motives. He possesses full and exact knowledge of what has happened in the past, or will happen in the future.
10. Life and death are completely under His control: He grants life to whomsoever He wills and brings death to whomsoever He wills.
11. The treasure houses of everything are with Allah: none can bestow anything on anyone whom He wills to deprive, and none can withstand anything from anybody whom He wills to favour.

12. Bestowing of gains or inflicting of losses is entirely in Allah's hands: none can ward off a misfortune that He wills one to suffer, and none can stop a good life that He wills one to enjoy.
13. Allah is the provider of every creature: all provisions of life are under His control. He is fully aware of the needs of His creations and provides them accordingly. He restricts His provisions or gives generously to whomsoever He wills.
14. Allah is just, all-knowing, all-wise: His decrees are just. He does not deprive anyone of his due. For Him good and evil are not equal: He will reward and punish everyone according to his deeds. He will neither punish a sinner unduly nor deprive a righteous worker of his rewards.
15. Allah has great love for His creatures: He forgives their sins, accepts their repentances and is ever merciful to them. A believer should never lose hope of His mercy and grace.
16. Allah alone deserves to be loved: one should seek only His pleasure and approval.
17. Allah alone deserves to be thanked, worshipped, adored and none else.
18. Allah alone has the right to be worshipped and His law obeyed unconditionally.
19. Allah alone deserves to be feared: He alone can fulfil hopes and grant prayers and give help and succour in difficulties and hardships.
20. Allah alone can show guidance: none can misguide the one whom Allah wills to guide, and none can show guidance to the one whom He has deprived of guidance.

Muslims would further reason that the worst people on the earth are those who disbelieve in Allah, reject His guidance, make others His associates and worship their own selves and desires instead of Him. As it says in the Qur'an:

> Those who disbelieve, and die while they are disbelievers; on them is the curse of Allah and of angels and of men combined.
> They ever dwell in it. The doom will not be lightened for them, neither will they be reprieved.
> (S2: 161–162)

Holding others as partners in Allah's Godhead is a falsehood and a most heinous sin. This is known as *shirk* (blasphemy). Allah will forgive all other sins but not the sin of *shirk*. As it says in the *Qur'an*:

> *Shirk* is the only sin that Allah does not forgive. He may forgive whosoever He will, other than this sin, for whose associate's partners with Allah does, in fact, go far astray into deviation.
> (S4: 116)

1.4 BELIEF IN DESTINY

The second Islamic Article of Faith is the belief in one's destiny as an integral part of one's belief in Allah's existence and His Attributes, and the *Qur'an* mentions it as such. The traditions (*Hadith*) of the Holy Prophet mention destiny as a separate and independent article of the faith.

Belief in destiny implies that all good and evil that takes place in the world, or will take place in future, is from Allah and in His knowledge. His knowledge is all-comprehensive and nothing of good or evil is outside it. Allah's knowledge comprehends all the good or evil deeds that humans will commit after their birth. Not a single particle moves anywhere in the universe unless its movement is within Allah's knowledge and in accordance with His will. No power can deprive or withhold from a creature anything that has been pre-ordained for it by Allah, and none can provide a creature with anything of which Allah has deprived it. Allah is the Maker of all destinies, good or otherwise.

In this regard, the teaching of Islam is that one should continue doing as much good as one can. One should avoid violating or neglecting religious commands and injunctions.

1.5 BELIEF IN ANGELS

The Islamic reasoning behind the third Article of Faith is as follows:

1. Angels have been created from light and are invisible, are of neither sex and have been appointed by Allah to carry out His Commands.
2. Angels are helpless creatures and cannot do anything out of their own will. They carry out, without question, all the Commands of Allah and dare not oppose or neglect them in any way.
3. They are engaged day and night in praising and glorifying Allah and are never tired of doing so.
4. They remain in awe of Him and can never so much as think of disobeying or revolting against Him.
5. They carry out their respective functions honestly, efficiently and responsibly, and are never guilty of shirking work.
6. The number of angels is only known to Allah Himself; four of them, however, are well-known, being nearest to Him in status and position. They are:
   Gabriel: whose duty has been to convey Allah's revelations and messages to the Prophets. He no longer performs this duty given that the institution of Prophet has come to an end with the arrival of The Holy Prophet Mohammed.
   Israfil: who by Allah's Command will blow into the trumpet on the Day of Judgement and bring the present system and order of the world to an end.
   Michael: whose duty is to arrange for rainfall and supply provisions to the creations of Allah, with His Command.
   Izra'il: who has been appointed to take the people's souls.
7. Two angels have been attached to every human being: one to record his good deeds and the other his bad deeds. They are called *Kiraman Katibin*.
8. Two angels, called Munkar and Nakir, are sent to the grave to question a person after his death.

1.6 BELIEF IN APOSTLES

The Islamic reasoning behind the fourth Article of Faith is as follows:

1. The arrangement made by Allah to convey His messages and commands for the guidance of mankind is called Apostleship, and those chosen for the mission are known as Apostles, Messengers or Prophets.
2. The Apostles have been conveying the Divine messages most scrupulously without tampering with them in any way.
3. Apostleship is God-given and cannot be acquired by effort and will.
4. All the Apostles have been men, and none of them was an angel, or *jinn* (evil spirit), or any other creature. Their only distinction was that God had chosen them as His Messengers and sent down His revelations to them.

5. The Apostles have faithfully practised what they presented and preached. They have been a perfect and true practical model of their teachings.

6. The Apostles were sent in every age and to every community and country. Muslims must believe in all the Apostles and reject none. They have to express complete faith in those of them who have been mentioned in the *Qur'an* and *Hadith* and hold them in the highest esteem.

7. All the Prophets gave the same message and invitation. Therefore rejection of one Prophet will indeed be rejection of all.

8. Belief in a Prophet implies that one should follow him in life faithfully and completely.

9. The institution of prophethood came to an end with the arrival of The Prophet Mohammed. He was the Last of the chain of Prophets. No Prophet is to appear after him. His prophethood, therefore, will last and remain effective until the Day of Judgement.

10. The personal example set by the Prophet Mohammed is the most perfect model for all his followers in all spheres of life. His verdict is decisive in all religious matters. A Muslim has to follow faithfully and sincerely all that he has enjoined and to avoid all that he has forbidden.

11. Obedience to the Prophet is obedience to Allah and disobedience of the Prophet is disobedience of Allah. Love of Allah, therefore, demands that one should obey the Prophet for that alone is the test of one's firmness in the faith.

12. Another proof of one's faith is the extent of honour and esteem in which one holds the Prophet generally. Any insolence or impudence shown with regard to the Prophet is destructive of all one's works of the lifetime. As it says in the Qur'an:

> O you who believe! Do not raise your voices above the Prophet's voice, nor speak loudly to him as you speak loudly to one another, lest your deeds become null, while you know not.
>
> (S.49: 2)

Muslims are honour-bound to regard the Holy Prophet dearer than their own parents, children and near and dear ones, even oneself. The *Qur'an* is explicit on this point:

> The Prophet is closer to the Believers than their own selves.
>
> (S.33: 6)

13. The belief in prophethood demands that Muslims should invoke Allah for His mercy and blessings on the Holy Prophet:

> O believers! Call for blessings on him and salute him with a (becoming) salutation.
>
> (S.33: 56)

1.7 BELIEF IN THE REVEALED BOOKS

The Islamic reasoning behind the fifth Article of Faith is as follows:

1. Allah sent down Scriptures for the guidance of humans to teach them how to live life in the right way. The Prophets demonstrated, by personal example, the meanings of these Scriptures.

2. Belief in all the revealed Books is necessary, for basically they all taught one and the same creed: to worship and serve Allah alone and to avoid blasphemy (*shirk*).

3. Five of the Scriptures revealed to five of the well-known Prophets are as follows:
   Sahifah Ibrahim: revealed to Prophet Abraham;

The *Torah*: revealed to Prophet Moses;

The Psalms: revealed to Prophet David;

The Gospel: revealed to Prophet Jesus;

The *Qur'an*: revealed to Prophet Mohammed.

4. Out of these revealed Books, Muslims believe that only the *Qur'an* is intact, exists in its original form and will remain so until the Last Day. Muslims believe that Allah has taken it on Himself to preserve it. As it says in the Qur'an:

> Surely We have sent down the *Qur'an*, and surely We are its Preserver.
>
> (S.15: 9)

5. The other four revealed Books have, Muslims reason, been irrevocably tampered with and none exist in their original form today. These Books were compiled long after the passing away of the Prophets and, Muslims reason, people inserted many things into them, which were opposed to their actual teachings. Thus the *Qur'an* is the only authentic and safe guide today in order to know and understand the practice of the original guidance sent down by Allah.

6. No one has the authority to effect any alteration in the *Qur'an* in any way. The Prophet himself was not authorised to do so; his only mission was to follow and practise it faithfully. To interpret the *Qur'an* according to one's personal whims and reading one's own meaning into its verses is highly sinful.

7. The *Qur'an* gives clear guidance for the solution of all human problems, personal and collective. Muslims believe that ignoring its guidance in any sphere of life or adopting and following other laws in preference to the *Qur'anic* Laws is sinful.

1.8 BELIEF IN THE HEREAFTER

The Islamic reasoning behind the sixth Article of Faith is as follows:

1. Life is not only this worldly life, but the real and eternal life is the life of the Hereafter that starts after death. The next worldly life will be blissful or painful and grievous depending on what one has earned and done in this worldly life. Belief in such a life is called belief in the Hereafter.

2. Every person is visited after death in the grave by two angels, called Munkar and Nakir, who put to the deceased the following questions:

Who is your Lord?

What is your religion?

What do you say about this man (pointing to the Holy Prophet Mohammed)?

This is the first of the tests in the accountability of the Hereafter.

3. On the first blowing of the Trumpet, the event which Muslims believe precedes the Day of Judgement, the present system and order of the universe will be upset and brought to an end. The earth will be shaken by a terrible earthquake, the mountains will be uprooted and shattered, the sun and the moon will collide, the stars will lose their brightness, and all living creatures will cease to live and the universe will be totally destroyed.

The Day of Judgement, Muslims believe, is the final day of life on earth and for the universe. At the same time it is the beginning of the eternal life in the Hereafter.

4. On the second blowing of the Trumpet, all the dead will be brought back to life by Allah's Command. This is the Day of Resurrection. A new order will be created in which all human beings will have eternal life and there will be no death. This will be a terrible and

dreadful Day. People will be in awe with downcast heads and eyes, awaiting the Divine verdict.

5. All humans will be gathered together before their Lord, Who will be the sole Judge and Ruler on that Day. As it says in the *Qur'an*:

> The day when all people will rise up (from their graves), nothing about them will remain hidden from Allah. (It will be asked): To whom belongs the sovereignty on this Day? (The whole world will cry out): To Allah, the One, the Almighty.
>
> (S.40: 16)

> The sovereignty on that Day rightly belongs to the Beneficent, and it will be a hard Day for the disbelievers.
>
> (S.25: 26)

No one will have the heart to utter a word except with Allah's permission. He will call upon each individual separately to account for all his deeds. Then Allah will deliver His verdict in full knowledge, justice and wisdom. Each individual will be recompensed justly and equitably for all his deeds and no one will be done any injustice whatever.

6. The righteous will be handed their life-scrolls in their right hand, and the sinners will be handed their life-scrolls in their left hand. The former will attain true success and the latter meet with failure. The former will exult in their success with bright and shining faces, while the latter will be burning inwardly with gloomy and dark faces. The righteous will be admitted to Paradise where they will enjoy Allah's favours and life of eternal bliss and peace. The criminals will be cast into Hell to suffer Allah's wrath and displeasure.

7. The Divine verdict on that Day will be final. None will be able to escape it by any trick, device or design; nor will any saint or prophet intercede for anyone, because intercession will not be possible except by Allah's leave and permission. Nor will it be possible for anyone to return to the world so as to work again to earn one's salvation.

8. All one's deeds and actions, verbal and practical, are being recorded by the angels of Allah in a manner so that nothing escapes their notice.

9. None of anyone's doings, big or small, remains hidden from Allah's sight.

10. The Believers will be blessed with such favours and bliss in Paradise that the like of these will never have been conceived by any eye, ear or mind.

11. The rebels of Allah will be cast into the blazing Hell from where they will have no escape. They will neither die to get rid of the everlasting torment nor live to enjoy the good things of life. They will desire death but death will disappoint them. The blaze of Hell will be ever brightening and unquenched. The dwellers will cry with thirst and be given molten metals for drink, which will scald their mouths and throats. They will have heavy collars around their necks and dresses of tar and fire on their bodies. They will be served with thorny bushes for food and will face Allah's wrath at every moment.

12. Who will be admitted to Paradise and who will suffer in Hell is known only to Allah. The Prophets of Allah, however, have clearly indicated and pointed out the works and deeds that enable one to deserve Paradise and the works that will lead one to Hell. It is, therefore, not possible in this world to predict with certainty as to who will be admitted to Paradise, except those who were given the good news of admission into Paradise by the Holy Prophet himself. One may, however, expect this from Allah: that He will admit one to Paradise on the basis of the good works that one is performing in this world.

13. Allah in His mercy will forgive any sin that He pleases but, according to the *Qur'an*, He will not forgive the sin of *shirk* and outright rejection of the Truth.

14. A person may believe and repent of sins any time in life; Allah is Gracious and Compassionate to His creatures and accepts their repentance most mercifully. No belief or repentance, however, is acceptable at the time one has reached the point of death and discerned, unmistakably, one's approaching end.

Given this background to Islam, the next chapter turns to the legal principles underlying Islamic banking and financial relationships: the *Sharia'a*.

2

Sharia'a Law and *Sharia'a* Boards: Roles, Responsibility and Membership

The first source of *Sharia'a* law is the Holy *Qur'an*. The second source is the *Sunnah* or the Practice of Prophet Mohammed who explained:

> I leave two weighty things for you. You will never go astray while holding them firmly. The Book of Allah and the *Sunnah* of His Prophet.
> The Hadith al – Thaqalayn

The third source, which may be classified as *Ijma*, is consensus of opinion of the *Ulema*, and the fourth source is *Qiyas*, analogical deductions.

2.1 DEFINITION OF THE *SHARIA'A*

Sharia'a is an Arabic word meaning the path to be followed. Literally it means the way to a watering place. It is the path not only leading to Allah (the Arabic word for God) but the path believed by all Muslims to be the path shown by Allah, the Creator Himself through His Messenger, the Prophet Mohammed. In Islam, Allah alone is sovereign and it is He who has the right to ordain a path for the guidance of mankind. Thus, Muslims believe, it is only *Sharia'a* that liberates humans from servitude to other than Allah. This is the reason why Muslims are obliged to strive for the implementation of that path, and no other path.

2.2 ALLAH IS THE LAW GIVER

In the *Sharia'a*, therefore, there is an explicit emphasis on the fact that Allah is the Law Giver and the whole *Ummah*, the nation of Islam, is merely His trustee. It is because of this principle that the *Ummah* enjoys a derivative rule-making power and not an absolute law-creating prerogative. The Islamic State consists of one vast homogeneous commonwealth of people who have a common goal and a common destiny and who are guided by a common ideology in all matters spiritual and temporal. The entire Muslim *Ummah* lives under the *Sharia'a* to which every member has to submit, with sovereignty belonging to Allah alone.

Every Muslim, who is capable and qualified to give a sound opinion on matters of *Sharia'a*, is entitled to interpret the law of Allah when such interpretation becomes necessary. In this sense Islam is a democracy. But, where an explicit command of Allah or His Prophet already exists, no Muslim leader or legislature, or any religious scholar, can form an independent judgement; not even all the Muslims of the world put together have any right to make the slightest alteration to it.

The *Sharia'a* is represented by the Council of Jurists (*Ulema* and *Fuqaha*) in whom the legislative function of deriving laws from the Book of Allah and the *Sunnah* is vested. New laws according to the needs of the time and circumstances are made only by these men, who are learned in the guiding principles of Islamic law. But the fundamental principles upon which the Islamic legal system rests is that the laws of Islam are not passed in a heated assembly by men who ardently desire the legislation in their interest against men who ardently oppose it again in their interest. The laws of Islam are firmly based upon the *Sharia'a* and are, therefore, deemed to be in the interest of the people as a whole. They are not the work of warring politicians, but of sober Jurists.

The difference between other legal systems and the *Sharia'a* is that, under the *Sharia'a*, its fountainhead is the *Qur'an* and *Sunnah*. The *Qur'an* and the *Sunnah* are the gifts given to the entire *Ummah*. Therefore, the *Ummah* as a whole is collectively responsible for the administration of justice.

The other important point in this regard is that under the *Sharia'a*, justice is administered in the name of Allah.

2.3 OBJECTIVES OF THE *SHARIA'A*

A flavour of the principles underlying *Sharia'a* law can be gained by the following *Ahadith* (traditional Islamic sayings):

> The basis of the *Sharia'a* is the wisdom and welfare of the people in this world, as well as the hereafter. This welfare lies in complete justice, mercy, well-being and wisdom. Anything that departs from justice to oppression, from mercy to harshness, from welfare to misery and from wisdom to folly, has nothing to do with the *Sharia'a*.
>
> *Ibn Al-Qayyim*

> The very objective of the *Sharia'a* is to promote the welfare of the people which lies in safeguarding their faith, their life, their intellect, their posterity and their property. Whatever ensures the safeguard of these objectives serves the public interest and is desirable.
>
> *Al-Ghazali*

2.3.1 *Sharia'a*: The Framework of Islamic Banking

The *Sharia'a*, or Islamic laws, sometimes referred to as Islamic Jurisprudence, is the origin and basis of Islamic banking. In the faith and belief of Muslims, Islam is the religion revealed by Allah to His last prophet, Mohammad. It is a complete religion, embracing all facets of a Muslim's mundane activities in this world and his state of affairs in the world hereafter. The teaching of Islam encompasses the essence of economic well-being and development of Muslims at the individual, family, society, state and *Ummah* (Islamic universal community) levels. Figure 2.1 illustrates the Islamic view of life of Muslims and the place of their economic activities, including banking and financial activities, within the framework of such a view.

As shown in Figure 2.1, Islam may be perceived as comprising three basic elements:

- The first element is *Aqidah*, which concerns all forms of faith and belief by a Muslim in Allah and His will, from the fundamental faith in His being to the ordinary beliefs in His individual commands (*ahkam*).
- The second element is *Sharia'a*, which concerns all forms of practical actions by Muslims manifesting their faith and belief.
- The third element is *Akhlaq*, which concerns behaviour, attitude and work ethics, within which Muslims perform their practical day-to-day activities.

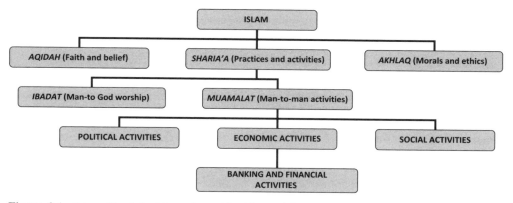

Figure 2.1   Islam, *Sharia'a*, *Muamalat* and banking and finance

Sharia'a, being the practical aspects of a Muslim's daily life, is then divided into two categories: *Ibadat* and *Muamalat*. *Ibadat* is concerned with the practicalities of a Muslim's worship to Allah, in the context of a man-to-Allah relationship, whereas *Muamalat* is concerned with the practicalities of a Muslim's mundane daily life, in the context of various forms of person-to-person relationships.

A significant segment of *Muamalat* is the conduct of a Muslim's economic activities within the economic system. Within the economic system one finds the banking and financial system, the place where people conduct their banking and financial activities. Thus, in the Islamic scheme of life and *Sharia'a* framework, a Muslim's banking and financial activities can be traced through his economic activities, back to *Muamalat*, to *Sharia'a*, to Islam, and finally to Allah. This is the root of Islamic banking and finance.

Sharia'a is the religious law of Islam. As Islam makes no distinction between religion and daily life, Islamic law covers not only the rituals but also every aspect of life. The actual codification of canonic law is the result of the concurrent evolution of jurisprudence proper and the so-called science of the roots of jurisprudence (*usul al-fiqh*).

A general agreement was reached, in the course of the formalisation of Islam, as to the authority of four such roots: the *Qur'an* in its legislative segments; the example of the Prophet as related in the *Hadith*; the consensus of the Muslims (*Ijma*), premised on a saying by Mohammed stipulating 'My nation cannot agree on an error'; and reasoning by analogy (*Qiyas*).

Another important principle is *Ijtihad*, the extension of *Sharia'a* to situations neither covered by precedent nor explicable by analogy to other laws. These roots provide the means for the establishment of prescriptive codes of action and for the evaluation of individual and social behaviour. The basic scheme for all actions is a fivefold division of categories and encompasses obligatory, meritorious, permissible, reprehensible and forbidden Islamic modes of conduct.

Numerous schools of jurisprudence (*Madhabs*) emerged in the course of Islamic history. Four coexist today within *Sunni* Islam, with one or more dominant in particular areas: *Maliki* (North and West Africa), *Hanafi* (Turkic Asia), *Shafii* (Egypt, East Africa, South-East Asia) and *Hanbali* (Saudi Arabia). *Shiite* jurisprudence is often referred to as *Jaafari*. Although these schools of jurisprudence vary on certain rituals and practices, they are perceived as being complementary rather than mutually exclusive. Box 2.1 provides an explanation of *Sharia'a* terminology.

Box 2.1 *Sharia'a* **terminology**

Sharia'a: A *Sharia'a* – compliant product must meet all the requirements of Islamic law. To facilitate this, a *Sharia'a* Supervisory Board is usually appointed. This board or committee is usually comprised of Islamic scholars available to the organisation, for guidance and supervision, for the development of *Sharia'a*-compliant products.

Sharia'a **adviser**: This means an independent professional, usually a classically trained Islamic legal scholar, appointed to advise an Islamic financial organisation on the compliance of its products and services with Islamic law, the *Sharia'a*. Although some organisations consult individual *Sharia'a* advisers, most establish a committee of advisers.

Sharia'a **compliant**: This means ensuring that the requirements of the *Sharia'a* law are being observed. The term is often used in the Islamic banking industry as a synonym for Islamic: for example, *Sharia'a*-compliant financing or *Sharia'a*-compliant investment.

To ensure that their financial activities are in conformity with the *Sharia'a* law, religious supervisory boards are mandatory for Islamic banks and Islamic financial institutions. The *Sharia'a* Supervisory Board (SSB), sometimes called the *Sharia'a* supervisory committee, examines contracts, dealings and transactions to assure that Islamic beliefs are being implemented.

The SSB guarantees, and certifies, that the banking activities are *halal* (permissible). The SSB is merely an advisory body, but nevertheless it has an authoritative and respected function because the bank entrusts the SSB with questions as to the permissibility of its activities.

Being part and parcel of Islamic *Muamalat*, banking and financial activities are therefore subject to the *Sharia'a* law on *Muamalat*.

2.4 SOURCES OF THE *SHARIA'A*

Muslims view the *Sharia'a* as the ideal code of conduct or pure way of life. It has much wider scope and purpose than an ordinary legal system in the Western sense of the term. The *Sharia'a* aims at regulating the relationship of man with Allah and with each other. This is why *Sharia'a* law cannot be separated from Islamic ethics. The process of revelation of various injunctions of the *Qur'an* shows that the revelation came down when social, moral or religious necessity arose, or when some of the Companions of the Prophet (*Sahaba*) consulted the Prophet concerning any significant problems that had wide repercussions on the lives of Muslims.

The *Qur'an* is the main source of the *Sharia'a*. The scholars of the *Qur'an* have enumerated varying number of verses of legal injunctions, but the number is approximately considered to be 500. These verses deal with marriage, polygamy, maintenance, rights and obligations of the spouses, divorce and various modes of dissolution of marriage, the period of retreat after divorce, fosterage, contracts, loans, deposits, weights and measures, oaths and vows, punishments for crime, wills, inheritance, equity, fraternity, liberty, justice to all, principles of an ideal state, fundamental human rights, laws of war and peace, judicial administration and so on.

The *Qur'anic* injunctions from which the *Sharia'a* is derived are further explained and translated into practice by the *Sunnah* of the Prophet. *Sunnah* literally means a way, practice or rule of life, and it refers to the exemplary conduct or the model behaviour of the Prophet in what he said, did or approved. Thus it became a very important source of the *Sharia'a*, second only in authority after the Holy *Qur'an*.

Besides the *Qur'an* and the *Sunnah*, the consensus of the opinion of the learned men and Jurists, known in the *Sharia'a* terminology as *Ijma*, plays an important role in Islamic law because it provides a broad vehicle reflecting progress and reconstruction. *Qiyas*, or analogical deduction, is also recognised as one of the sources of the Islamic legal system because it gives an instrument to cope with the growing needs and requirements of society. Such analogical deduction is based on very strict, logical and systematic principles.

Alongside these four sources, the *Sharia'a* takes into consideration *Istihsan* or the juristic preference or equity of a Jurist as against *Qiyas*, which helps in providing elasticity and adaptability to the entire Islamic legal system. The concept of *al-Masalih al Mursalah* (matters that are in the public interest and which are not specifically defined in the *Sharia'a*) has also become part of the *Sharia'a* system.

The basic principles of *Sharia'a* can be summed up as follows:

- The larger interest of society takes precedence over the interest of the individual.
- Although relieving hardship and promoting benefit are among the prime objectives of the *Sharia'a*, the former takes precedence over the latter.
- A bigger loss cannot be inflicted to relieve a smaller loss or a bigger benefit cannot be sacrificed for a smaller one. Conversely, a smaller harm can be inflicted to avoid a bigger harm or a smaller benefit can be sacrificed for a larger benefit.

2.4.1 *Qur'an*: The Primary Source of the *Sharia'a*

The *Qur'an* is believed to be the miracle of Mohammed, the proof of his prophethood and a testimony to its divine origin.

Being the verbal noun of the root word *qara'a* (to read), *Qur'an* literally means reading or recitation. It may be defined as 'the book containing the speech of God revealed to the Prophet Mohammed in Arabic and transmitted to us by continuous testimony'. It is a proof of the prophecy of Mohammed, the most authoritative guide for Muslims, and the primary source of the *Sharia'a*. The *Ulema* (religious scholars) are unanimous on this point, and some even say that it is the only source and that all other sources are explanatory of the *Qur'an*. The salient attributes of the *Qur'an* that are indicated in this definition may be summarised as the following five points:

- it was revealed exclusively to the Prophet Mohammed;
- it was put into writing;
- it is all *mutawatir* (universally accurately reported);
- it is the inimitable speech of God;
- it is recited in *salah* (ritual prayer).

The first revelation of the *Qur'an* began on the 15th night of the month of Ramadan in the 41st year of the Prophet's life. Its first *surah* (chapter) was revealed in the Cave of Hira:

Recite in the name of thy Lord and Cherished who created man out of a (mere) clot of congealed blood. Proclaim and thy Lord is Most Bountiful.

(S.96: 1–3)

The *Qur'an* was revealed to mankind gradually, over about 23 years, through the mediation of the archangel Gabriel.

There are 114 *suras* (chapters) and 6235 *ayat* (verses) of unequal length in the *Qur'an*. The shortest of the *suras* consist of four *ayat* and the longest of 286 *ayat*. Each chapter has a separate title. The longest *suras* appear at the beginning of the Qur'an and the *suras* become shorter as the text proceeds. Both the order of the *ayat* within each *sura*, and the sequence of the *suras*, were re-arranged and finally determined by the Prophet, in the year of his demise.

The *Qur'an* consists of manifest revelation, which is defined as communication from God to the Prophet Mohammed, conveyed by the angel Gabriel, in the very words of God. The Prophet received this revelation in a state of wakefulness, and thus no part of the *Qur'an* originated in internal inspiration or dreams. God inspired the Prophet and the latter conveyed the concepts in his own words. All the sayings, or *Hadith*, of the Prophet fall into the category of internal revelation and, as such, are not included in the *Qur'an*.

The *Ulema* are in agreement that the entire text of the *Qur'an* is *mutawatir*; that is, its authenticity is proven by universally accepted testimony. It has been retained both in memory and as a written record throughout the generations.

During the lifetime of the Prophet, the text of the *Qur'an* was preserved not only in memories, but also in inscriptions on such available materials as flat stones, wood and bones, which would explain why it could not have been compiled in a bound volume. Initially, the first Caliph, Abu Bakr, collated the *Qur'an* soon after the battle of Yamamah, a battle which led to the death of at least 70 memorisers of the *Qur'an*. Zayd ibn Thabit, the scribe of the Prophet, was employed in the task of compiling the text, which he accomplished between AD 623 and 626 (11 and 14 AH). But several versions soon crept into use. Hence the third Caliph, 'Uthman, again used the services of Zayd to verify the accuracy of the text, and compiled it into a single volume. All remaining variations were then destroyed. As a result, only one authentic text has remained in use to this day.

Out of more than 6200 *ayat*, less than one-tenth relate to law and jurisprudence: the rest largely concern matters of belief and morality, the five pillars of the faith and a variety of other themes. On the whole, the concept of economic and social justice, including its legal contents, is subsidiary to the *Qur'an's* religious call.

2.4.2 *Sunnah*: The Second Primary Source of the *Sharia'a*

Literally, *Sunnah* means a clear path or a beaten track, but it is also used to imply normative practice or an established course of conduct. In pre-Islamic Arabia, the Arabs used the word *Sunnah* in reference to the ancient and continuous practices of the community that they inherited from their forefathers. In the *Qur'an*, the word *Sunnah* is used to imply an established practice or code of conduct.

As mentioned earlier the primary source of the religion of Islam is the *Qur'an*: the word of Allah to all Muslims. The Prophet had nothing to do with its words; it was revealed to him as it is now read. Although the *Qur'an* gives Muslims a primary rule of life, it says nothing about many matters where guidance for practical living is necessary. In such cases the obvious solution was to follow the custom or usage of the Prophet (such as *Sunnah*). There were ancient customs that could be accepted in some matters, but on matters peculiar to the religion of Islam there was the custom of the earliest believers who had been the contemporaries and companions of the Prophet. Presumably the earliest believers would act in matters of religion according to the custom of the Prophet himself. Eventually statements came into existence as to what the *Sunnah* of the earliest Muslims was on a variety of matters.

As *Sunnah* means a way of acting or mode of life, a class of scholars arose in Islam who made it their business to investigate and hand down the minutest details concerning the life of the Prophet.

After his death, reports of the Prophet's sayings and behaviour began to circulate. The reports continued to increase from time to time as they were collected from the *Sahaba*, the Companions of the Prophet, and became subject to standardization and selection. The records of the sayings, therefore, were called *Hadith*; the rest, as a whole, was called *Sunnah* (custom or usage).

The *Hadith* is the second primary source (after the *Qur'an*) upon which all Muslims rest the fabric of their faith and life. The body of traditions circulated orally for some time, as indicated by the word *Hadith*, commonly used in the sense of a tradition. *Hadith* literally means a saying conveyed to humans through hearing of or witnessing an event. The term is also used to denote conversation or the telling of something new.

To the *Ulema* of *Hadith*, *Sunnah* refers to all that is narrated from the Prophet, his acts, his sayings and whatever he tacitly approved, plus all the reports that describe his physical attributes and character.

Notwithstanding the fact that the *Ulema* have used *Sunnah* and *Hadith* almost interchangeably, the two terms have meanings of their own. Literally, *Hadith* means a narrative, communication or news consisting of the factual account of an event. The word occurs frequently in the *Qur'an* (23 times) and in all cases it carries the meaning of a narrative or communication. In none of these instances is *Hadith* used in its technical, exclusive sense, that is, as the sayings of the Prophet. In the early days of Islam, following the demise of the Prophet, stories relating to the life and activities of the Prophet dominated all other kinds of narratives, and so the word began to be used almost exclusively for a narrative from, or a saying of, the Prophet.

Hadith differs from *Sunnah* in that *Hadith* is a narration of the conduct of the Prophet whereas *Sunnah* is the example or the law that is deduced from it. *Hadith* in this sense is the vehicle or the carrier of *Sunnah*, although *Sunnah* is a wider concept, especially before its literal meaning gave way to its juristic usage. *Sunnah* thus refers not only to the *Hadith* of the Prophet but also to the established practice of the community.

2.4.2.1 Qur'an *and* Sunnah *Distinguished*

The *Qur'an* was recorded in writing from beginning to end during the lifetime of the Prophet, and he ascertained that the *Qur'an* was preserved, as he received it, through divine revelation. The Prophet clearly expressed the concern that nothing of his own *Sunnah* should be confused with the text of the *Qur'an*. This was, in fact, the main reason why he discouraged his Companions, at the early stage of his mission, from reducing the *Sunnah* into writing, lest it be confused with the *Qur'an*. The *Sunnah*, on the other hand, was mainly retained in memory by the Companions who did not, on the whole, keep a written record of the teachings of the Prophet. There were perhaps certain exceptions because the relevant literature suggests that some, though a small number, of the Companions held collections of the *Hadith* of the Prophet, which they wrote and kept in their private collections. The overall impression, however, is that this was done on a fairly limited scale.

2.4.2.2 *Priority of the* Qur'an *over the* Sunnah

As *Sunnah* is the second source of the *Sharia'a* after the *Qur'an*, the *mujtahid* (Scholar of Islamic law) is bound to observe the order of priority between the *Qur'an* and *Sunnah*. Hence in his search for a solution to a particular problem, the Jurist must resort to the *Sunnah* only when he fails to find any guidance in the *Qur'an*. Should there be a clear text in the *Qur'an*, it must be followed and be given priority over any ruling of the *Sunnah* that may happen to be in conflict with the *Qur'an*. The priority of the *Qur'an* over the *Sunnah* is partly a result of the fact that the *Qur'an* consists wholly of manifest revelation whereas the *Sunnah* mainly consists of internal revelation and is largely transmitted in the words of the narrators themselves. The other reason for this order of priority relates to the question of authenticity: the authenticity of the *Qur'an* is not open to doubt. It is, in other words, decisive in respect of authenticity and must therefore take priority over the *Sunnah*.

2.4.3 *Ijma* (Consensus): The First Secondary Source of the *Sharia'a*

The primary sources of the *Sharia'a* are the *Qur'an* and the *Sunnah*. The secondary sources are *Ijma*, *Qiyas* and *Ijtihad*, which are derived from the legal injunctions of the Holy *Qur'an* and the *Sunnah* of the Prophet. The final sanction for all intellectual activities in respect of the development of *Sharia'a* comes from nowhere else but the *Qur'an*. Any *Hadith* that goes contrary to the *Qur'an* is not to be considered as authentic.

Ijma refers to the consensus of juristic opinions of the learned *Ulema* of the *Ummah* after the death of the Messenger of Allah, the Prophet Mohammed. *Ijma* can be defined as the consensus of opinion of the Companions of the Prophet *(Sahaba)* and the agreement reached on the decisions taken by the learned *Muftis*, or Jurists, on various Islamic matters.

Unlike the *Qur'an* and *Sunnah*, *Ijma* does not directly partake of divine revelation. *Ijma* is the verbal noun of the Arabic word *ajma'a*, which means to determine and to agree upon something. The second meaning of *Ijma* often subsumes the first, in that whenever there is a unanimous agreement on something, there is also a decision on that matter. Whereas a decision can be made by one individual or by many, unanimous agreement can only be reached by a plurality of individuals. *Ijma* is defined as the unanimous agreement of the Muslim community for any period, following the demise of the Prophet Mohammed, on any matter.

It is clear from its definition that *Ijma* can only occur after the demise of the Prophet. During his lifetime, the Prophet alone was the highest authority on *Sharia'a*; hence the agreement or disagreement of others did not affect the overriding authority of the Prophet. In all probability *Ijma* occurred for the first time among the Companions in the city of Medina. Following the demise of the Prophet, the Companions used to consult each other about the problems they encountered, and their collective agreement was accepted by the community. After the passing of the Companions, this leadership role passed on to the next generation, the Successors, and then to the second generation of Successors. When the latter differed on a point, they naturally referred to the views and practices of the Companions and the Successors. In this way, a fertile ground was created for the development of the theory of *Ijma*.

The essence of *Ijma* lies in the natural growth of ideas. It begins with the personal view of individual Jurists and culminates in the universal acceptance of a particular opinion over a period of time. Differences of opinion are tolerated until a consensus emerges. *Ijma* represent authority. Once an *Ijma* is established it tends to become an authority in its own right.

2.4.4 *Qiyas* (Analogical Reasoning): The Second Secondary Source of the *Sharia'a*

Literally, *Qiyas* means measuring or ascertaining the length, weight or quality of something. The term also means comparison, with a view to suggesting equality or similarity between two things. *Qiyas* thus suggests an equality or close similarity between two things, one of which is taken as the criterion for evaluating the other.

Technically, *Qiyas* is the extension of a position from the *Sharia'a* to a new case, on the grounds that the latter has the same effective cause as the former. The original case is regulated by a given text, and *Qiyas* seeks to extend the same textual ruling to the new case. It is by virtue of the commonality of the effective cause (*'illah*), between the original case and the new case that the application of *Qiyas* is justified. Recourse to analogy is only warranted if the solution of a new case cannot be found in the *Qur'an*, the *Sunnah* or a definite *Ijma*.

Qiyas is defined, in Islamic theological parlance, as analogy, or analogical deduction. In other words, *Qiyas* is the legal principle introduced in order to derive a logical conclusion of a certain law on a certain issue that has to do with the welfare of Muslims. In exercising this, however, it must be based on the *Qur'an*, *Sunnah* and *Ijma*.

This legal principle was introduced by *Imam* Abu Hanifah, the founder of the Hanafi School in Iraq. Its introduction was intended to curb the excessive thinking and digression of the people from strict Islamic principles.

During the period of the Abbasids (AD 750–1258), the people engaged themselves in reading various text books on logic, philosophy, etymology, linguistics, literature from various places and foreign text books. Some argued that this reading tended to corrupt minds and lead them astray. The people wanted to apply what they had studied in these foreign text books to Islamic jurisprudence. Many new Muslims from overseas had brought with them their philosophical outlook, their culture and even some religious notions on the role of Islam. Abu Hanifah introduced *Qiyas* so as to curb this excessive thinking and to ensure that Islamic principles were upheld.

During the lifetime of the Companions of the Prophet they arrived at various decisions using analogical deductions. To take an example concerning the punishment that should be given to a drunkard, Sayyidna Ali concluded by saying:

> He who drinks gets drunk; he who gets drunk raves; he who raves accuses people falsely and he who accuses people falsely should be given eighty strokes of cane. Therefore, he who drinks should be given eighty strokes of cane.

It is perfectly acceptable, in using *Qiyas*, to derive a logical conclusion in *Sharia'a* law in as much as that conclusion does not go against the injunctions of the *Qur'an* or the *Sunnah* of the Prophet.

2.4.5 *Ijtihad*

The Arabic word *Ijtihad* literally means an effort or exercise to arrive at one's own judgement. In its widest sense, it means the use of human reason in the elaboration and explanation of *Sharia'a* law. It covers a variety of mental processes, ranging from the interpretation of texts of the *Qur'an* and the assessment of the authenticity of the *Ahadith*. *Qiyas* or analogical reasoning, then, is a particular form of *Ijtihad*, the method by which the principles established by the *Qur'an*, *Sunnah* and *Ijma* are to be extended and applied to the solution of new problems not expressly regulated before.

Ijtihad, therefore, is an exercise of one's reasoning to arrive at a logical conclusion on a legal issue undertaken by the Jurists, to deduce a conclusion as to the effectiveness of a legal precept in Islam.

Any form of *Ijtihad* must have as its starting point a principle of the *Qur'an*, *Sunnah* or *Ijma* and cannot be used to achieve a result that contradicts a rule established by any of these three fundamental sources. Whenever a new issue presents itself, reasoning by *Qiyas* with an original case covered by the *Qur'an*, the *Sunnah* or *Ijma* is possible provided that the effective cause (*'illah*) is common to both cases.

2.4.6 Compliance with the Scheme of *Sharia'a* Laws

Within the Islamic scheme of life, Islam imposes its *ahkam* (laws) – in modern terminology norms or values – on its believers. These laws or values are not constructed by humans; they are ordained by Allah and derived from the two primary sources of the *Sharia'a*: the *Qur'an* and *Sunnah*.

As derived from the above sources, these laws are arranged into the following five-level scheme:

1. *Fard* or *Wajib*: an obligatory duty, the omission of which is punishable Islamically.
2. *Mandub* or *Mustahab*: an action that is rewarded Islamically, but the avoidance of which is not punishable.
3. *Jaiz* or *Mubah*: an action that is permitted, with the law being indifferent.
4. *Makruh*: an action disliked Islamically, and yet not punishable, but the avoidance of which is rewarded.
5. *Haram*: an action that is absolutely forbidden and punishable Islamically.

2.5 *SHARIA'A* ISLAMIC INVESTMENT PRINCIPLES

A good illustration of the application of the *Sharia'a* is to look at Islamic investment prohibitions. It is forbidden for any Islamic institution or investment fund to deal in the following goods:

- alcoholic drinks and related activities;
- pork, ham, bacon and related by-products;
- dead animals (or those not slaughtered according to the rules of the *Sharia'a*);
- products associated with gambling such as gambling machines;
- tobacco and other drugs;
- activities associated with pornography;
- gold and silver except for spot cash;
- armaments and destructive weapons.

According to the principles of Islamic jurisprudence the payment and receipt of interest is a grave sinful act, for which the participant is responsible in the Hereafter. Since almost all companies deal with some form of interest or otherwise prohibited activity, some *Sharia'a* advisory boards have determined an upper limit as to what percentage of a company's income can be earned through interest and/or such activities. It would be unacceptable to invest in a firm that exceeds these limits, which are evolving and, as a result, becoming more sophisticated and nuanced. Companies that may have been excluded under simplistic models a few years ago (for example, due to large cash holdings) may now be acceptable under newer *Sharia'a* models.

2.6 CONDITIONS FOR INVESTMENT IN SHARES

In the light of the foregoing discussion, dealing in equity shares can be acceptable in *Sharia'a* subject to the following conditions:

- The main business of the company is not in violation of *Sharia'a*. This means that it is not permissible to acquire the shares of companies providing financial services associated with interest, such as conventional banks and insurance companies. Companies involved in some other business not approved by the *Sharia'a*, such as those manufacturing, selling or offering alcohol, pork or *haram* (forbidden) meat, or involved in gambling, night club activities, pornography and so on are forbidden.
- If the main business of the company is *halal* (permitted), such as computers, cars and house building, but the company involved deposits its surplus cash in an interest-bearing account or borrows money paying interest, Muslim shareholders must express their disapproval against such dealings. This should preferably be done by raising their voice against such activities in the annual general meeting of the company.
- If some income from interest-bearing accounts is included in the income of the company, the proportion of such income in the dividend paid to the shareholder must be given to charity, and must not be retained by the investor. For example if 5% of the total income of a company has come out of interest-bearing deposits, then 5% of the dividend must be given to charity.

  In other words, where profits are earned through dividends a certain proportion of the dividend, which corresponds to the proportion of interest earned by the company, must be given to charity. Islamic scholars have termed this process 'purification'.

  Sharia'a scholars have different views about whether purification is necessary where profits are made through capital gains (such as by purchasing the shares at one price and selling them at a higher price). Some scholars are of the view that, even in the case of capital gains, the process of purification is necessary because the market price of the share may reflect an element of interest related leverage and so interest payments have boosted the performance of the company. Other scholars reason that no purification is required if the share is sold, even if the activity results in a capital gain.
- The shares of a company are negotiable (and can be freely invested in) only if the company owns some nonliquid assets. If all the assets of a company are in liquid form, or in the form of money that cannot be purchased or sold, except at par value, then these shares cannot be purchased. In this case the shares represent money only and, Islamically, money cannot be traded except at par.

  What should be the exact proportion of nonliquid assets of a company enabling the negotiability of its shares? Contemporary scholars have different views about this question. Some scholars are of the view that the ratio of nonliquid assets must be 51% at the very least. They argue that if such assets are less than 50%, most of the assets are in liquid form, and therefore, all its assets should be treated as liquid, on the basis of the Juristic principle 'the majority deserves to be treated as the whole of a thing'. Other scholars have opined that even if the nonliquid assets of a company are 33%, its shares can be treated as negotiable.

2.7 *SHARIA'A* SUPERVISORY BOARD (SSB)

As mentioned earlier in Section 2.3.1, to ensure conformity with *Sharia'a* law and that Islamic beliefs are being implemented, *Sharia'a* Supervisory Boards (SSB) are mandatory.

2.7.1 Function and Responsibilities

The three central responsibilities of an SSB are

- to make sure that banking facilities and services offered are in accordance with Islam;
- to guarantee that the bank's investments and involvement in projects are *Sharia'a*-compliant;
- to ensure that the bank is managed in concordance with Islamic values.

In its articles of association, the Faisal Bank of Egypt states that 'A Religious Supervisory Board shall be formed within the Bank to observe conformance of its dealings and actions with the principles and rulings of the *Sharia'a*'.

The International Association of Islamic Banks (IAIB) has chosen a more scrupulous clarification of the duties imposed on its supervisory committee.

In Article 2 of the Board's Statute, the IAIB has entrusted its SSB with the following duties:

- to study previously issued *Fatawa* (religious rulings), assess its constituency with the *Sharia'a* and, when appropriate, base its own rulings on these decisions;
- to supervise the activities of the bank in order to guarantee conformity with the *Sharia'a* law;
- to issue religious opinions on banking and financial questions;
- to clarify legal religious rulings on new economic issues.

2.7.2 *Sharia'a* Boards: Roles and Scope of Responsibilities

Sharia'a advisers have both supervisory and consultancy functions. Categorically, the overall applications of the *Sharia'a* by these advisors have a two-fold objective. Firstly, the *Sharia'a* advisers review the operations of the institutions participating in the Islamic financial markets, ensuring that they comply with the requirements of the *Sharia'a*. This is, to a large extent, equivalent to a supervisory role.

Secondly, in the increasingly complex and sophisticated world of modern and dynamic Islamic finance, *Sharia'a* advisers endeavour to answer any issues or concerns for a particular transaction or product conformation with the *Sharia'a*. Where deemed necessary, they offer constructive, creative and/or alternative recommendations. This is, to a large extent, a consultancy role.

Institutions participating in the Islamic financial markets are required to establish operating policies and procedures to ensure that their activities, investments and operations are undertaken in line with *Sharia'a* requirements. *Sharia'a* advisers are expected to participate and engage themselves actively in deliberating the *Sharia'a* issues put before them. Among the duties and responsibilities of the *Sharia'a* advisers that are prevalent in the Islamic financial markets are the following:

- *Review the products and services to ensure conformity with Sharia'a requirements.* In the Islamic investment industry, *Sharia'a* advisers are responsible for ensuring that the funds they oversee are managed and administered in accordance with the principles of the *Sharia'a*. This also includes the responsibility to provide expertise and guidance to the investment management companies and fund managers in all matters relating to the principles of the

Sharia'a pertaining to the fund, including the trust deed, the prospectus, the investments of the fund and other operational and administrative matters.

- *Review and endorse relevant documents.* In order to be *Sharia'a*-compliant, Islamic financial market products and services need to undergo a pre-defined vetting and endorsement process by *Sharia'a* advisers. The adviser's role is to advise on all aspects of Islamic securities, including documentation, structuring and investment as well as other administrative and operational matters, and to ensure compliance with applicable *Sharia'a* principles and relevant resolutions. A basic principle which must be adhered to in the course of reviewing and endorsing the documentation is that no other person is competent enough to ensure that the documentation conforms and is consistent with the contemplated *Sharia'a* transaction, other than the *Sharia'a* adviser.

- *Supervise investments made by the institutions in the Islamic financial markets.* The *Sharia'a* adviser supervises and ensures that the investments made by these institutions comply with the *Sharia'a*. In this case, the *Sharia'a* adviser must ensure that the fund managers invest only in securities classified as *Sharia'a*-approved by the *Sharia'a* board.

- *Deliberate on Sharia'a issues pertaining to the day-to-day operations of the institutions and provide advice accordingly.* In the everyday operations of these institutions, there are various *Sharia'a* issues that practitioners will come across, particularly with regard to the practice and implementation of financial transactions. These issues are usually not covered by text books or the theoretical framework of a particular transaction. Thus, *Sharia'a* advisers are compelled to understand and resolve these issues. By and large, this requires them to be closely involved with the actual practice and implementation side, because this gives them a more comprehensive and deeper understanding of the issues with which they are dealing.

- *Conduct research and development of new products.* As the financial system advances, the need for Islamic financial institutions to compete, not only with existing but also upcoming conventional products, requires *Sharia'a* advisers to develop or approve innovative new products that are competitive and acceptable to all the stakeholders. Some of the more complex financial areas requiring *Sharia'a*-compliant innovation are risk management, hedging tools, derivatives and hybrid financing facilities. When *Sharia'a* advisers are equipped with the essentials of both the *Fiqh* (Islamic law) and the *Muamalat*, especially concerning capital and asset management principles, it is intended that they develop Islamically-acceptable financial products.

- *Provide training and education on Muamalat, based on Sharia'a contracts.* The large growing pool of Islamic-finance practitioners must be well informed and systematically educated in order to prepare them with the necessary knowledge for managing Islamic financing activities. In the course of developing the Islamic financial market its dynamic nature must be recognised and complacency should be avoided. The dissemination process must be continuous, in order to train as many practitioners as possible, so as to provide successors who are well trained prior to succeeding their superiors. Since the *Sharia'a* advisers possess the knowledge in *Muamalat*, it is pertinent that they lead the way in imparting knowledge to these practitioners as well as to society in general. This is vital towards achieving a true and accurate understanding of the *Sharia'a* and the application of the nominate contracts in *Muamalat*.

- *Assist related parties on Sharia'a matters and provide advice upon request.* The related parties of the institutions in the Islamic financial market, such as their legal counsels, auditors and consultants, may seek advice on *Sharia'a* matters from the advisers. The latter are expected to provide the necessary assistance so that full compliance with *Sharia'a* principles can be assured. Over and above this, they must also explain the *Sharia'a* issues and the recommendations offered for a particular decision. These opinions must be supported by the relevant *Sharia'a* jurisprudential literature from established sources.

2.7.3 Dubai Islamic Bank (DIB)

At DIB, the *Fatwa* and *Sharia'a* supervision board oversees the application of different aspects of the *Sharia'a* and also ensures that all the transactions are in strict compliance with the *Sharia'a* principles. The board is further empowered with the right of reversing any violating procedures, if found. The board of directors is obligated to obey the *Fatawa*, irrespective of whether a unanimous or a majority consensus secured the decision (clause 78 of the Bank's Memorandum & Articles of Association). *Sharia'a* board meetings are held periodically or whenever the need arises. The rights of the board are enshrined in Article Seven of the Bank's Memorandum & Articles of Association (Clauses 74–84). Box 2.2 provides details of the functions of the DIB's *Sharia'a* board.

Box 2.2 Duties of the DIB *Sharia'a* board

- As an expert source on Islamic principles (including *Fatawa*), the board, through a representative (usually the general secretary of the board), supervises the *Sharia'a* compliance of all the transactions in the bank.
- To devote time and effort to devising more *Sharia'a*-compliant transactional procedures, templates and banking products that enable the bank to adapt to market trends, while maintaining a competitive edge in deposit procedures, investments, and banking services. At the same time, the board gives its opinion on proposed new templates and banking transactions.
- Analysing unprecedented situations that are not covered by *Fatawa* in the bank's transactional procedures or those reported by different departments, branches and sometimes the customers. This is to ensure *Sharia'a* compliance before the bank develops any new products or implements any new procedures.
- Analysing contracts and agreements concerning the bank's transactions, as submitted by the chairman of the board of directors or any department or branch within the bank or requested by the board itself in order that *Sharia'a* compliance can be evaluated and maintained.
- Ensuring *Sharia'a* compliance in the implementation of all banking transactions and correcting any breaches.
- Analysing administrative decisions, issues and matters that require the board's approval.
- Supervising *Sharia'a* training programmes for the bank's staff.
- Preparing an annual report on the bank's balance sheet, with respect to its *Sharia'a* compliance.
- The *Fatwa* and *Sharia'a* board submits a complete annual report for the board of directors, summarising all the issues referred to the board, as well as its opinion on the bank's transactional procedures.

Source: DIB

2.8 *SHARIA'A* BOARD SCHOLAR QUALIFICATIONS

The qualifications necessary to become a *Sharia'a* scholar are not defined in any formalised manner from, say, some central institution, as one would find in most professional bodies such as solicitors, architects and so on. A glance, however, at the CVs of some of the better known scholars, listed in this section, provides a flavour of the qualifications needed to be a *Sharia'a* board scholar. The following nine abbreviated CVs of prominent *Sharia'a* board scholars indicate the depth of experience needed by *Sharia'a* board members. The *Sharia'a* board requirements for the State Bank of Pakistan are also described.

2.8.1 Dr Hussain Hamid Hassan

Dr Hussain Hamid Hassan received his PhD from the Faculty of *Sharia'a* at Al Azhar University in Cairo, Egypt, in 1965. He also holds two degrees in law from the International Institute of Comparative Law, University of New York and two degrees in Law and Economics from Cairo University. He served as Assistant Professor, Associate Professor and Professor of *Sharia'a* in the Faculty of Law and Economics at Cairo University between 1960 and 2002.

Dr Hassan chairs, or is member of, the *Sharia'a* supervisory committees of many Islamic financial institutions, including Emirates Islamic Bank, DIB, National Bank of Sharjah, Islamic Development Bank, Dubai Islamic Insurance and Re-Insurance (Aman), Tamweel, AMLAK, the Liquidity Management Centre and the Accounting and Auditing Organisation for Islamic Financial Institutions. Dr Hassan is the author of 21 books on Islamic law, finance, economics, social studies and art. In addition, he has also written more than 400 research articles on these subjects.

2.8.2 Dr Ali AlQaradaghi

Dr Ali AlQaradaghi received his PhD in the area of contracts and financial transactions from Al Azhar University in Cairo, Egypt, in 1985. He is currently a Professor of Islamic financial contracts and heads the Department of Islamic jurisprudence in the College of *Sharia'a* and Islamic studies at the University of Qatar.

Dr Ali AlQaradaghi presently serves on the *Sharia'a* boards of many Islamic financial institutions in and outside Qatar including Emirates Islamic Bank and DIB in the UAE, Investment House and Investors Bank in Bahrain and First Investment in Kuwait.

He is a founding member of numerous charitable organisations and international Islamic jurisprudence bodies and the author of many research articles in contemporary issues in Islamic finance and banking. He has more than eight books published.

2.8.3 Dr Mohamed Elgari

Dr Elgari received his PhD in economics from University of California (USA), and is currently serving as a Professor of Islamic economics at King Abdulaziz University (Jeddah), Saudi Arabia. He is a *Sharia'a* advisor to many Islamic financial institutions including HSBC Amanah, Abu Dhabi Islamic Bank, Bahrain Islamic Bank, Dow Jones Islamic Index, National Commercial Bank, Saudi American Bank and Saudi Fransi Bank. He is a prolific writer and has published in a number of scholarly journals and authored several books.

2.8.4 Dr Mohd. Daud Bakar

Dr Mohd. Daud Bakar received his PhD from the University of St Andrews, UK. He was the former Associate Professor in Islamic law and Deputy Rector at the International Islamic University, Malaysia. Dr Bakar is the Chief Executive Officer of the International Institute of Islamic Finance. His areas of specialisation include Islamic legal theory, Banking and Finance, Law of *Zakat* and Medieval Law. Dr Bakar is a member of the *Sharia'a* supervisory committees of many financial institutions in Malaysia and around the world, including the Central Bank of Malaysia, Securities Commission of Malaysia, International Islamic Financial Market, Accounting and Auditing Organisation for Islamic Financial Institutions and numerous other institutions. He has published more than 30 articles in academic journals and presented more than 120 papers in various conferences.

2.8.5 Sheikh Nizam M.S. Yaquby

Sheikh Nizam M.S. Yaquby received a BA from McGill University Montreal, Canada, in Economics and Comparative Religion. He has studied traditional Islamic studies under the guidance of eminent scholars, including Sheikh Abdulla al-Farisi, Sheikh Yusuf al-Siddiqi, Sheikh Muhammed Saleh al-Abbasi, Sheikh Muhhamed Yasin al Fadani (Makkah), Sheikh Habib-ur-Rahman A. Zaini (India), Sheikh Abdulla bin Al-Siddiq Al-Ghumar (Morocco) and others.

His areas of specialisation include Khatib in Bahrain Mosques (1981–1990). He also taught *Tafsir*, *Hadith* and *Fiqh* in Bahrain. He is a member of the *Sharia'a* supervisory boards for the Islamic Investment Banking Unit of The Ahli United Bank (UK) PLC London, Abu Dhabi Islamic Bank and numerous other Islamic banks and institutions. He has participated in many Islamic *Da'wah* and *Fiqh* international meetings. His publications include *Risalah fi al Tawbah* (in Arabic), *Qurrat al-Ainayn fi Fada il Birr al-Walidayn* (in Arabic) and *Irshad al-Uqala ila Hukm al Qira h min al-Mushaf fi al-Salah* (in Arabic). He has also participated in over 500 lectures, sermons and training sessions and audio cassette recordings. He speaks Arabic, English and Persian.

2.8.6 Sheikh Muhammed Taqi Usmani

Sheikh Muhammed Taqi Usmani earned an MA in Arabic with distinction from the Punjab University in 1970 and was awarded an LLB with distinction from Karachi University in 1967. His BA is from Karachi University in 1964. In 1961 he earned Takhassus in Ifta from Darul Uloom Karachi. He was awarded an Alimiyyah from Darul Uloom Karachi in 1959 and the Fazil-e-Arabi with distinction from the Punjab University in 1958.

He recently retired as Judge *Sharia'a* Appellate Bench, Supreme Court of Pakistan (where he had been since 1982). He is deputy chairman/permanent member of the International Islamic Fiqh Academy Jeddah (sponsored by the Organisation of Islamic Conference (OIC)) and Vice President of Darul Uloom Karachi. He has been chairman of the Centre for Islamic Economics Pakistan since 1991 and the chairman of the *Sharia'a* boards for Saudi American Bank, Jeddah; Robert Fleming Oasis Fund, Luxembourg; and *Sharia'a* Council, AAOIFI.

He also worked for the Citi Islamic Investment Bank, Bahrain and Amana Investments Ltd, Sri Lanka. He was vice chairman of the *Sharia'a* board of the Abu Dhabi Islamic Bank, Abu Dhabi. He was also a member of the *Sharia'a* boards for The Ahli United Bank (UK) PLC,

London; Al-Baraka Group, Jeddah; and First Islamic Investment Bank, Bahrain. His other accomplishments include:

- being a member of the Commission for Islamization of Economy, Government of Pakistan;
- teaching several branches of Islamic studies for over 40 years;
- participating in many Islamic, *Da'wah* and *Fiqh* meetings across the world.

His publications include over 50 works published in English (including *Islamic Modes of Financing*), Arabic and Urdu. He speaks Arabic, English, Urdu and Farsi.

2.8.7 Sheikh Abdullah Bin Suleiman Al-Maniya

Sheikh Abdullah Bin Suleiman Al-Maniya has been a member of the Senior Ulema Board since its inception in 1971 (1391 AH). He was formerly Judge of the Cassation Court in Makkah Al Mukarramah. He has supervised a number of PhD theses. By delegation he was appointed president of the courts of the Makkah Al Mukarramah. He has compiled a number of *Fatawa* (interpretive opinions) and published several books.

2.8.8 Sheikh Dr Abdullah bin Abdulaziz Al Musleh

Sheikh Dr Abdullah bin Abdulaziz Al Musleh established the branch of Al-Imam Muhammad bin Saud Islamic University in Abha (Saudi Arabia) and was its rector from 1976 until 1994 (1396–1415 AH). He was Dean of the Faculty of *Sharia'a* and Principles of Religion at the Imam Muhammad bin Saud Islamic University, in addition to his work as rector of the University's branch in Abha. At the Faculty he also established the Islamic Economics Division. He was also Director General of the Panel of Scientific Miracles in the *Qur'an* and *Sunnah*. He has published numerous research studies and books.

2.8.9 Sheikh Dr Muhammad Al-Ali Al Qari bin Eid

Sheikh Dr Muhammad Al-Ali Al Qari bin Eid worked as Professor of Islamic Economics at King Abdulaziz University in Jeddah and was an expert at the Fiqh Academy of the Organisation of Islamic Conference in Jeddah. He was also director of the National Administrative Consultancy Centre in Jeddah. He has several publications and books to his name.

2.9 STATE BANK OF PAKISTAN (SBP): PROPER CRITERIA FOR APPOINTMENT OF *SHARIA'A* ADVISORS

According to the State Bank of Pakistan, *Sharia'a* advisors needs the following minimum qualification and experience:

- A minimum of five years experience giving religious rulings.
- A knowledge of, or familiarity with, the banking industry.
- A minimum qualification of Dars-e-Nizami. In higher education, a qualification such as an MA in Islamiat, economics or in the discipline of banking and finance may be an added bonus.

- Where a *Sharia'a* advisor has experience as a teacher of Islamic *Fiqh* in a reputable institution, other than banking institutions, for a period of not less than three years with a proven track record, the number of years of experience necessary may be relaxed.

As well as the above qualifications and experience, *Sharia'a* advisors must have an impeccable track record in the companies with which they have served in the capacity of an employee or director or chief executive or as chairperson. Advisors must not have had their employment terminated or dismissed in the capacity of employee, director or chairman of a company.

2.9.1 Solvency and Financial Integrity

Sharia'a advisors must not be associated with any illegal activity relating to banking business. They must not have been in default of payment of dues owed to any financial institution and/or default in payment of any taxes in an individual capacity or any partnership firm or in any private unlisted and listed company. They must also have sufficient means to discharge financial obligations.

2.9.2 Personal Integrity, Honesty and Reputation

Sharia'a advisors must be honest and have no criminal convictions or have been involved in fraud or forgery or any other financial crime. They must not have been subject to any adverse findings or any settlement in civil or criminal proceedings particularly with regard to financial or business investments, misconduct, fraud, formation or management of a corporate body and so on. They must not have contravened any of the requirements and standards of regulatory system or the equivalent standards of requirements of other regulatory authorities, or been involved with a company, firm or other organisation that has been refused registration or licence to carry out trade or business. Nor must they have been involved with a company or firm whose registration or licence has been revoked or cancelled or gone into liquidation. *Sharia'a* advisors must not have been debarred for giving religious rulings by any religious institution or body.

They must have no conflict of interest; for example, the person cannot be a *Sharia'a* advisor for any other financial institution. The term financial institution includes any bank, investment finance company, nonbanking finance company, venture capital company, housing finance company, leasing company or *Mudaraba* company. The conflict of interest does not apply if a *Sharia'a* advisor is nominated by the SBP to its own *Sharia'a* board.

Source: State Bank of Pakistan

3
Definition of Islamic Banking

The central tenet of Islamic banking, the prohibition of interest (*riba*), stems from the following *Qur'anic* quotation:

> S. 275. Those who eat riba will not stand (on the Day of Resurrection) except like the standing of a person beaten by Shaitân (Satan) leading him to insanity. That is because they say: 'Trading is only like riba', whereas Allah has permitted trading and forbidden riba. So whosoever receives an admonition from his Lord and stops eating riba shall not be punished for the past; his case is for Allah (to judge); but whoever returns [to riba], such are the dwellers of the Fire – they will abide therein.
>
> The *Qur'an* – Al-Baqarah S. 275–281

The prohibition of interest (*riba*) is in fact mentioned in four different revelations in the *Qur'an*. The first revelation emphasises that interest deprives wealth from God's blessings. The second revelation condemns it, placing interest in juxtaposition with wrongful appropriation of property belonging to others. The third revelation enjoins Muslims to stay clear of interest for the sake of their own welfare. The fourth revelation establishes a clear distinction between interest and trade, urging Muslims to take only the principal sum and forgo even this sum if the borrower is unable to repay. It is further declared in the *Qur'an* that those who disregard the prohibition of interest are at war with God and His Prophet.

3.1 CONVENTIONAL BANKERS AND ISLAMIC BANKING

A conventional banker, when asked about Islamic banking, may mumble something about religion and perhaps, 'well they can't charge interest but they use something else which is the same thing'. The 'something else', incidentally, is never defined. The banker may then describe Islamic banking as being about smoke and mirrors, and conclude by profoundly announcing that, with a few tweaks, it is what he does every day anyway.

If pushed to describe an Islamic financial instrument, or some Islamic terminology such as *Murabaha*, *Mudaraba* or so on, the banker's eyes will start to gloss over.

Frankly this stereotyped image of Islamic banking is all too prevalent within the conventional banking world. In an endeavour to both enlighten conventional bankers and broaden the understanding of Islamic banking principles, this chapter goes back to basics. It will highlight the key characteristics of Islamic banking that differentiate it from conventional banking.

Islamic banking is not about smoke and mirrors. It is in fact about banking based on Islamically-ethical principles which are, in many ways, very different indeed from conventional banking principles.

So what exactly is Islamic banking all about? Islamic financial institutions are those based, in their objectives and operations, on *Qur'anic* principles. They are thus set apart from conventional institutions, which have no such religious preoccupations. Islamic banks provide commercial services that comply with the religious injunctions of Islam. Islamic banks provide services to their customers free from interest (the Arabic term for which is *riba*). The giving and taking of interest is prohibited in all transactions. This prohibition makes an Islamic banking system differ fundamentally from a conventional banking system.

Technically, *riba* refers to the addition in the amount of the principal of a loan according to the time for which it is loaned and the amount of the loan. In earlier historical times there was a fierce debate as to whether *riba* relates to interest or usury, although there now appears to be a consensus of opinion among Islamic scholars that the term extends to all forms of interest.

The term *riba*, in Islamic law (the *Sharia'a*), means an addition, however slight, over and above the principal. According to the Federal *Sharia'a* Court of Pakistan, this means that the concept

- covers both usury and interest;
- is not restricted to doubled and redoubled interest;
- applies to all forms of interest, whether large or small, simple or compound, doubled or redoubled.

Therefore, the Islamic injunction is not only against exorbitant or excessive interest, but also against a minimal rate of interest. Financial systems based on Islamic tenets are therefore dedicated to the elimination of the payment and receipt of interest in all forms. This taboo makes Islamic banks and other financial institutions differ, in principle, from their conventional counterparts.

There are a range of modern interpretations of why *riba* is considered *haram* (forbidden) but these are strictly secondary to the religious underpinnings.

The fundamental sources of Islam are the Holy *Qur'an* and the *Sunnah*, a term that in Ancient Arabia meant ancestral precedent or the custom of the tribe, but which is now synonymous with the teachings and traditions of the Prophet Mohammed as transmitted by the relaters of authentic tradition. Both of these sources treat interest as an act of exploitation and injustice and, as such, it is inconsistent with Islamic notions of fairness and property rights. Although it is often claimed that there is more than the prohibition of interest to Islamic banking – such as its contribution towards economic development and a more equitable distribution of income and wealth, its increased equity participation in the economy and so on – nevertheless it derives its specific *raison d'être* from the fact that there is no place for the institution of interest in the Islamic order.

This rejection of interest poses the central question as to what replaces the interest rate mechanism in an Islamic framework. Financial intermediation is at the heart of modern financial systems, and so if the paying and receiving of interest is prohibited, how do Islamic banks operate? Here profit and loss sharing (PLS) comes in, substituting PLS for interest as a method of resource allocation and financial intermediation.

The basic idea of Islamic banking can be simply stated. The operations of Islamic financial institutions primarily are based on a PLS principle. An Islamic bank does not charge interest but rather participates in the yield resulting from the use of funds. The depositors also share in the profits of the bank according to a predetermined ratio. There is thus a partnership between the Islamic bank and its depositors, on one side, and between the bank and its investment clients, on the other side, hereby acting as a manager of depositors' resources in productive uses. This is in contrast with a conventional bank, which mainly borrows funds paying interest on one side of the balance sheet and lends funds, charging interest, on the other. The complexity of Islamic banking comes from the variety (and nomenclature) of the instruments employed, and in understanding the underpinnings of Islamic law.

3.2 SIX KEY ISLAMIC BANKING PRINCIPLES

Six key principles drive the activities of Islamic banks:

- predetermined loan repayments as interest (*riba*) is prohibited;
- profit and loss sharing is at the heart of the Islamic system;
- making money out of money is unacceptable: all financial transactions must be asset-backed;
- speculative behaviour is prohibited;
- only *Sharia'a*-approved contracts are acceptable;
- contracts are sacred.

These principles, as applied to Islamic banking and finance, are set out below.

3.2.1 Predetermined Payments are Prohibited

Any predetermined payment over and above the actual amount of principal is prohibited. Islam allows only one kind of loan and that is *qard al hassan* (literally meaning good loan), whereby the lender does not charge any interest or additional amount over the money lent. Traditional Muslim Jurists have construed this principle so strictly that, according to one Islamic scholar

> the prohibition applies to any advantage or benefits that the lender might secure out of the *qard* (loan) such as riding the borrower's mule, eating at his table or even taking advantage of the shade of his wall.

The principle, derived from this quotation, emphasises that any associated or indirect benefits that could potentially accrue to the lender, from lending money, are also prohibited.

3.2.2 Profit and Loss Sharing

The principle here is that the lender must share in the profits or losses arising out of the enterprise for which the money was lent. Islam encourages Muslims to invest their money and to become partners in order to share profits and risks in a business instead of becoming creditors. Islamic finance is based on the belief that the provider of capital and the user of capital should equally share the risk of business ventures, whether those are industries, service companies or simple trade deals. Translated into banking terms, the depositor, the bank and the borrower should all share the risks and the rewards of financing business ventures.

This is unlike the interest-based commercial banking system, where all the pressure is on the borrower who must pay back the loan, with the agreed interest, regardless of the success or failure of his venture.

The central principle is that under any Islamic financing arrangement the financier is only entitled to returns if risk is involved. If a return is expected there must be risk. If there is no relationship between risk and return, then this financial arrangement is not permitted Islamically. It is this lack of risk, which takes place with allowing *riba*, that makes interest so anathema to Muslims.

The resulting principle is that in order to ensure that investments are made into productive enterprises, Islam encourages particular types of investments so that the community may ultimately benefit. However, Islam is not willing to allow a loophole to exist for those who do not wish to take risks with their investment but are instead intent on hoarding money or depositing money in a bank in return for receiving interest (*riba*) on these funds for no risk (other than the bank becoming insolvent).

Accordingly, under Islam, people invest with risk or suffer loss by keeping their money idle. Islam encourages the notion of higher risks and higher returns and promotes it by leaving no other avenue available to investors. The objective of all this is to encourage investments and thereby provide a stimulus to the economy and encourage entrepreneurs to maximise their efforts to make them succeed.

3.2.2.1 Risk Sharing

As mentioned above one of the most important features of Islamic banking is that it promotes risk sharing between the providers of funds (investors) and the users of funds (entrepreneurs). By contrast, under conventional banking, the investor is assured of a predetermined rate of interest.

In conventional banking, all the risk is borne by the entrepreneur. Whether the project succeeds and produces a profit or fails and produces a loss, the owner of capital is still rewarded with a predetermined return. In Islam, this kind of unjust distribution of risk is not allowed. In pure Islamic banking both the investor and the entrepreneur share the results of the project in an equitable way. In the case of profit, both share this in pre-agreed proportions. In the case of loss, all financial loss is borne by the capital supplier with the entrepreneur being penalised by receiving no return (wages or salary) for his endeavours, at least for the *Mudaraba* mode of Islamic finance (as described in Chapter 5).

3.2.2.2 Emphasis on Productivity as Compared to Credit-worthiness

Under conventional banking, almost all that matters to a bank is that its loan and the interest thereon are paid on time. Therefore, in granting loans, the dominant consideration is the credit-worthiness of the borrower. Under PLS banking, the bank will receive a return only if the project succeeds and produces a profit. Therefore, it is reasoned, an Islamic bank will be more concerned with the soundness of the project and the business acumen and managerial competence of the entrepreneur.

3.2.3 Making Money Out of Money is Not Acceptable

Making money from money is not Islamically acceptable. Money, in Islam, is only a medium of exchange, a way of defining the value of a thing. It has no value in itself, and therefore should not be allowed to generate more money, via fixed interest payments, simply by being deposited in a bank or lent to someone else.

The human effort – that is, the initiative – and risk involved in a productive venture become more important than the money used to finance it. Muslim Jurists consider money as potential capital rather than capital, meaning that money becomes capital only when it is invested in business. Accordingly, money advanced to a business as a loan is regarded as a debt of the business and not capital. As such, it is not entitled to any return (such as interest).

Muslims are encouraged to spend and/or invest in productive investments and are discouraged from keeping money idle. Hoarding money is regarded as being Islamically unacceptable. In Islam, money represents purchasing power, which is considered to be the only proper use of money. This purchasing power (money) cannot be used to make more purchasing power (money) without undergoing the intermediate step of it being used for the creation of goods and services.

3.2.4 Uncertainty is Prohibited

Gharar (uncertainty, risk or speculation) is also prohibited, and so any transaction entered into should be free from these elements. Contracting parties should have perfect knowledge of the counter-values intended to be exchanged as a result of their transactions. In this context the term counter-values is used in the sense of something being deferred, either the price paid or the commodity delivered. Deferral of payment is an acceptable form of debt under Islam, in contrast to predetermined debt in conventional finance. Also, parties cannot predetermine a guaranteed profit. The rationale behind the prohibition of *gharar* is the wish to protect the weak from exploitation. Therefore, options and futures, considered to be very risky, are deemed to be forbidden as are forward foreign exchange transactions, given that forward exchange rates are determined by interest rate differentials.

3.2.5 Only *Sharia'a*-Approved Contracts are Acceptable

Conventional banking is secular in its orientation. In contrast, in the Islamic system, all economic agents have to work within the ethical system of Islam. Islamic banks are no exception. As such, they cannot finance any project that conflicts with the Islamic moral value system. For example Islamic banks are not allowed to finance a wine factory, a casino, a night club or any other activity prohibited by Islam or *known* to be harmful to society.

3.2.6 Sanctity of Contract

Many verses in the Holy *Qur'an* encourage trade and commerce, and the attitude of Islam is that there should be no impediment to honest and legitimate trade and business. It is a duty for Muslims to earn a living, support their families and give charity to those less fortunate.

Just as Islam regulates and influences all other spheres of life, so it also governs the conduct of business and commerce. Muslims have a moral obligation to conduct their business activities in accordance with the requirements of their religion. They should be fair, honest and just towards others. A special obligation exists upon vendors because there is no doctrine of *caveat emptor* in Islam. Monopolies and price-fixing are prohibited.

The basic principles of the law are laid down in the four root transactions of

- sales (*bay*): transfer of the ownership or corpus of property for a consideration;
- hire (*Ijara*): transfer of the usufruct (right to use) of property for a consideration;
- gift (*hiba*): gratuitous transfer of the corpus of property;
- loan (*ariyah*): gratuitous transfer of the usufruct of property.

These basic principles are then applied to the various specific transactions of, for example, pledge, deposit, guarantee, agency, assignment, land tenancy, *waqf* foundations (religious or charitable bodies) and partnerships.

Islam upholds contractual obligations and the disclosure of information as a sacred duty. This feature is intended to reduce the risk of asymmetric information and moral hazard, defined in the next section, which are potentially major problems for Islamic banks.

3.3 DEFINITION OF ASYMMETRIC INFORMATION

Asymmetric information can be defined as information that is known to one party in a transaction but not to the other. The classical argument is that some sellers with inside information about the quality of an asset will be unwilling to accept the terms offered by a less informed buyer. This may cause the market to break down, or at least force the sale of an asset at a price lower than it would command if all buyers and sellers had full information. This is known as the lemon market problem in valuation, with the term lemon referring to a poor quality item, company or borrower.

This concept has been applied to both equity and debt finance as follows:

• For equity finance, shareholders demand a premium to purchase shares of relatively good firms to offset the losses arising from funding lemons. This premium raises the cost of new equity finance faced by managers of relatively high-quality firms above the opportunity cost of internal finance faced by existing shareholders.
• In debt markets, a borrower who takes out a loan usually has better information about the potential returns and risk associated with the investment projects for which the funds are earmarked. The lender on the other side does not have sufficient information concerning the borrower.

Lack of sufficient information creates problems before and after the transaction is entered into, which is potentially a major problem with Islamic profit-sharing financial contracts. The presence of asymmetric information normally leads to adverse selection and moral hazard problems.

3.3.1 Adverse Selection

Adverse selection refers to a situation in which sellers have relevant information that buyers lack (or vice versa) about some aspect of product quality. The term refers to the problem created by asymmetric information *before* the transaction occurs. It occurs when the potential borrowers are the ones most likely to produce an undesirable (adverse) outcome. Bad credit risks are the ones who most actively seek out a loan and are thus most likely to be selected. This is potentially problematic with Islamic profit-sharing financial contracts.

3.3.2 Moral Hazard

Moral hazard is the consequence of asymmetric information *after* the transaction occurs. The lender runs the risk that the borrower will engage in activities that are undesirable from the lender's point of view because they make it less likely that the borrower will repay the loan.

The conventional debt contract is a contractual agreement by the borrower to pay the lender a fixed amount of money at periodic intervals. When the firm has high profits, the lender receives the contractual payments and does not need to know the exact profits of the borrower. If the managers are pursuing activities that do not increase the profitability of the firm, the lender does not care as long as the activities do not interfere with the ability of the firm to make its debt payments on time. Only when the firm cannot meet its debt payments, thereby being in a state of default, is there a need for the lender to verify the state of the firm's profits.

But if debt interest payments are not being made, as under Islamic financing principles, the moral hazard problem is embedded within the system.

3.4 ORIGINS OF ASYMMETRIC RISK WITHIN ISLAMIC BANKING

The principle of PLS stipulates that the partners are free to determine the extent of their profit-sharing ratio regardless of their capital contributions. Losses, on the other hand, are to be shared strictly in proportion to their capital contributions, with *Musharaka* (discussed in detail in Chapter 6). Collateral cannot be provided with PLS activities in the event that the project fails due to business risk. So in the event of the project failing the Islamic bank is exposed to financial loss. The result is that Islamic banks are subject to asymmetric risk.

To ensure timely payment of the repayment obligations plus the institution's share of the profits (if any), the bank could impose a fine on those borrowers who do not pay on time. To conform with the principles of the *Sharia'a* these fines must be deposited with a charity, rather than being given to individual financial institutions. So if the borrower defaults there is no explicit protection for the Islamic bank. Again this is asymmetric risk.

Since PLS emphasises distribution of both risk and profits between the lender and the borrower when a loan is made, the lending institution should, in an ideal world, need only worry about the profitability of the proposed project for which the loan is requested rather than the credit-worthiness of the firm to which they are lending. This should lead to the lender making more conservative decisions and to the need for more careful monitoring of the borrower.

In the conventional banking model, bank regulation and the availability of deposit insurance have replaced the need for monitoring bank activities by depositors. Consequently, as far as small depositors are concerned, deposits in one bank are very similar to deposits in another bank, and hence there is no need to monitor bank activities.

The Islamic, interest-free system, on the other hand, imposes the burden on depositors of gathering information about the safety, soundness, riskiness and profitability of the bank. Again asymmetric risk is a problem.

3.5 *RIBA* IN THE *QUR'AN* AND *SUNNAH* OR *HADITH*

There are two major kinds of *riba*:

- *Riba Al-Nasiah*: Interest on borrowed money.
- *Riba Al-Fadl*: Taking a superior thing of the same kind of goods by giving more of the same kind of goods of inferior quality, for example dates of superior quality for dates of inferior quality.

The literal meaning of interest or *riba*, as it is used in Arabic, means an excess or increase. In the Islamic terminology interest means effortless profit. *Riba* has been described as a loan with the condition that the borrower will return to the lender more than the amount borrowed. One of the main concerns of Muslims, when it comes to financial transactions, is to avoid *riba* in any of its forms. This is despite the fact that the basic foundation of modern business and finance involves interest-based transactions.

The Prophet foretold of a time when the spread of *riba* would be so overwhelming that it would be extremely difficult for Muslims to avoid it. This situation calls for Muslims to be extra cautious before deciding on what financial methods to use in any personal or business transaction. To understand why the ban on interest is so central to Islamic finance it is necessary to examine the textual evidence.

3.5.1 Textual Evidence for the Ban on Interest

The textual evidence comes from both of the primary sources of *Sharia'a* law: the *Qur'an* and the *Hadith*. The following passage comes from the *Qur'an* – *Al-Baqarah* S. 275–281:

> S. 275. Those who eat *riba* will not stand (on the Day of Resurrection) except like the standing of a person beaten by *Shaitân* (Satan) leading him to insanity. That is because they say: 'Trading is only like *riba*', whereas Allah has permitted trading and forbidden *riba*. So whosoever receives an admonition from his Lord and stops eating *riba* shall not be punished for the past; his case is for Allah (to judge); but whoever returns [to *riba*], such are the dwellers of the Fire – they will abide therein.
>
> S. 276. Allah will destroy *riba* and will give increase for *Sadaqah* (deeds of charity, alms, etc.) And Allah likes not the disbelievers, sinners.
>
> S. 277. Truly those who believe, and do deeds of righteousness, and perform *as-Salat* (*Iqâmat-as-Salât*), and give *Zakat*, they will have their reward with their Lord. On them shall be no fear, nor shall they grieve.
>
> S. 278. O you who believe! Be afraid of Allah and give up what remains (due to you) from *riba* (from now onward), if you are (really) believers.
>
> S. 279. And if you do not do it, then take a notice of war from Allah and His Messenger but if you repent, you shall have your capital sums. Deal not unjustly (by asking more than your capital sums), and you shall not be dealt with unjustly (by receiving less than your capital sums).
>
> S. 280. And if the debtor is in a hard time (has no money), then grant him time till it is easy for him to repay, but if you remit it by way of charity, that is better for you if you did but know.
>
> S. 281. And be afraid of the Day when you shall be brought back to Allah. Then every person shall be paid what he earned, and they shall not be dealt with unjustly.

The following is taken from the *Qur'an* – *Al-Imran* S3: 130:

> O you who believe! Eat not riba doubled and multiplied, but fear Allah that you may be successful.

The following two quotes are from the *Hadith*:

> My father bought a slave who practised the profession of cupping (defined below). My father broke the servant's instruments of cupping. I asked my father why he had done so. He replied, 'The Prophet forbade the acceptance of the price of a dog or blood, and also forbade the profession of tattooing, or getting tattooed and receiving or giving riba, and cursed the picture makers'.
> (Cupping means letting out bad blood that is beneath the skin. It is a type of medical treatment.)
> Hadith – Sahih Bukhari, Volume 3, No. 299; Narrated 'Aun bin Abu Juhaifah, r.a.

> He speaks of in a dream related to the Prophet that there is a river of blood and a man was in it, and another man was standing at its bank with stones in front of him, facing the man standing in the river. Whenever the man in the river wanted to come out, the other one threw a stone in his mouth and caused him to retreat back into his original position. The Prophet was told that these people, in this river of blood, were people who dealt in riba.
> Hadith – Sahih Bukhari, 2.468, Narrated Samura bin Jundab, r.a.

The following three *Ahadith* (sayings) have been taken from Mishkat-ul-Masabih under the section on interest. The English version is by Al Hajj Moulana Fazl Karim (218–227, vol. 11):

> Hazrat Jabir has reported that the Messenger of Allah cursed the devourer of usury, its payer, its scribe and its two witnesses. He also said that they were equal (in sin).
> Hazrat Abu Hurairah reported that the Prophet said: A time will certainly come over the people when none will remain who will not devour usury. If he does not devour it, its vapour will overtake him. [Ahmed, Abu Dawood, Nisai, Ibn Majah].

Hazrat Abu Hurairah reported that the Messenger of Allah said: I came across some people in the night in which I was taken to the heavens. Their stomachs were like houses wherein there were serpents, which could be seen from the front of the stomachs. I asked: O Gabriel! Who are these people? He replied these are those who devoured usury. [Ahmed, Ibn Majah].

Finally, Hazrat Al-Khudri reported that the Prophet said:

Gold in exchange for gold, silver in exchange for silver, wheat in exchange for wheat, barley in exchange for barley, dates in exchange for dates, salt in exchange for salt is in the same category and (should be exchanged) hand to hand, so whoever adds or demands increase he has practised usury. The giver and taker are the same.

It is evident from the textual evidence that interest is *haram* (prohibited) for Muslims. Allah has declared war on the user. Islam encourages people to earn their own provision and provide for their families on condition that the earnings are in accord with the *Sharia'a*.

3.5.2 Islamic Rationale for Banning Interest (*Riba*)

One of the main features that distinguish Islamic financial institutions from their conventional banking counterparts is that Islamic institutions adhere closely to the Islamic creed (*aqidah*). Since those institutions are first and foremost Muslim institutions, they share the fundamental Islamic drive to avoid what Allah has forbidden. In this regard, the *Qur'an* contains clear and eternal prohibitions of all kinds of *riba*, whether sales or loan related.

In this context we read, as mentioned earlier: 'But indeed Allah has permitted trading and forbidden *riba*' (S2: 275). The *Qur'an* also states that Allah has ordered Muslims to abandon and liquidate all remaining *riba* (regardless of how large or small): 'O you who believe, fear Allah and give up what remains of *riba*, if you are indeed believers' (S2: 278). And He has declared war on those who devour it: 'If you do not, take notice of a war from Allah and his Messenger; but if you turn back then you shall have your principals without inflicting or receiving injustice' (S2: 279). To deserve such a declaration of war is the severest punishment in all of Islam, providing further proof that *riba* is one of the most severely forbidden of transgressions.

There is no ambiguity about the impermissibility of *riba* within the Islamic financial system. Although the basic source of the ban on the use of interest is the divine authority of the Holy *Qur'an*, somewhat surprisingly no explicit rationale was provided for why this was indeed the case.

The primary rationale for abolishing interest and introducing Islamic banking principles is a religious one, and it is therefore difficult to evaluate the reasoning in purely secular terms. Nevertheless, Islamic scholars have sought to provide a theoretical basis for the prohibition in terms of morality and economics, as discussed in the following section.

3.6 FIVE REASONS FOR THE PROHIBITION OF *RIBA*

Islamic scholars have put forward five reasons for the prohibition of *riba*:

- it is unjust;
- it corrupts society;
- it implies improper appropriation of other people's property;
- it results in negative economic growth;
- it demeans and diminishes human personality.

3.6.1 Interest is Unjust

Among the most important reasons that have been emphasised by most Islamic scholars is that interest is prohibited because it is unjust (*zulm*). A contract based on interest involves injustice to one of the parties, sometimes to the lender and sometimes to the borrower.

Sura 2: 279 of the *Qur'an* clearly states that taking an amount in excess of the principal would be unjust. It also recognises the right of the lender or creditor to the principal without any decrease because that too would be unjust. The *Qur'an* does not rationalise, however, as to why it is unfair to take an excess in the case of a loan. Presumably it relies on the notions of equality and reciprocity inherent in the Islamic concept of justice. The unacceptability of injustice and unfairness was never in dispute between the *Qur'an* and its audience.

What is not so understandable to non-Muslims is the *Qur'anic* stand that taking anything in excess of the principal amounts to injustice.

The *riba* contract is deemed to be unjust to the borrower because if somebody takes a loan and uses it in his business he may earn a profit or he may end up with a loss. In the case of a loss the entrepreneur has received no return for his time and work. In addition to this loss, the borrower has to pay interest and capital to the lender. The lender, or the financier, in spite of the fact that the business has ended up making a loss, has his capital returned as well as his interest. It is in this context that *riba* is deemed unjust.

The *Qur'an* makes clear that individuals having difficulty paying their debts should have their obligations made easier for them and not more difficult. Such individuals may actually deserve charity and it is deemed to be a morally offensive practice to start demanding that they be punished for their failure to pay on time.

Riba, derived from this rationalisation, based on the Prophet's Farewell Address, is the crime of a person or institution that is owed money demanding an 'increase in a debt' owed as a compensation for late payment. The reason for this delay may be that the borrower has suffered some problem but, Islamic scholars argue, a judge must consider the debtor's situation first. If payment is late without good reason and there was no difficulty in making the payment, then demands of payment of additional damages may be legitimate, but this is a matter of judgement for a judge and it is not for one party to be able to impose his desired punishment on the other, it is argued. Automatic penalties built into contracts are also unjust for the same reason. It is argued that for damages to be legitimate, they must be based on the claim of wilful breach of contract, and decided by a judge. Failure to pay may be due to difficulty of circumstances and therefore not something willed by the debtor.

There are thus two related aspects to the practice of *riba* as referred to by the Prophet and the *Qur'an* that make it unjust:

- punishing someone for default is unjust;
- a judge should decide the amount of any compensation for a default, not the party to whom the debt is owed.

The latter aspect is crucial, it is argued, because once a jurisdiction allows for contracts to impose punishments for default, then the law itself becomes nothing but the slave of such contracts and any crime may be legitimised as a form of punishment of the 'debt-slave'. The relationship of one party imposing punishment on another has, it is argued, become that of a master and slave. A transaction in which one party buys something from another should be a relationship of equals. Allah has allowed buying and has forbidden imposed increases in debt (*riba*).

3.6.2 Interest Corrupts Society

The argument here is that there is an association between charging interest with *fasad*, loosely translated as corruption. This argument is revealed in the *Qur'an*, Chapter 30, *Surah Rum*, verses 37–41, along with some of the preceding and following verses. These read:

> That which you give in usury in order that it may increase in other people's property has no increase with Allah; but that which you give in charity, seeking Allah's countenance, has increased manifold. Allah is He Who created you and then sustained you, then causes you to die, then gives life to you again. Is there any of your (so called) partners (of Allah) that does aught of that? Praised and exalted be He above what they associate with him. Corruption does appear on land and sea because of (the evil) which men's hands have done, that He may make them taste a part of that which they have done, in order that they may return.

Within the framework of the general message that *fasad* in society results from people's own (wrong) behaviour, Muslims would read the sub-message that charging interest is one of those facets of wrong behaviour that corrupts society. In fact this may have been the first time, chronologically speaking, that *riba* is mentioned in the *Qur'an*. It was in the fitness of things to highlight its negative social role long before the practice of charging interest was banned.

3.6.3 Interest Implies Unlawful Appropriation of Other People's Property

The reasoning here is indicated in the *Qur'an*, Chapter Four, Surah al-Nisa', where the Jews are admonished for 'taking usury when they were forbidden it, and of their devouring people's wealth by false pretences' (S4: 161). Significantly, the *Qur'an* relates the tendency to appropriate other people's wealth without any justification, to some more serious crimes. In (S9: 34) *riba* is associated with hoarding and (S4: 29) seems to put it at par with murder.

Considering the serious dimensions of *fasad* to which *riba* has been related, the message seems to be clear: charging interest belongs to a mindset that leads to the disruption of civil society. The argument is that interest on money is regarded as representing an unjustified creation of instantaneous property rights. It is unjustified, because interest is a property right claimed outside the legitimate framework of recognised property rights. It is instantaneous, because as soon as the contract for lending upon interest is concluded, a right to the borrower's property is created for the lender.

3.6.4 Interest-Based Systems Result in Negative Growth

The fourth reason is implied in the *Qur'an*'s declaration that *riba* is subject to destruction (S2: 276), which means decrease after decrease, a continuous process of diminishing. That sounds a little odd as it runs counter to the commonly observed fact of people growing rich by applying the power of compound interest. Once we leave out the improbable interpretation of individual wealth amassed through *riba* business being subject to continuous decrease, we have to turn to an alternative interpretation, namely to its effect on social wealth.

Riba, even when it is increasing in numerical terms, it is argued, fails to spur growth in social wealth. That role is played by charitable giving mentioned in the next half of S2: 276. Charitable giving transfers purchasing power to the poor and the needy that are dependent upon it. The destination of interest earnings is not that certain.

Interest, it is argued, also has many adverse consequences for the economy. It results in an inefficient allocation of society's resources, and can contribute to the instability of the system. In an interest-based system the major criteria for the distribution of credit is the credit-worthiness of the borrower. In an Islamic finance sharing system the productivity of the project is more important, thereby encouraging finance to go to more productive projects. In this way, instead of resources going to low-return projects for borrowers with better credit-worthiness, bank lending is more likely to flow to high-return projects even if the credit-worthiness of the borrower is somewhat lower. Therefore the Islamic sharing system is more efficient in allocating resources. It is also deemed to be more efficient because the return to the bank is now linked to the success of the project. In the interest-based system banks do not have to care as much, it is argued, about project evaluation since they obtain a return on their loans irrespective of the success of the project.

Also in conventional banking, if security is provided then a return is guaranteed (or at least part guaranteed) even if the project is a disaster. Although conventional banks, of course, make losses, the argument is that interest-based systems force borrowers to continue to repay loans even when their circumstances are ill-suited to making such repayments, ultimately exacerbating the problem and resulting in default. Interest-based banking systems, therefore, it is argued, may accentuate downturns in the business cycle.

3.6.5 Interest Demeans and Diminishes Human Personality

The fifth reason behind the prohibition of *riba* is inferred from S2: 275, quoted above on page 38. This verse draws a picture of 'those who devour usury' as well as stating the reason why they got into that pitiable mould. That reason is their being trapped into the false economics that equate trade – the act of selling and buying – with the practice of charging interest.

In many cases, the charging of interest may also be demeaning. For example, if the loan is for procuring things necessary for survival, charging interest violates the nature of social life that requires cooperation, care and help for the needy by those who can spare the money.

One may legitimately ask how earning interest can affect your personality. A plausible answer lies in the generally rising level of anxiety in modern interest-based societies. The fact of the matter is that in the complex modern economy the relationship between the one who pays interest and the one who receives interest is not as direct and visible as in the primitive agricultural societies or merchant communities of old. It is mediated by numerous agencies and institutions, which makes it impersonal, potentially raising anxiety levels.

4

Murabaha as a Mode of Islamic Finance

The *Murabaha* contract refers to the sale of goods with a pre-agreed profit mark-up on the cost. *Murabaha* sale is of two types. In the first type, the Islamic bank purchases the goods and makes them available for sale without any prior promise from a customer to purchase them. In the second type, the Islamic bank purchases the goods ordered by a customer from a third party and then sells these goods to the same customer. In the latter case, the Islamic bank purchases the goods only after a customer has made a promise to purchase them from the bank.

Murabaha to the purchase orderer

The *Murabaha* contract, which involves the customer's promise to purchase the item from the institution, is called '*Murabaha* to the purchase orderer'. By this it is distinguished from the normal type of *Murabaha*, which does not involve such a promise by the customer. The *Murabaha* to the purchase orderer is the sale of an item by the institution to a customer (the purchase orderer) for a pre-agreed selling price, which includes a pre-agreed profit mark-up over its cost price. This element has been specified in the customer's promise to purchase. Normally, a *Murabaha* to the purchase orderer transaction involves the institution granting the customer a *Murabaha* credit facility.

A *Murabaha* to the purchase orderer transaction typically involves deferred payment terms, but such deferred payment is not one of the essential conditions of the transaction. A *Murabaha* can be arranged with no deferral of payment. In this case, the mark-up will only include the profit the institution will receive for a spot sale and not the extra charge it will receive for deferral of payment.

Source: Accounting and Auditing Organisation for Islamic Financial Institutions (AAOIFI)

4.1 *MURABAHA* TRANSACTIONS

Murabaha is a term of Islamic *Fiqh* (Islamic jurisprudence). It refers to a particular kind of sale having nothing to do with financing, in its original sense. If a seller agrees with the purchaser to provide him with a specific commodity with a certain profit being added to his cost, it is called a *Murabaha* transaction. The basic ingredient of *Murabaha* is that the seller discloses the actual cost he has incurred in acquiring the commodity, and then adds some profit thereon. This profit may be in a lump sum form or may be based on a percentage.

Murabaha, in its original Islamic connotation, is simply a sale. The only feature distinguishing it from other kinds of sale is that the seller in *Murabaha* expressly tells the purchaser how much cost he has incurred and how much profit he is going to charge, in addition to the cost. If a person sells a commodity for a lump sum price without any reference to the cost, this is not a *Murabaha*, even though he is earning some mark-up profit on his cost, because the sale is not based on a 'cost-plus' concept. In this case, the sale is called *Musawamah*.

Murabaha is sometimes referred to as '*Murabaha* to the purchase-orderer'. In this version the seller (the bank) does not buy and stock goods, but rather waits for buyers to 'order' him to buy goods and then sells them these goods on a *Murabaha* basis.

Murabaha to the purchase-orderer could be defined as an 'arrangement wherein two parties negotiate, agree to specific terms of a sale contract and promise each other to consummate it'. According to this contract, one party 'orders' another to buy a specific commodity and then sell it to him on a *Murabaha* basis. There are four elements to this contract, as follows:

- An order by a prospective buyer to a seller to buy a specific commodity promising to buy it for a profit. Sharia'a scholars consider this order as an invitation to do business. It is not a commitment.
- If the seller accepts this invitation, he is bound to ensure that he can locate the commodity, buy and own it via a true and legitimate contract.
- The seller then makes an offer to the prospective buyer after the commodity has been bought and owned by the seller.
- The prospective buyer has the option to buy the commodity or renege on his promise. If he agrees to buy, then a *Murabaha* contract is formed.

The validity of a *Murabaha* contract depends on various conditions which should be duly observed to make them acceptable in the *Sharia'a*.

In order to understand these conditions correctly, one should, in the first instance, appreciate that *Murabaha* is a sale with all its implications, and that all the basic ingredients of a valid sale contract, under the *Sharia'a*, should also be present in *Murabaha*.

4.1.1 Definition of *Musawama*

Musawama is a general kind of sale in which the price of the commodity to be traded is stipulated between the seller and the buyer without any reference to the price paid or cost incurred by the seller. Thus it is different from *Murabaha* in respect of the pricing formula.

Unlike *Murabaha*, the seller in *Musawama* is not obliged to reveal his costs. All other conditions relevant to *Murabaha* are valid for *Musawama*. *Musawama* can be a preferred mode of finance where the seller is not in a position to ascertain precisely the costs of commodities that he is offering to sell.

4.1.2 Some Terminological Issues

Murabaha is one type of trust sales (*buyu' al-amanah*) where the purchaser puts his trust on the seller to disclose the latter's real cost of buying the subject matter. Based on the cost disclosed by the seller, the purchaser (with agreement between them) buys the subject matter adding a mark-up as a profit to the seller. The strict definition is a cash sale with payment being made promptly.

Bai' Muajjal, in contrast, is a deferred payment sale. In other words, the sold item is given to the purchaser promptly in the *majlis al-aqd* (session or place of contract), but the price is paid to the seller later or as credit. It is also called an *Bai' Bithaman Ajil* (literally meaning a sale with a deferred payment).

In the Malaysian Islamic financial market, *Murabaha* is used for short-term contracts and *Bai' Bithaman Ajil* (popularly used in Malaysia instead of *Bai' Muajjal*) is used for short-term financing. The Central Bank of Malaysia (Bank Negara) recommends that the parties involved differentiate between the two types of contract, to ease the understanding of Islamic financing for business and the public.

However, *Murabaha* and *Bai' Bithaman Ajil* (as practised by the Malaysian Islamic financial institutions) is similar from a *Fiqh* point of view.

4.2 WHAT MAKES *MURABAHA SHARIA'A* COMPLIANT?

In a *Murabaha* transaction, the bank finances the purchase of a good or asset by buying the item on behalf of its client and adding a mark-up before reselling the item to the client, on a cost plus profit basis contract.

It may appear, at first glance, that the mark-up is just another term for interest as charged by conventional banks. Interest, it could be argued, is thus being admitted through the back door. Yet the legality of the traditional type of *Murabaha* is not questioned by any of the schools of *Sharia'a* law.

What makes the traditional *Murabaha* transaction in *Fiqh* books Islamically legitimate is that the bank first acquires the asset for resale at profit, so that a commodity is sold for money and the operation is not a mere exchange of money for money. In the process the bank assumes certain risks between purchase and resale: for example, a sudden fall in price could see the client refusing to accept the goods at the agreed higher price. That is, the bank takes responsibility for the good before it is safely delivered to the client. The services rendered by the Islamic bank are therefore regarded as quite different from those of a conventional bank, which simply lends money to the client to buy the goods.

Understanding the Islamic position involves stepping back from conventional Western thinking regarding the trading of commodities and money in normal commercial transactions. In the conventional financial system, when it comes to matters of trading, money and commodities are both treated at par. Both can be traded. Both can be sold at whatever price the parties agree upon. One can sell one dollar for two dollars on the spot as well as in the future, just as one can sell a commodity valuing one dollar for two dollars. The only condition is that it should be with mutual consent.

Islamic economic principles, however, do not subscribe to this theory. According to these principles, money and commodities have different characteristics and therefore they are treated differently. The basic points of difference between money and commodities, as set out by Usmani (1999) are as follows:

1. Money has no intrinsic utility. It cannot be used for fulfilling human needs directly. It can only be used for acquiring goods or services. Commodities, on the other hand, have intrinsic utility. They can be used directly without exchanging them for some other thing.
2. Commodities can be of different qualities, whereas money has no other quality except that it is a measure of value or a medium of exchange. Therefore, all the units of money, of the same denomination, are 100% equal to each other. An old and dirty bank note of Rs. 1000 has the same value as a brand new bank note of Rs. 1000, unlike commodities that may have different qualities. Obviously an old and used car may be worth much less in value than a brand new car.
3. When it comes to commodities, the transaction of sale and purchase is effected on a particular individual commodity, or at least, on the commodities having particular specifications. If 'A' purchases a particular car by pinpointing it and the seller agrees, 'A' expects to receive

that same car. The seller cannot compel 'A' to take delivery of another car, even of the same type or quality.

4. Money, on the contrary, cannot be pinpointed in an exchange transaction. If 'A' purchases a commodity from 'B' by showing 'B' a particular bank note of Rs. 1000, 'A' can still pay 'B' with another bank note of the same denomination, while 'B' cannot insist that he will only accept the same bank note that was shown to him earlier.

4.3 ISLAM TREATS MONEY AND COMMODITIES DIFFERENTLY

Keeping these differences in mind, Islam has traditionally treated money and commodities differently. Since money has no intrinsic utility, but is only a medium of exchange, the exchange of a unit of money for another unit of the same denomination cannot be effected except at par value. If a currency bank note of US$1,000 is exchanged for another bank note of US dollars, it must be of the value of US$1,000. The price of the former bank note can neither be increased nor decreased from US$1,000 even in a spot transaction, because the currency bank note has no intrinsic utility nor a different quality (recognised legally).

Therefore any excess on either side is without consideration. Hence it is not allowed in the *Sharia'a*. As this is true in a spot exchange transaction, it is also true in a credit transaction where there is money on both sides, because if some excess is claimed in a credit transaction (where money is exchanged for money) it will be against nothing but the time value of money. Charging for the time value of money is deemed to be *riba* and is not acceptable Islamically.

The position when trading commodities is different, from an Islamic perspective. Since commodities have intrinsic utility and have different qualities, the owner is at liberty to sell them at whatever price he wants, subject to the forces of supply and demand. As long as the seller does not commit fraud or a misrepresentation, he can sell a commodity at a price higher than the market rate with the consent of the purchaser. If the purchaser agrees to buy it at that increased price, the excess charged from him is quite permissible for the seller. When he can sell his commodity at a higher price in a cash transaction, he can also charge a higher price in a credit sale, subject only to the condition that he neither deceives the purchaser, nor compels him to purchase, and the buyer agrees to pay the price under his free will.

4.3.1 Commodity Transactions with Credit can Involve an Excess

The upshot of this discussion is that when money is exchanged for money, from an Islamic perspective, no excess is allowed, either in cash or credit transactions. However where a commodity is sold for money, the price agreed upon by the parties may be higher than the market price, both in cash and credit transactions. The time of payment may act as an ancillary factor to determine the price of a commodity, but it cannot act as an exclusive basis for and the sole consideration of an excess claimed in exchange of money for money.

This position is accepted unanimously by all the four schools of *Sharia'a* law and the majority of the Muslim Jurists. The unanimous view is that if a seller determines two different prices for cash and credit sales, the price of the credit sale being higher than the cash price, it is allowed in the *Sharia'a*. The only condition is that at the time of the actual sale, one of the two options must be determined, leaving no ambiguity in the nature of the transaction.

For example, it is allowable for the seller, at the time of bargaining, to say to the purchaser, 'if you purchase the commodity on cash payment, the price would be US$100 and if you purchase it on credit over six months, the price would be US$110'. But the purchaser must select one of the two options: for example, he must say agree to purchase on credit for US$110 if taking the credit option. Thus, at the time of the actual sale, the price must be known to both parties.

4.4 *MURABAHA* AND THE *SHARIA'A*

Murabaha cannot be traced back to the *Qur'an* or to the *Sunnah*. Jurists have justified the use of the principle on other grounds. The Maliki school of jurisprudence has acknowledged the method because it claims that it has always been the practice of the people in Medina. The *Shafii* school and the *Hanafi* School justify the *Murabaha* technique on other grounds, but it is evident that all the schools of jurisprudence accept the usage. As long as it is employed in its original meaning, they consider it to be in conformity with the *Sharia'a*. Evidence from the *Ahadith* is usually used to justify the application of *Murabaha*:

* The legality of a *Murabaha* sale can be justified from

    It is no crime in you if you seek of the bounty of your Lord.

    Al-Baqarah 198

    This is because *Murabaha* represents looking for more. It is also subsumed under the general rule that legalises sale. *Allah sayeth* 'Allah hath permitted trade'.
* The Prophet permitted the sale of the commodity for more than its purchase price. He said: 'if the two commodities are different, buy and sell as you wish'.

4.5 PRACTICALITIES OF IMPLEMENTING *MURABAHA*

In the light of the aforementioned principles, Usmani (1999) sets out the stages and principles that a financial institution should apply when implementing *Murabaha* as a mode of finance:

1. The client and the institution sign an overall agreement whereby the institution promises to sell and the client promises to buy the commodities with an agreed ratio of profit being added to the cost. This agreement may specify the limit up to which the facility may be availed.
2. When a specific commodity is required by the customer, the institution appoints the client as its agent to purchase the commodity on its behalf, and an agency agreement is signed by both the parties.
3. The client purchases the commodity on behalf of the institution and takes possession as an agent of the institution.
4. The client informs the institution that it has purchased the commodity on its behalf, and at the same time, makes an offer to purchase it from the institution.
5. The institution accepts the offer and the sale is concluded whereby the ownership as well as the risk of the commodity is transferred to the client.

All five stages are necessary to effect a valid *Murabaha*. If the institution purchases the commodity directly from the supplier (which is preferable), it does not need any agency agreement. In this case, the second stage is dropped and at the third stage the institution itself purchases the commodity from the supplier. The fourth stage is then restricted to making an offer by the client. *The most essential element of the transaction is that the commodity must remain at the risk of the institution during the period between the third and the fifth stage.*

This is the key feature of *Murabaha* that distinguishes it from an interest-based transaction. Therefore, it must be observed with due diligence at all costs, otherwise the *Murabaha* transaction becomes invalid, according to the *Sharia'a*.

It is also a necessary condition for the validity of Murabaha that the commodity is purchased from a third party. The purchase of the commodity from the same person on a buy-back agreement is not allowed in the *Sharia'a*. *Murabaha* based on a buy-back agreement is effectively an interest-based transaction.

The above mentioned procedure of *Murabaha* financing is a complex transaction whereby the parties involved have different capacities at different stages.

At the first stage, the institution and the client promise to sell and purchase a commodity in future. This is not an actual sale. It is just a promise to effect a sale in future on *Murabaha* basis. Thus at this stage the relation between the institution and the client is that of a Promisor and a Promisee.

At the second stage, the relation between the parties is that of a principal and an agent.

At the third stage, the relation between the institution and the supplier is that of a buyer and seller.

At the fourth and fifth stage, this relationship of buyer and seller comes into operation between the institution and the client. Since the sale is effected on a deferred payment basis, the relationship of a debtor and creditor also emerges between them simultaneously.

All these capacities must be kept in mind and be applied with all their consequential effects, each at its relevant stage. These different capacities should never be mixed up or confused with each other.

The bank may ask the client to furnish some security to its satisfaction for the prompt payment of the deferred price. It may also ask the client to sign a promissory note or a bill of exchange, but this must be after the actual sale takes place, that is at the fifth stage mentioned above. The reason for this is that the promissory note is signed by a debtor in favour of his creditor, but the relationship of debtor and creditor between the institution and the client begins only at the fifth stage, whereupon the actual sale takes place between them.

In the case of default by the buyer when it comes to payment at the due date, the price cannot be increased. However, if the buyer has undertaken, in the agreement to make a donation for a charitable purpose, he is liable to pay the amount undertaken by him. But the amount so recovered from the buyer cannot form part of the income of the seller or financier. The seller is obliged to donate the funds for a charitable purpose as determined by the *Sharia'a* board.

As part of the *Murabaha* transaction, the client will be asked to present some security to the bank at the time of signing the pledge. This security can be in the form of cash or in any other liquid asset, equivalent to about 5% to 10% of the value of the deal. This is called, in Islamic banking jargon, Earnest Money (*Seriousness Margin*), thereby evidencing that the client is serious. This will be used to compensate the bank in the event the buyer failed to honour his commitment to purchase the goods. It is to be noted that this is not a down-payment, because the sale contract is yet to be concluded. In the *Sharia'a* no sale is to be made unless the seller actually has the goods to be sold under his custody.

4.6 *SHARIA'A* RULES CONCERNING *MURABAHA*

Murabaha is not a loan provided in exchange for the charging of interest but is the sale of a commodity. Therefore it has to fulfil all the contractual conditions necessary for a valid *Sharia'a* sale.

Sale is defined in the *Sharia'a* as: the exchange of a thing of value by another thing of value with mutual consent. Islamic jurisprudence has laid down a large number of rules governing the contract of sale, and the Muslim Jurists have written an extensive number of books, in a number of volumes, to elaborate them in detail. Although there are many rules regarding contract of sale, the following three, set out by Usmani (1999), are the most important ones deemed necessary to make any sale valid:

- **The subject of sale must exist at the time of sale.** An item that has not yet come into existence cannot be sold. If a nonexistent item has been sold, even though by mutual consent, the sale is void according to the *Sharia'a*. For example, if 'A' sells the unborn calf of his cow to 'B', this sale is void.
- **The subject of sale must be owned by the seller at the time of sale.** Thus, what is not owned by the seller cannot be sold. If he sells something before acquiring its ownership, the sale is void. For example: 'A' sells 'B' a car that is presently owned by 'C', but 'A' is hopeful that he will buy it from 'C' and deliver it to 'B' subsequently. This sale is void because the car was not owned by 'A' at the time of sale.
- **The subject of sale must be in the physical or constructive possession of the seller when he sells it to another person.** 'Constructive possession' means a situation where the possessor has not taken the physical delivery of the commodity, but the commodity has come into his control, and all the rights and liabilities of the commodity are passed on to him, including the risk of its destruction. For example 'A' has purchased a car from 'B'. After identifying the car, 'B' places it in a garage to which 'A' has free access and allows him to take delivery from that place whenever he wishes. Thus the risk of the car has passed to 'A' and the car is in the constructive possession of 'A'. If 'A' sells the car to 'C' without acquiring physical possession, the sale is valid.

4.7 REASONING BEHIND *SHARIA'A* RULES

The gist of the *Sharia'a* rules, mentioned above, is that a person cannot sell a commodity unless

- It has come into existence.
- It is owned by the seller.
- It is in the physical or constructive possession of the seller.

There is a vast difference between an actual sale and a mere promise to sell. The actual sale cannot be effected unless the above three conditions are fulfilled. A person can, however, promise to sell something that he does not yet own or possess. This promise initially creates only a moral obligation on the Promisor to fulfil his promise, which is normally not enforceable in law.

Nevertheless, in certain situations, especially where such a promise has burdened the promise with some liability, it can be enforceable through a *Sharia'a*-based court of law. In such cases the court may force the Promisor to fulfil his promise, that is, to effect the sale. And if he fails to do so, the court may order him to pay the Promisee the actual damages he has incurred due to the default of the Promisor.

4.7.1 Important Exceptions to *Sharia'a* Rules

The *Sharia'a* rules mentioned above are relaxed with respect to two types of sale:

- *Istisna'a* sale (a contractual agreement for manufacturing goods and commodities, allowing cash payment in advance and future delivery or future payment and delivery – discussed in Chapter 8).
- *Salam* sale (a contract in which advance payment is made for goods to be delivered later – discussed in Chapter 9).

4.8 PRACTICAL EXAMPLES OF THE APPLICATION OF *MURABAHA*

Practical examples of the application of *Murabaha* help to illustrate clearly this mode of finance. The following illustrations are outlined:

- mortgages;
- working capital;
- syndicated credits;
- GSM licences;
- letters of credit;
- car purchase.

4.8.1 Mortgages

Murabaha has been used on the retail level as a technique for financing home sales in accordance with *Sharia'a* requirements. A British bank recently joined with an Islamic bank from the Gulf to organise a facility that would enable clients of the Islamic institution to finance the purchase of homes in the UK. Generally, the facility involves the purchase of a designated residence at a specified price by the British bank which, in turn, resells the property to the consumer, with the purchase price (including a profit component) to be paid in instalments over a period of five years.

4.8.2 Working Capital

In 2005, ABC Islamic Bank and Emirates Islamic Bank were given the joint mandate for a US$70 million, three-year *Murabaha* financing facility for Esfahan Steel Company (ESCO) in Iran.

The proceeds of the facility were to be used for financing ESCO's purchases of raw materials, machinery and equipment for the completion of its coking coal production expansion project. The facility has been guaranteed by the Iranian Mines and Mining Industries Development and the Renovation Organisation of Iran.

4.8.3 Syndicated Credits

Murabaha is mainly used in the context of trade financing. However, it has been used by Islamic and conventional banks to provide a short-term facility to an independent power project in Pakistan called the Hub River project. Using *Murabaha*, several Islamic and conventional banks, including Citibank, formed a syndicate to provide a six-month US$110 million facility to the Hub River Power Company. The facility was used by the company to finance, on a deferred basis, the purchase of equipment needed for the project. The lead manager was Islamic Investment Company of the Gulf, a wholly-owned subsidiary of Dar Al-Maal Al-Islami.

The most significant aspect of this deal was the demonstration that Western banks and Islamic financial institutions could work together in a financing. Relying upon the same technique, Citibank arranged a syndicated facility in July 1994 to provide a six-month US$115 million *Murabaha* financing to the Pakistan Water and Power Development Authority that was used to buy engineering equipment. Since that time many similar deals have been concluded.

4.8.4 Financing of GSM Licences

When a consortium led by Emirates Telecommunications Corporation (Etisalat), the United Arab Emirates telecoms operator emerged in 2007 as the winning bidder in an auction of a second GSM licence in Saudi Arabia, it chose to use Islamic finance facilities to part fund the subsequent roll out of the network. Given the size of the transaction, this decision is viewed as having a significant impact on the future growth of Islamic financing.

The size of the bid was SR12.21 billion (approximately US$3.256 billion) for the GSM licence. The bid also covered a separate licence to operate Saudi Arabia's first 3G network valued at SR753.8 million (US$201 million). Besides Etisalat, the winning consortium included Saudi Arabian partners the General Organisation for Social Insurance (GOSI), Al-Jomaih Holding, Abdul-Aziz al-Saghyir Commercial Investment, Rana Investment, Abdullah & Said Binzagr and Riyadh Cables Group.

Requiring bank finance to fund its licence payment, the Etisalat Consortium ran a competition for the arranger role between two sets of regional and international banks. The favoured group of mandated lead arrangers was chosen and comprised Samba Financial Group, National Commercial Bank, Citigroup, Emirates Bank International, Abu Dhabi Islamic Bank, Al-Rajhi Banking & Investment Corporation, Bank al-Jazira, Dubai Islamic Bank and Kuwait Finance House.

The facilities to be put in place were split into two tranches – tranche A was for an amount of US$1.6 billion to be used for the part-financing of the licence while tranche B worth US$750 million was to be used to acquire equipment for the roll out of the network. Both tranches are *Murabaha* facilities and, in each case, National Commercial Bank was the *Mudarib* (managing partner).

4.8.5 Letters of Credit

An interesting application of *Murabaha* is in the issuing of a letter of credit (L/C). At the Dubai Islamic Bank, L/Cs are opened in the following manner:

1. The customer requests the bank to open a L/C to import goods from abroad through an application enclosing a pro-forma invoice and providing all the necessary details and information.

2. After securing the necessary guarantee and scrutinising the application, the bank opens a L/C in favour of the client and sends copies to the correspondent bank abroad and to the exporter.
3. The customer endorses a 'Promise to Buy' the merchandise. The parties negotiate the cost of the goods and the conditions of delivery.
4. The exporter makes arrangements to export the goods and delivers the documents to the correspondent bank abroad. The shipment of the goods takes place and the correspondent bank advises the bank and sends the documents.
5. After the confirmation of the bank's ownership of the goods in question through the acquisition of related documents, it signs an Agreement of Sale with the client.

4.8.6 Car and House Purchase

At many of the Gulf Cooperation Council (GCC) banks, *Murabaha* is used to finance the purchase of goods, such as cars, that are subject to mortgage. The individual submits an application to the bank requesting the purchase of a car. He promises to buy it at a later stage. The bank issues an invoice to the seller who registers the car in the name of the bank. The seller submits the required document to the bank and receives his payment. The bank sells the car to the purchaser, with the registration in the name of the purchaser, on a deferred payment basis after getting an appropriate guarantee. The guarantee condition may stipulate the mortgage of the car to the bank. *Murabaha* is also applied to the purchase of land and buildings in a similar manner. Meezan Bank, in Pakistan, has similar schemes.

4.9 KEY ISSUES ASSOCIATED WITH *MURABAHA*

Usmani (1999) has set out in detail many of the more controversial issues involved with *Murabaha*. They revolve around the following:

- Can *Murabaha* be benchmarked against an interest rate?
- What about problems of *Gharar* (uncertainty, risk or speculation)? As the required commodity is not owned by the bank at the time of the contract, how can it be allowed to sell it Islamically?
- Given that there are risks associated with the transaction, is it Islamically acceptable to mitigate them?
- Can a bank ask for guarantees?
- Can default penalties be invoked?
- Are roll-overs permissible with *Murabaha*?
- Are rebates for early repayment permissible?
- Subject matter issues.
- Rescheduling issues.
- Securitisation issues.

4.9.1 Use of an Interest Rate as a Benchmark

Many institutions financing by way of *Murabaha* determine their profit or mark-up on the basis of the current interest rate, mostly using London Inter-Bank Offered Rate

(LIBOR) as the benchmark. For example, if LIBOR is 6%, they determine their mark-up on *Murabaha* equal to LIBOR or some percentage above LIBOR. This practice is often criticised on the ground that profit based on a rate of interest should be prohibited as being interest itself.

There is no doubt that the use of the rate of interest for determining a *halal* profit cannot be considered desirable. It certainly makes the transaction resemble an interest-based financing, at least in appearance. Keeping in view the severity of the prohibition of interest, even this apparent resemblance should be avoided as far as possible. But one should not ignore the fact that the most important requirement for the validity of *Murabaha* is that it is a genuine sale with all the Islamic ingredients and necessary consequences.

If a *Murabaha* transaction fulfils all the conditions enumerated, merely using the interest rate as a benchmark for determining the profit of *Murabaha* does not render the transaction invalid, *haram* or prohibited, because the deal itself does not contain interest. The rate of interest has been used only as an indicator or as a benchmark.

4.9.1.1   Benchmarking Against LIBOR is Permitted in Islamic Financial Transactions

A question is often raised as to why Islamic banks, more often than not, base the *Murabaha* mark-up on fluctuating conventional interest benchmarks such as LIBOR. Why not pre-fix the *Murabaha* mark-up at the outset for the entire term? There are two main reasons for this benchmarking:

- The absence of an internationally acceptable Islamic profit benchmark, as compared to LIBOR in conventional banking.
- Apprehension in the customer's mind that he may end up paying higher *Murabaha* mark-up if it is fixed as compared to the fluctuating benchmark-based interest rate charged by a conventional bank.

As there are relatively few Islamic banks as against a very large number of conventional ones, it becomes important, on the part of Islamic banks, to remain competitive and, as such, adjust their profit earnings close to the market. By not adopting market standards, they may not be able to achieve the purpose of adding value to the trusted investments of their shareholders and depositors when acting as *Mudarib*.

The objection raised against the LIBOR benchmarking is that, by subjecting the *Murabaha* mark-up payments as being equal to a rate of interest, the transaction may be rendered akin to an interest-based financing.

The reply to this argument is that as long as all the other *Sharia'a* parameters are fulfilled, the *Murabaha* agreement may use any benchmark for merely determining the amount of periodical mark-up.

Mere use of the conventional benchmark does not render the contract invalid from a *Sharia'a* perspective, because it is simply meant to determine the *Murabaha* mark-up for the underlying asset and is not interest on lending, since nothing is being lent by the bank.

Another question sometimes raised is that given that future variation in the LIBOR rate is unknown, the *Murabaha* mark-up thus tied to it may be uncertain and, in this, case there is an element of *Gharar*. *Gharar* is not allowed under the *Sharia'a* because all considerations in a contract must be clearly known and understood to the parties entering into it. It is true that the *Sharia'a* does not condone a contract with the element of uncertainty in it, primarily to avoid any dispute in future. However, this aspect is absent in *Murabaha* mark-up based on a well defined benchmark since both parties agree that it will serve as criterion for determining the mark-up. As such, whatever *Murabaha* mark-up is ascertained, based on this benchmark, it will be acceptable.

4.9.2 *Gharar* Issues

Another important issue in *Murabaha* financing, which has been the subject of debate among contemporary *Sharia'a* scholars, is that the bank or financier cannot enter into an actual sale at a time when the client seeks *Murabaha* financing, because the required commodity is not, at this stage, owned by the bank. This issue raises questions around what is known as *gharar* (contractual uncertainty). Under the *Sharia'a* rules, one cannot sell a commodity not owned by the potential seller, and nor can the financier effect a forward sale. The bank is therefore bound to purchase the commodity from the supplier. Only then can he sell it to the client after having its physical or constructive possession.

The problem here, for the financier, is that if the client is not bound to purchase the commodity after the financier has purchased it from the supplier, the financier may be confronted with a situation where he has incurred huge expenses to acquire the commodity, but the client refuses to purchase it. The commodity may be of such a nature that it has no other buyer in the market and the buyer may find it is very difficult to dispose of. In this case the financier may suffer an unacceptable loss.

The solution to this problem is sought in the *Murabaha* arrangement by asking the client to sign a promise to purchase the commodity when it is acquired by the financier. Instead of being a bilateral contract usually associated with a forward sale, it is a unilateral promise from the client which binds himself rather than the financier. Being a one-sided promise, it is distinguishable from a bilateral forward contract.

This solution, however, must then be subjected to the objection that a unilateral promise creates a moral obligation but cannot be enforced, according to the *Sharia'a*, by the courts of law. This then leads us to the question as to whether or not a one-sided promise is enforceable in the *Sharia'a*. The general impression, derived from many scholars is that it is not. However, it is important to examine this view in the light of the primary sources of the *Sharia'a*.

A thorough study of the relevant material in the books of Islamic jurisprudence would show that the *fuqahah* (the Muslim Jurists) have different views on the subject. Many of the scholars are of the opinion that fulfilling a promise is a noble quality and it is advisable for the promisor to observe it, and its violation is reproachable, but it is neither mandatory (*wajib*), nor enforceable through the courts. This view is attributed to Imam Abu Hanifah, Imam al-Shafii, Imam Ahmad and to some *Maliki* Jurists. However, many other *Hanafi*, *Maliki* and some *Shafii* Jurists do not subscribe to this view.

4.9.2.1 *Promises, Promises...*

This is not a question pertaining to the *Murabaha* mode of finance alone. If promises are not enforceable in commercial transactions, it may seriously jeopardise other commercial activities. If somebody orders a trader to obtain for him certain goods and promises to purchase it from him, on the basis of which the trader obtains the goods, how can it be allowable for the former to refuse to purchase them? Nothing in the *Qur'an* or *Sunnah* prohibits the making of such promises enforceable.

The Islamic Fiqh Academy, in Jeddah, has made promises in commercial dealings binding on the Promisor with the following conditions:

- It should be a one-sided promise.
- The promise must have caused the Promisee to incur some liabilities.
- If the promise is to purchase something, the actual sale must take place at the appointed time by the exchange of offer and acceptance. A mere promise itself should not be taken as a concluded sale.
- If the Promisor backs out of his promise, the *Sharia'a* court may force him either to purchase the commodity or pay actual damages to the seller. The damages will include the actual monetary loss suffered by him, but cannot include the time value of money, nor the opportunity cost incurred.

On these bases, it is allowable that the client promises the financier that he will purchase the commodity after the latter acquires it from the supplier. This promise will be binding on him and may be enforced through the *Sharia'a* courts. This promise does not amount to the actual sale. It will be simply a promise and the actual sale will take place after the commodity is acquired by the financier for which an exchange of offer and acceptance will be necessary.

4.9.3 Collateral Provisions Against the *Murabaha* Payment

Another issue regarding *Murabaha* financing revolves around the fact that the *Murabaha* payment is payable at a later date. The seller or financier naturally wants to make sure that the price will be paid at the due date. For this purpose he may ask the client to furnish some acceptable security. The security may be in the form of a mortgage or a hypothecation or some other kind of lien or charge.

The question then arises as to whether the security can be claimed rightfully where the transaction has created a liability or a debt. The *Sharia'a* rule here is that no security can be requested from a person who has not incurred a liability or debt. The procedure of *Murabaha* financing comprises different transactions carried out at different stages, as discussed earlier. In the earlier stages of the procedure the client does not incur a debt. It is only after the commodity is sold to him by the financier on credit that the relationship of a creditor and a debtor comes into existence. The correct procedure in a *Murabaha* transaction would be that the financier asks for security after he has actually sold the commodity to the client and the price has become due on him because, at this stage, the client incurs a debt.

However, it is also permissible that the client furnishes security at earlier stages, but after the *Murabaha* price is determined. In this case, if the security is possessed by the financier, it will remain at his risk. Therefore, if the commodity is destroyed before the actual sale to the client, he will have either to pay the market price of the mortgaged asset, and cancel the agreement of *Murabaha*, or sell the commodity required by the client and deduct the market price of the mortgaged asset from the price of the sold property.

4.9.4 Guaranteeing the *Murabaha*

The seller in a *Murabaha* financing can also ask the purchaser or client to furnish a guarantee from a third party. In the case of default regarding the payment at the due date, the guarantor will be liable to pay the amount guaranteed by him. The *Sharia'a* rules regarding guarantees as set out in the books of Islamic *Fiqh*, however, do specify certain rigorous restrictions associated with these guarantees. They are not something to be entered into lightly.

4.9.5 Penalty of Default

Murabaha is a sale transaction, irrespective of the mode of payment, and the sale price is fixed. Hence, if a client defaults on payment on the due date, the sale price cannot be increased. This is a major problem in *Murabaha* financing in that, if a client defaults, the price cannot be increased. In interest-based loans, the amount of loan continues increasing according to the length of the period of default. In *Murabaha* financing, however, once the price is fixed, it cannot be increased. This *Sharia'a*-based restriction is sometimes exploited by dishonest clients who deliberately avoid paying on the due date, because they know that they will not have to pay any additional amount on account of default.

In contrast to conventional finance, the concept of compensation in such circumstances is not accepted by the majority of the present day *Sharia'a* scholars. It is their considered opinion that the concept of compensation does not conform to the principles of *Sharia'a* and is not designed to solve the problem of default.

In favour of charging compensation, it is argued that the Prophet condemned the person who delays the payment of his dues without a valid cause. According to the well-known *Hadith* he said:

> The well-off person who delays the payment of his debt, subjects himself to punishment and disgrace.

The argument here being that the Prophet permitted the infliction of a punishment on such a person. The punishments may be of different kinds, including the imposition of a monetary penalty. But this argument overlooks the fact that even if it is assumed that imposing a fine or a monetary penalty is allowed in the *Sharia'a*, it is imposed by a court of law and is normally paid to the government. It has rarely been the case that an aggrieved party imposes a fine on its own (and for its own benefit) without a judgement of a court, competent to decide the matter. The outcome of this is that debtors have an incentive, with *Murabaha*, to default, hence the need for guarantees and collateral provision as security.

If the financing is repaid on time the transaction is terminated. If there is delay in repayment, scholars are of the opinion that since the transaction is a sale and purchase, the seller cannot claim anything over and above the agreed price. But in order to discourage wilful delays by the client, most of the banks claim a penalty for non-fulfilment of promise, equal to the average rate of return for the *Mudaraba* accounts of the bank, but they must use the amount for charitable purposes and *qard al hasan* (a benevolent loan). There is, however, no penal interest such as conventional banks would normally charge, nor is the penalty clause, appearing in the *Murabaha* Agreement, enforced if the delay is for reasons beyond the control of the client.

4.9.5.1 *Exploitation Issues*

It is common knowledge that this *Sharia'a* restriction has been intentionally exploited by some elements, knowing full well that their repayment obligation to an Islamic bank will retain its status quo even if they delay repayment. The problem in the *Murabaha* contract, as envisioned by contemporary Jurists, is that they refuse to give an explicit value to the deferral element of the price. Accordingly, if an individual buys an asset at a deferred price on day one, payable in 10 years, and then goes bankrupt on day two, the individual becomes liable for the entire amortised purchase price, even though only one day has elapsed since entering the contract.

Under conventional finance, the individual would only be liable for one day of interest, not 10 years of interest, as would be the case when treating a delayed price independently of the time element. In a resolution passed by the Organisation for Islamic Conference (OIC) Fiqh Committee, the committee said that in this situation the parties can bargain the debt to a discount after bankruptcy, but not agree to one prior to bankruptcy per an amortisation schedule.

This situation results in a bilateral monopoly giving the creditor unjustified leverage not only over his debtor, but also relative to other creditors whose debts are of shorter term, thereby allowing longer-term debtors to extract a larger claim of the bankrupt's estate than they would otherwise be entitled to. Ironically, if there is a rule of mandatory acceleration upon bankruptcy without discounting the debt to present value, the creditor might be better off, at least in some cases, to have his debtor go bankrupt.

4.9.6 No Roll-Over in *Murabaha*

In an interest-based financing, if a customer of the bank cannot pay at the due date for any reason, he may request the bank to extend the facility for another term. This facility is known as a roll-over. If the bank agrees, the facility is rolled over on the terms and conditions mutually agreed at that point of time, whereby the newly agreed rate of interest is applied to the new term. The practical result is that another loan of the same amount is re-advanced to the borrower.

A *Murabaha* transaction, however, cannot be rolled over for a further period. *Murabaha* is not a loan. It is the sale of a commodity the price of which is deferred to a specific date. Once the commodity is sold, its ownership is passed onto the client. It is no longer the property of the seller. What the seller can legitimately claim is the agreed price which has become a debt payable by a buyer. Therefore, there is no question of effecting another sale on the same commodity between the same parties. Any roll-over in *Murabaha*, it is argued, would be purely interest, because it is an agreement to charge an additional amount on the debt created by the *Murabaha* sale.

4.9.7 Rebate on Earlier Payment

Sometimes the debtor may want to pay earlier than the specified date. In this case the debtor usually wants to earn a discount on the agreed deferred price. The question is whether it is permissible to allow the debtor a rebate for paying early.

This question has been discussed by the classical Jurists in detail. The issue is known in the Islamic legal literature and translated from Arabic as 'give the discount and receive soon'. The majority of Muslim Jurists, including the four recognised schools of Islamic jurisprudence, do not allow it if the discount is held to be a condition for earlier payment.

In a *Murabaha* transaction effected by an Islamic bank or institution, no such *rebate* can be stipulated in the agreement, nor can the client claim it as his right. However, if the bank or a financial institution gives the client a rebate on its own volition, this is not deemed objectionable, especially where the client is a needy person. For example, if a poor farmer has purchased a tractor or fertiliser on the basis of *Murabaha*, and wants to repay early, the bank is advised to give him a voluntary discount.

4.9.8 Subject Matter of *Murabaha*

All commodities that can be the subject matter of sale with profit can be the subject matter of *Murabaha*, given that it is a particular kind of sale. Conversely, no *Murabaha* can be effected on things that cannot be the subject matter of sale. For example *Murabaha* is not possible in the exchange of currencies, because it must be spontaneous or, if deferred, on the exchange rate prevalent on the date of transaction. Similarly commercial paper, representing a debt receivable by the holder, cannot be sold or purchased except at par value. Therefore, no *Murabaha* can be effected in respect of such paper. Any commercial paper entitling the holder to receive a specified amount of money from the issuer cannot be negotiated. The only way it can be sold is to transfer it at face value. The effect is that this type of commercial paper cannot be sold on a *Murabaha* basis.

4.9.9 Rescheduling of the Payments in *Murabaha*

If the purchaser or client in *Murabaha* financing is not able to pay, according to the dates agreed upon in the *Murabaha* agreement, he may request the seller or the bank to reschedule the instalments. In conventional banks, the loans are normally rescheduled on the basis of additional interest. This is not possible in *Murabaha* payments. If the instalments are rescheduled, no additional amount can be charged for rescheduling. The *Murabaha* price must remain the same.

4.9.10 Securitisation of *Murabaha*

Murabaha is a transaction that cannot be securitised thereby creating a negotiable instrument to be sold and purchased in the secondary market. The reason follows from the earlier discussion. If the purchaser or client in a *Murabaha* transaction signs a financial document to evidence his indebtedness towards the seller or financier, the document will represent a monetary debt receivable from him. In other words, it represents money payable by him. Therefore, the transfer of this commercial paper to a third party will mean the transfer of money.

As mentioned earlier where money is exchanged for money (in the same currency) the transfer must be at par value. The commercial paper cannot be sold or purchased at a lower or higher price. Therefore, the commercial paper representing a monetary obligation, arising out of a *Murabaha* transaction, cannot create a negotiable instrument. If the commercial paper is transferred, it must be at par value.

4.10 COMPARISON OF *MURABAHA* WITH INTEREST-BASED FINANCE

The best way of illustrating the differences is as shown in Figure 4.1; that is, to observe the working mechanics of a conventional bank and its relationship with depositors and borrowers, and to then compare this with *Murabaha* finance in an Islamic bank.

4.11 *MURABAHA* DIFFERENCES FROM THE OTHER ISLAMIC FINANCING TECHNIQUES

There are several ways to classify Islamic finance modes of finance. In this context the contracts are broken down into two groups (see Figure 4.2).

- Islamically permissible deferred sales contracts;
- profit and loss share contracts.

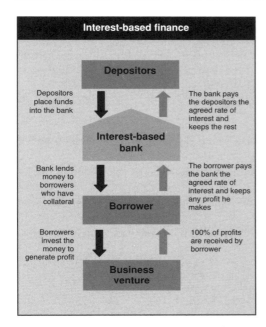 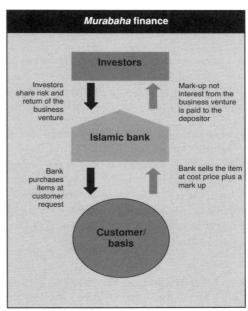

Figure 4.1   Conventional interest-based finance as compared with *Murabaha* finance

4.11.1 Islamically Permissible Deferred Sales Contracts

Jurists have ruled it valid to sell an object immediately, with a deferred price, possibly paid in instalments, greater than its cash price. All the major *Madhabs* (Schools of Islamic jurisprudence), *Shafiis*, *Hanafis*, *Malikis* and *Hanbalis* have agreed to this. The rationale is that the seller of an object for a price to be paid in instalments, in the future, is sacrificing a benefit in order to make the object available to the person who is buying it with a deferred payment.

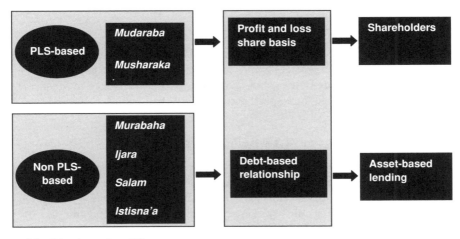

Figure 4.2   Islamic modes of finance

This sacrifice is based on the fact that the seller gets paid at a later date. Thus the seller is making a sacrifice in that he is not able to get paid today and thereby purchase something else or simply have the cash today. Thus, the increase in the deferred price may be viewed as compensation to the seller. The Jurists ruled these sales valid as long as the contract is independently specified and contains no ignorance (*jahala*).

Islamically permissible deferred sales create deferred obligations using the concept of counter-values and were discussed in Chapter 3:

- *Murabaha*: sale with a known profit. The object of sale is delivered at the contract time but the price becomes due as debt.
- *Salam* sale. The price is paid at the time of contract but the object of sale becomes due as debt-in-kind.
- *Istisna'a* sale. The price is paid at the time of contract and the object of sale is to be manufactured and delivered later.
- *Ijara*. Sale of the rights to use assets where assets are delivered to the user, who in turn pays periodical rentals later.

4.11.2 Profit and Loss Share (PLS) Contracts

A PLS contract means that the outcome is sharing-based and cannot be predetermined. Shareholders are only repaid if profits are made and if no profits are made then no payouts take place. The two types of PLS contracts are described below.

4.11.2.1   Mudaraba *PLS Contracts*

The *Mudaraba* contract is a contract between two parties: an Islamic bank as an investor (*Rab ul Mall*) who provides a second party, the entrepreneur (*Mudarib*), with financial resources to finance a particular project. Profits are shared between the parties in a proportion agreed in advance. Losses are the liability of the Islamic bank and the *Mudarib* sacrifices only its efforts and expected share in the profits.

4.11.2.2   Musharaka *PLS Contracts*

The *Musharaka* PLS contract is an equity participation contract. The bank is not the sole provider of funds to finance a project. Two or more partners contribute to the joint capital of an investment. Profits are shared between the parties in a proportion agreed in advance. Losses are shared strictly in relation to the respective capital contributions.

4.12 SUMMARY

The *Murabaha* financing mode comprises more than 75% of Islamic banks' financing activities. (To help clarify *Murabaha* further, see the flow chart in Figure 4.3.) Although Islam encourages PLS-based solutions, these account for only 10% or so of total assets. The PLS principle is rarely strictly applied. Since Islamic banks appear to survive primarily on non-PLS financing techniques, this has been referred to as a legal embarrassment for purists in the Islamic finance industry.

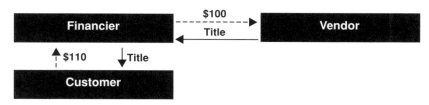

Figure 4.3   Murabaha – cost plus financing

That so many banks and clients prefer the *Murabaha* method of financing is, however, not particularly surprising. The bank with PLS projects is taking larger risks, and must often cope with excessive project evaluation costs. At the same time, since the amount owed to the bank in a profit-sharing contract often exceeds the amount to be paid in a *Murabaha* contract, the borrowers also face potentially higher borrowing costs in PLS-mode financing, when the project succeeds. Accordingly, banks and borrowers often choose the mark-up mode. This development is often referred to as the '*Murabaha* syndrome'.

Another concern is that Islamic banks have significantly twisted the principle of *Murabaha*. They have, on occasions and on Islamically dubious grounds, justified *Sharia'a*-contrary behaviour: for example, the allowance of time-value of money and the enforcement of penalty fees on clients who are unable to pay. Many scholars now demand that the banks reduce their use of synthetic *Murabaha* transactions, on the grounds that they very much resemble interest-based lending.

Other scholars insist that the *Murabaha* concept should not be employed at all, because they consider both the concept itself, as well as the widespread practice of complicated contractual texts in *Murabaha* transactions, to be a shameful face of Islamic banking. The application, they say, is no more than a dishonest method to avoid the *riba* proscription. PLS contracts, they claim, should always be applied.

A related issue is the sell-and-buy-back contract (*bai-al-inah*), which is a variation on the commissioned purchase model of *Murabaha*. A number of classical schools of law consider this transaction to be a device merely designed to circumvent the prohibition of *riba*. Other schools, for instance the *Shafii* School, consider it as a valid contract of sale, notwithstanding the intention of the parties, which the *Shafii* School views as irrelevant. Malaysia has opted for the *Shafii* School and therefore consents to the application of the sell-and-buy-back contract.

Meanwhile the *Sharia'a* Appellate Bench of the Supreme Court of Pakistan condemns the sell-and-buy-back contract, saying it is to '. . . make fun of the original concept' and claiming it to be '. . . repugnant to the Holy *Qur'an* and *Sunnah*'.

REFERENCE

Usmani, T.U. (1999). *An Introduction to Islamic Finance*. Idaratul-Ma'arif, Karachi, Pakistan.

5

Mudaraba as a Mode of Islamic Finance

Mudaraba is a partnership in profit between capital and work. It is conducted between investment account holders, as owners of capital, and the Islamic bank as a *Mudarib* (managing partner).

The Islamic bank announces its willingness to accept the funds of investment account holders with the sharing of profits being as agreed between the two parties and the losses being borne by the owner of funds unless they were due to misconduct, negligence or violation of the conditions agreed upon by the Islamic bank.

A *Mudaraba* contract may also be concluded between the Islamic bank, as a provider of capital on behalf of itself or on behalf of investment account holders, and business owners.

Source: Accounting and Auditing Organisation for Islamic Financial Institutions (AAOIFI)

5.1 DEFINITION OF *MUDARABA*

The term refers to a form of business contract in which one party brings capital and the other brings personal effort and time to a business transaction. The proportionate share in profit from the business deal is determined by mutual agreement. But the loss, if any, is borne only by the owner of the capital, in which case the entrepreneur gets no share of the profits for his labour. The financier is known as *Rab ul Mall* and the entrepreneur as *Mudarib*.

As a financing technique adopted by Islamic banks, it is a contract in which all the capital is provided by the Islamic bank while the other party manages the business for an agreed wage. The profit is shared in pre-agreed ratios, and any loss, unless caused by negligence or violation of terms of the contract by the *Mudarib*, is borne by the Islamic bank. The bank passes on this loss to the depositors, known as investment account holders.

To repeat, there is no loss sharing in a *Mudaraba* contract. Profit and loss sharing is what takes place with the *Musharaka* contract (discussed in detail in Chapter 6). The *Mudaraba* contract may better be represented by the expression 'profit sharing'. *Mudaraba* is an Islamic contract in which one party supplies the finance and the other party provides management expertise in order to undertake a specific business transaction. The party supplying the capital is called the owner of the capital. The other party is referred to as the worker or agent (the *Mudarib*) who actually runs the business. Under Islamic jurisprudence, different duties and responsibilities have been assigned to each of these two parties.

As a matter of principle the owner of the capital does not have a right to interfere in the management of the business enterprise. This is the sole responsibility of the agent. However, he has every right to specify such conditions that would ensure better management of his money, which is why *Mudaraba* is sometimes referred to as a sleeping partnership.

An important characteristic of *Mudaraba* is the arrangement of profit sharing. The profits in a *Mudaraba* agreement may be shared in any proportion agreed between the parties beforehand. However, the loss is to be completely borne by the owner of the capital. In the case of loss, the capital owner must bear the monetary loss and the agent sacrifices the reward for all his effort. Box 5.1 illustrates the terminology used when discussing *Mudaraba*.

Box 5.1 *Mudaraba* terminology

- *Mudarib*: Working partner (brings effort and entreprenenial skills)
- *Ras ul Mall*: Investment funds
- *Rab ul Mall*: Investor (brings capital)
- *Wakeel*: Agent
- *Ameen*: Trustee
- *Kafeel*: Guarantor

5.1.1 Types of *Mudaraba*

There are two types of *Mudaraba*:

- *Mudaraba Al Muqayyadah* (restricted *Mudaraba*). Under this scheme the *Rab ul Mall* may specify a particular choice of business or a particular place of business for the *Mudarib*, in which case he must invest the money in that particular business or place.
- *Mudaraba Al Mutlaqah* (unrestricted *Mudaraba*). Under this scheme the *Rab ul Mall* gives full freedom to the *Mudarib* to undertake whatever business it deems fit. Without the consent of the *Rab ul Mall*, however, the *Mudarib* cannot invest money with anyone. The *Mudarib* is authorised to do whatever is normally done in the course of business, but cannot undertake something beyond the normal routine of the business without the express permission of the *Rab ul Mall*.

The *Mudarib* is also not authorised to

- keep (work with) another *Mudarib* or a partner;
- mix its investment in that particular *Mudaraba* without the consent of the *Rab ul Mall*. To help clarify the *Mudaraba* arrangement, please see the flow chart in Figure 5.1, which depicts a two-tiered contract as described in the next section.

5.1.2 Two-tier *Mudaraba* and the Asset and Liability Structure of an Islamic Bank

Islamic bankers have adapted and refined the *Mudaraba* concept to form what is known as the two-tier *Mudaraba*. In this arrangement, the *Mudaraba* contract has been extended to include three parties: the depositors as financiers, the bank as an intermediary and the entrepreneur who requires funds. The bank acts as an entrepreneur or *Mudarib* when it receives funds from depositors and as a financier (*Rab ul Mall*) when it provides the funds to entrepreneurs.

The main conditions associated with a Two-tier *Mudaraba* contract are as follows:

1. The bank receives funds from the public on the basis of unrestricted *Mudaraba*. These funds are also called 'unrestricted investment accounts'. There are no constraints imposed on the bank concerning the kind of activity, duration and location of the enterprise wherein it invests the finance. However, a *Mudaraba* contract cannot be applied to finance *haram*

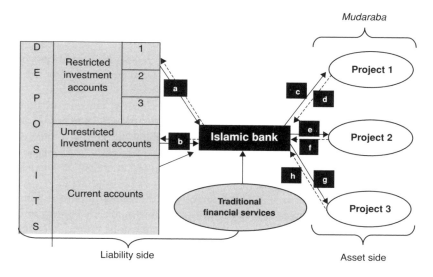

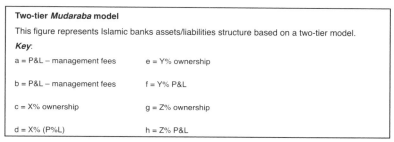

Figure 5.1   Mudaraba flow chart

activities (that is, those forbidden by Islam). Such a contract would be considered null and void.

2. The bank has the right to aggregate and pool the profit from different investments, and share the net profit (after deducting administrative costs, capital depreciation and Islamic tax) with depositors, according to a specified formula. In the event of losses, the depositors lose a proportional share or the entire amount of their funds. The return to the financier has to be strictly maintained as a share of profits.

3. The bank applies the restricted form of *Mudaraba* when funds are provided to specified entrepreneurs. The bank has the right to determine the kind of activities, the duration and the location of the projects, and to monitor the investments. However, these restrictions may not be formulated in a way so as to harm the performance of the entrepreneur. When a project is undertaken, the bank cannot interfere with the management of the investment nor take part in the daily operation of the business. Thus loan covenants and other such constraints, considered usual in conventional bank lending, are not allowed in PLS-based Islamic banking.

4. Under a *Mudaraba*, the *Rab ul Mall* cannot demand any guarantee from the *Mudarib*, such as insisting on a return of the capital with a fixed profit, because the relationship between

the investor and the *Mudarib* is a fiduciary one: that is, a legal relationship between the parties. The *Mudarib* is deemed to be a trustworthy person. Accordingly, the bank cannot require any guarantee such as security and collateral from the entrepreneur in order to insure its capital against the possibility of an eventual loss. Such a condition would make the *Mudarib's* contract null and void. But a guarantee from an independent third party is allowable.

5. The *Mudaraba* contract should assign a profit rate for each party. The rate should be a ratio, and not a fixed amount. Assigning a fixed amount to either party invalidates the *Mudaraba* due to the possibility that the profit realised may not equal the sum so stipulated. Before arriving at a profit figure the *Mudaraba* venture should be converted to a monetary amount and the capital should be set aside. The *Mudarib* is entitled to deduct all business-related expenses from the *Mudaraba* capital.

6. The liability of the financier is limited exclusively to the capital provided. On the other hand, the liability of the entrepreneur is also restricted, but in this case solely to his labour and effort. Nevertheless, if negligence or mismanagement can be proven, the entrepreneur may be liable for any financial loss and be obliged to remunerate the financier accordingly.

7. The entrepreneur shares the profit with the bank according to a previously agreed profit division. Until the investment yields a profit, the bank is able to pay a salary to the entrepreneur. This salary is determined on the basis of the ruling market salary rates.

5.1.3 Sources of Finance for an Islamic Bank

An Islamic bank is traditionally organised as a joint stock company with the shareholders supplying the initial capital. It is managed by the shareholders through their representatives on the board of directors. Its main business is to obtain funds from the public on the basis of *Mudaraba* and to supply funds to entrepreneurs on the same basis. Its gross income comprises the share in the actual profits of the fund users, in accordance with an agreed ratio of profit sharing. That income, after deducting the expenses incurred in managing the funds, is distributed pro rata to the shareholders as dividends. The bank retains, in favour of its shareholders, part of the profits according to deposits, in accordance with the predetermined profit-sharing ratio.

In addition to the unrestricted *Mudaraba* investment deposits mentioned earlier, there can also be restricted *Mudaraba* investment accounts in which deposits are made for investments in particular projects. These are sometimes known as special investment accounts, in which deposits are made on condition that they be invested in particular business activities, for example, trade financing on a *Murabaha* (mark-up) basis, or leasing, and so on.

Another financing alternative is current accounts in which deposits are made that can be withdrawn at any time. These are current accounts on which banks pay no profit, but they are allowed to use these deposits profitably at their own risk. Current accounts are regarded as loans to banks whose repayment is guaranteed.

An Islamic bank's funds comprise share capital, current accounts and various types of *Mudaraba* investment deposits.

The main feature of the Two-tier model is that it replaces interest by profit sharing on both the liabilities and the assets side of the bank's balance sheet. This change brings about, it is argued, a number of positive effects for the efficiency, equity and stability of the banking system. The structure of the activities of an Islamic bank is represented in Figure 5.2.

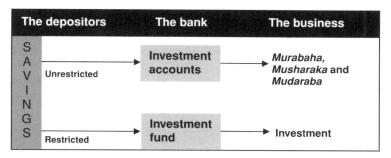

Figure 5.2   A stylised Islamic banking model

5.1.4 *Mudaraba* as Limited Recourse Debt Finance

Mudaraba can usefully be thought of as limited recourse debt finance. The entrepreneur is indebted to the *Rab ul Mall* in the sense that the *Rab ul Mall* has a first priority claim on the cash flows of the enterprise until it recovers its initial investment. After this time the profit share element takes place. The debt is limited recourse, however, because the *Rab ul Mall* has no claim to the assets of the entrepreneur in the event that the cash flows of the enterprise fail to generate sufficient return to pay back its initial investment.

This situation differs from limited recourse debt investments primarily on the upside. Instead of the investor getting a priority claim on the profits of the venture (in exchange for a fixed cap on the absolute amount of those profits, for example, 5% annually), the investor and the entrepreneur share the profits pro rata according to a fixed formula. In other words, *Mudaraba* mimics a debt investment on the downside, because the investor is given a first priority claim on the investment's assets up to the point where the investment reaches the breakeven point. At this point it becomes an equity investment and the investor's priority disappears.

The hybrid debt-equity structure of *Mudaraba* is reflected in the *Maliki* term for this investment vehicle, *qirad*, which is derived from *qard* (loan), because the investor lends money to the entrepreneur to invest it on his behalf.

5.2 WHAT MAKES *MUDARABA SHARIA'A* COMPLIANT?

In order to establish what makes *Mudaraba Sharia'a* compliant, it is important first to examine the origin of the term, before continuing to demonstrate how it complies with the *Sharia'a*.

5.2.1 Origin of the Term *Mudaraba*

The word *Mudaraba* is derived from the Arabic term *darb fi al-ard*, which means those 'who journey through the earth (*yadribuna fi al-ard*) seeking the bounty of Allah' (*Qur'an*, S. 73: 20). Because of his work and travel, the *Mudarib* becomes entitled to part of the profits of the venture. In terms of the *Sunnah*, Jurists rely on the precedent of the contract of *Mudaraba* concluded by the Prophet Mohammed with Khadija prior to his marriage to her, as a result of which he travelled to Syria. Thus the legal evidence employed in support of the *Mudaraba* mode of finance comes from both the *Qur'an* and the *Sunnah*.

5.2.1.1   *Evidence of Legality Under the* **Sharia'a (Hadith)**

It was proved in the *Sira* biography of the Prophet, that before prophethood, he travelled to Syria as a *Mudarib* using the capital of Khadija, and the Messenger of Allah related that he approved it.

The Companions of the Prophet transacted, using *Mudaraba*, and none of them was reported to have an adverse opinion of the contract. There has also been a consensus among the *Ummah*, for many generations, on the permissibility of *Mudaraba*.

> Others travelling through the land Seeking of Allah's bounty.
>
> Al-Muzzammil 20

> It is no crime in you if ye seek of the bounty of your Lord.
>
> Al-Baqara 198

5.3 PRACTICALITIES OF IMPLEMENTING *MUDARABA*

There are several stages of the *Mudaraba* contract to be implemented:

1. The establishment of a *Mudaraba* project: the bank provides the capital as a capital owner. The *Mudarib* provides the effort and expertise for the investment of capital in exchange for a share in the agreed upon profits.
2. The results of *Mudaraba*: the two parties calculate the earnings and divide the profits at the end of the *Mudaraba*. This can be done periodically, in accordance with the agreement, along with observance to the *Sharia'a* rules.
3. The participation in capital: the bank recovers the *Mudaraba* capital it contributed before dividing the profits between the two parties given that profit is deemed in the *Sharia'a* as the 'protection of capital'. In the case of an agreement to distribute profits periodically, before the final settlement, it must be on account until the return of the capital is assured.

5.4 *SHARIA'A* RULES CONCERNING *MUDARABA*

The *Sharia'a* rules have been set out by Usmani (1999):

1. It is a condition in *Mudaraba* that capital must be specific, given that its return to the owner is mandatory at the settlement of the *Mudaraba*. So its amount must be known at the outset of the contract. Uncertainty about the amount of capital necessarily leads to uncertainty about the amount of profit.
2. It is a condition that capital must be the normal currency in circulation. However it can be merchandise, under the condition that it is evaluated at the outset of the contract, and the agreed upon value becomes the capital of the *Mudaraba*.
3. It is a condition that the capital must not be a liability or debt on the *Mudarib*. The Mudarib is a trustee.
4. It is permissible for a *Mudarib* to mix its own private capital with the capital of the *Mudaraba*. Thus it becomes a partner, as well, and its disposal of capital on the basis of *Mudaraba* is permissible.
5. It is a condition that the capital of *Mudaraba* must be delivered to the *Mudarib* because not delivering it imposes constraints on the *Mudarib* and restricts its power of disposal.

Some of the Jurists permit the capital owner to withhold capital and to release it gradually, according to the needs of the *Mudarib*.

6. If two or more Islamic banks are involved the distributable profits are divided between them, and the owner, proportionate to the amount of capital provided by each.

7. It is permissible to impose restrictions on the *Mudarib* if the restriction is beneficial and does not constitute a constraint on the agent achieving the profit required and is not counterproductive to the purpose of the *Mudaraba*.

8. It is permissible for the *Mudarib* to hire an assistant.

9. The disposal of the *Mudarib* is confined to what is conducive to the *Mudaraba*. It must lend or donate nothing of the *Mudaraba* capital. The *Mudarib* is also not allowed to purchase, for the *Mudaraba*, with more than its capital, nor is it allowed to go into partnership with others using the *Mudaraba* capital. All of the above, however, is permissible if the capital owner consents and authorises the agent to use its discretion.

10. No security on the *Mudarib* shall be stated in the *Mudaraba* contract except in the case of negligence or trespass, because the *Mudarib* is a trustee on what is under its control. Capital is judged to be a deposit. It is permissible to take a surety or mortgage from the *Mudarib* to guarantee the payment in case of negligence, trespass or violation of the conditions. But it is impermissible to take that as a guarantee for capital or profit, because it is impermissible for the *Mudarib* to guarantee capital or profit.

11. It is a condition that profit should be specific, because it is the subject of the contract and it being unknown abrogates the contract. The contracting parties should stipulate, in the contract, the profit shares in a percentage form for each party. It is impermissible to stipulate a lump sum as profit to either party.

12. Profit in *Mudaraba* is distributed according to the agreement of the two contracting parties. They may agree on specific ratios, whatever they consensually agree. It is a condition that the capital owner alone bears the loss. The *Mudarib* bears none of the loss because a loss is a decrease in capital and the capital belongs to the owner.

13. The *Mudarib* collects its share of the profit only after obtaining the permission of the capital owner. Also the *Mudarib* is entitled to collect its share of profit only after the capital is recovered, because the *Sharia'a* principle states that 'profit is protection to capital'.

14. The ownership of the *Mudarib* becomes secure after the liquidation of the *Mudaraba* and the capital owner has recovered its capital. Some of the Jurists hold the view that auditing is like division and possession. If two parties reach a final settlement after the liquidation of the assets and then leave the *Mudaraba*, it is considered to be a new *Mudaraba* and neither one makes good the loss of the other.

15. The *Mudaraba* is terminated if one of the two parties rescinds it, given that it is an optional not a binding contract. Some Jurists hold the view that *Mudaraba* is binding and it cannot be rescinded if the *Mudarib* has commenced work.

5.5 PRACTICAL EXAMPLES OF *MUDARABA*

Mudaraba is considered to be the essential mode accredited by the Islamic banks in their relationship with the depositors who tender their moneys to the bank as capital owners to be invested by the bank as *Mudarib*. This is on the basis of profit sharing according to specific ratios agreed upon. See Table 5.1 for a representative example of profit payout ratios for Tier 1 *Mudaraba* accounts.

Table 5.1 Tier 1 *Mudaraba* accounts (unrestricted investment account holders)

Profit paid to *Mudaraba* depositors by Islamic Banks (%)

(Percent per annum)

Nature of deposits	Islami Bank Bangladesh 2004	Al-Arafa Bank 2003	Social Investment Bank 2004	Oriental Bank 2003	Shahjalal Islamic Bank 2003	Shamil Bank 2003
1. *Mudaraba* savings deposits	5.28	6.31	6.85	6.50	8.50–9.00	3.00–5.50
2. *Mudaraba* term deposits						
a) Three years	7.05	8.74	9.50	9.00	8.50–9.50	8.50–9.00
b) Two years	6.91	8.55	9.30	9.00	8.50–9.50	8.00–8.50
c) One year	6.76	8.35	9.20	9.00	8.50–9.50	7.50–8.50
d) Six months	6.48	7.96	8.85	8.50		6.50–8.00
e) One month	6.20	7.57	8.50	8.00		6.00–7.00
3. *Mudaraba* special notice deposits	3.88	4.00				5.75
4. *Mudaraba* short term deposits			5.60	5.00		
5. *Mudaraba Hajj* savings deposits: MMPDR or *Hajj*						
a) Deposit (monthly)	9.51	9.33	9.50		11.00	
b) Cash *Waqf*		9.72				

5.5.1 Target Profit Rates and *Mudaraba*

Most banks will enter into a PLS contract with a profit target that is stated in the *Mudaraba* contract. An illustration of a standard *Mudaraba* deal is given in Box 5.2. In this example, the contract includes a profit distribution clause that states that the net profit will be distributed equally among the partners (50:50). In the event that the bank's share of the profit exceeds the stated target of say 11% per annum, the bank has the option to reward the other party, for good performance, a percentage of the amount that exceeds the target profit rate. This percentage can be between 90–97% of the additional sum depending on the market and the bank's internal pricing and risk-taking policies.

Box 5.2 Standard *Mudaraba* transaction

Assume the following:

Main contract value: US$250,000
Mudaraba value: US$180,000
Profit sharing: 50:50 (50–50%)
Profit target: 11%
11% profit based on the calculation: US$12,986
Award to the contractor for good performance: 95%
The profit amounts are calculated as follows:
Main contract value: US$250,000
Mudaraba value: US$180,000
Net profit: US$70,000
Bank's profit: US$35,000
Contractor's profit: US$35,000

The bank will award the contractor:

$$US\$35,000 - US\$12,986 = US\$22,014$$

Bank's share over 11%

$$US\$1,101$$

Bank's overall profit

$$US\$12,986 + US\$1,101 = US\$14,087$$

Contractor's overall profit

$$US\$35,000 + US\$20,913 = US\$55,913$$

Bank's overall profit percentage

$$20.2\%$$

Contractor's overall profit percentage

$$79.8\%$$

Source: Qatar Islamic Bank

Islamic banks use the same mode with businesses seeking finance whether they are dentists, physicians, engineers, traders or whatever. The bank provides the necessary finance as a capital owner in exchange for a share in the profit to be agreed upon.

It is worth noting that this mode is a high risk for the bank because the bank delivers capital to the *Mudarib* who undertakes the work and management and the *Mudarib* is only a guarantor in case of negligence and trespass. Islamic banks usually take the necessary precautions to decrease the risk.

In Iran, *Mudaraba* is considered a short-term commercial partnership between a bank and an entrepreneur. All financial requirements of the project are provided by the bank and the managerial input is provided by the entrepreneur. Both parties of the *Mudaraba* agreement share in the net profits of the project in an agreed proportion. Iranian banks are directed by the monetary authorities to give priority in their *Mudaraba* activities to cooperatives.

Furthermore, commercial banks in Iran are not allowed to engage in the *Mudaraba* financing of imports by the private sector. Article 9 of the Law of Usury Free Banking provides for banks to expand their commercial activities through *Mudaraba*, within the overall framework of the commercial policy of the government.

5.6 KEY ISSUES ASSOCIATED WITH *MUDARABA*

Mudaraba is a high-risk mode of finance. It is so risky that it is almost unthinkable to conventional bankers. This is because the bank, under this scheme, is expected to provide capital to the client relying completely on his integrity, ability and good management. The bank is not only risking the expected return but also the capital itself. This high degree of moral hazard is present in the classical form of *Mudaraba*.

Recently, however, many Islamic banks are developing *Sharia'a*-based forms of *Mudaraba* with significantly reduced degrees of risk. For example:

- *Mudaraba* is used with public limited companies, where a reasonable degree of transparency is possible, for example, when audited accounts and quarterly-reported performance is available.
- Guarantees are introduced in the contract, but not against profit or payment of capital. Rather these are used only against loss due to negligence or mismanagement.
- Only those economic activities in which the bank can easily see what the money is being used for, can easily be financed on a *Mudaraba* basis. For example, a car dealer who buys cars from a manufacturer, and then sells them on instalments, is a reasonably transparent activity.

5.7 COMPARISON OF *MUDARABA* WITH THE CONVENTIONAL BANKING EQUIVALENT

One way of illustrating *Mudaraba* is to observe the working mechanics of a conventional bank and its relationship with depositors and borrowers and compare them with *Mudaraba* finance in an Islamic bank (see Figure 5.3). Although profit sharing and interest-based lending may seem alike, the differences are clearly more than semantic ones. The yield is not guaranteed in the profit-sharing mode. In addition, in interest-based lending the loan is not contingent on the profit or loss outcome, and is usually secured, so that the debtor has to repay the borrowed

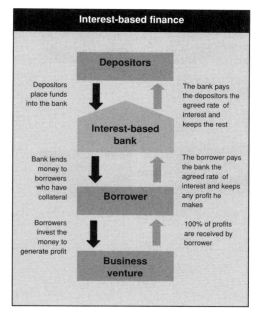
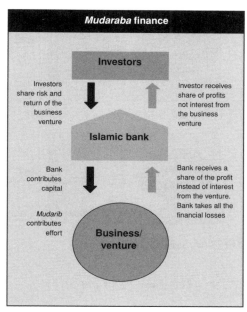

Figure 5.3   Conventional interest-based finance as compared with *Mudaraba*

capital plus the fixed (or predetermined) interest amount regardless of the resulting yield of the capital. Thus, with interest-based lending, the financial losses fall most directly upon the borrower.

Under *Mudaraba*, financial losses are borne completely by the lender. The entrepreneur, as such, sacrifices his time and effort invested in the enterprise and the reward for his labour. This distribution effectively treats human capital equally with financial capital.

5.8 *MUDARABA*: DIFFERENCES FROM THE OTHER ISLAMIC FINANCING TECHNIQUES

There are several ways to classify Islamic finance modes of finance. In this context the contracts are broken down into two groups:

- PLS contracts;
- Islamically permissible deferred sales contracts.

5.8.1 Profit and Loss Share (PLS) Contracts

A PLS contract means that the outcome is sharing based and cannot be predetermined. Shareholders are only repaid if profits are made; if no profits are made then no payouts take place. There two types of PLS contracts.

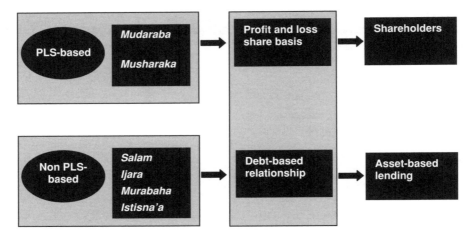

Figure 5.4   Islamic modes of finance

5.8.1.1   Mudaraba *PLS Contracts*

The *Mudaraba* contract is a contract between two parties: an Islamic bank as an investor (*Rab ul Mall*) who provides a second party, the entrepreneur (*Mudarib*), with financial resources to finance a particular project. Profits are shared between the parties in a proportion agreed in advance. Losses are the liability of the Islamic bank and the *Mudarib* sacrifices only its efforts and expected share in the profits.

5.8.1.2   Musharaka *PLS Contracts*

The *Musharaka* PLS contract is an equity participation contract. The bank is not the sole provider of funds to finance a project. Two or more partners contribute to the joint capital of an investment. Profits are shared between the parties in a proportion agreed in advance. Losses are shared strictly in relation to the respective capital contributions. The flow chart depicted in Figure 5.4 illustrates these modes of finance.

5.8.2 Islamically Permissible Deferred Sales Contracts

Jurists have ruled it valid to sell an object immediately, with a deferred price, possibly paid in instalments, greater than its cash price. All the major *Madhabs* (Schools of Islamic jurisprudence), *Shafiis*, *Hanafis*, *Malikis* and *Hanbalis* have agreed to this principle. The rationale is that the seller of an object for a price to be paid in instalments, in the future, is sacrificing a benefit in order to make the object available to the person who is buying it with a deferred payment.

This sacrifice is based on the fact that the seller gets paid at a later date. Thus the seller is making a sacrifice in that he is not able to get paid today and thereby purchase something else or simply have the cash today. Thus, the increase in the deferred price may be viewed as compensation to the seller. The Jurists ruled these sales valid as long as the contract is independently specified and contains no ignorance (*jahala*).

Islamically permissible deferred sales create deferred obligations using the concept of counter-values described in Chapter 3:

- *Murabaha*: sale with a known profit. The object of sale is delivered at the contract time but the price becomes due as debt.
- *Salam* sale. The price is paid at the time of contract but the object of sale becomes due as debt-in-kind.
- *Istisna'a* sale. The price is paid at the time of contract and the object of sale is to be manufactured and delivered later.
- *Ijara*. Sale of the rights to use assets where assets are delivered to the user, who in turn pays periodical rentals later.

5.9 SUMMARY

One major drawback of the *Mudaraba* mode of finance is that there is no legal framework in the contemporary commercial laws of most countries, especially non-Islamic countries, which can be relied upon in the case of a dispute. As such the *Mudaraba* Agreement must be comprehensive and cover all the details.

The other major shortcoming is that to specify a time limit (timeframe) in the *Mudaraba* makes it null and void, because the principle of *Mudaraba* is that it continues until the other partner completes the work for which the agreement has been established and its proceeds are collected. This, of course, leads the bank to have difficulties planning the actual cash flow and profit accrual and it would therefore be advisable to deal with *Mudaraba* as either a medium or long-term investment, even though it may be possible to conclude it before that.

There is a *Sharia'a* ruling that it is not permissible for the bank to interfere in the running of the work in order to administer the execution of the project. The bank will normally only use contractors in which it has full confidence as regards their honesty and technical capabilities. This is difficult to achieve without examining all aspect of the contract and the contractor.

In addition the bank must have, or endeavour to establish, the technical capability to carry out the necessary duties and to exercise due diligence and make the proper credit and technical follow-up to ensure that the project execution is going according to schedule. It is also advisable to have contingency plans and strategies for intervening in the event that the contractor fails to carry out its commitments.

Wrongful use of funds is a risk which banks need to be aware of and mitigate against, by establishing a drawdown mechanism that ensures the funds are spent on the project itself and not any other work that the contractor may be carrying out at the same time.

A mismatch between the amount of money withdrawn and the completed work could happen. This may lead to over-spending at the end of the project, especially if the contractor is either not using all the money for the specific project (the subject of the *Mudaraba*) or not properly managing the spending as he should. In either case the bank must step in to correct the situation as soon as it notices any indication of such mismatch.

Project cancellation completely or partially may also happen during the course of the project. To make sure that the bank's investment is not lost, it should ensure that it is aware of all developments throughout the life of the project and has direct access to the project owner. In addition, careful monitoring of spending will help in minimising the bank's losses.

Project withdrawal may take place, especially when the contractor is accused of major negligence. In such a case the *Mudaraba* Agreement must cover this possibility and also be clear and specific in terms of how such a situation should be dealt with, bearing in mind that in the *Mudaraba* Agreement the contractor is not responsible or accountable for losses or damages that are beyond his control. In such a case the bank risks losing its money unless it can prove that the contractor is negligent and, as such, is responsible for such loss.

In conclusion, *Mudaraba* can be used as a type or mode of finance that is heavily dependent on the bank accepting the performance risk of the contractor to perform the work successfully within the project's budget and timeframe limitations.

The *Mudaraba* Agreement must be comprehensive and detailed in order to cover all aspects of the work and be clear as to how to deal with each possible risk that may occur. The financial structuring should be appropriate to the type of project in hand in order to minimise the possibility of mismatch between spending and work completion and the misappropriation of funds.

Mudaraba is not without risk, and the success of the *Mudaraba* largely depends on how well the bank manages this risk. Therefore the bank must examine all matters that are directly or indirectly related to the project: the contractor, the project owner and any matter that may have positive or negative future influences on the project or the agreement.

REFERENCE

Usmani, T.U. (1999). *An Introduction to Islamic Finance*. Idaratul-Ma'arif. Karachi, Pakistan.

6

Musharaka as a Mode of Islamic Finance

Musharaka is a form of partnership between an Islamic bank and its clients whereby each party contributes to the partnership capital, in equal or varying degrees, to establish a new project or share in an existing one, and whereby each of the parties becomes an owner of the capital on a permanent or declining basis and is owed its due share of profits. Losses, however, are shared in proportion to the contributed capital. It is not permissible to stipulate otherwise.

Constant *Musharaka*

This is a *Musharaka* in which the partners' shares in the capital remain constant throughout the period, as specified in the contract.

Diminishing *Musharaka*

This is a *Musharaka* in which an Islamic bank agrees to transfer gradually to the other partner its (the Islamic bank's) share in the *Musharaka*, with the effect that the Islamic bank's share declines and the other partner's share increases until the latter becomes the sole proprietor of the venture.

Source: Accounting and Auditing Organisation for Islamic Financial Institutions (AAOIFI)

6.1 DEFINITION OF *MUSHARAKA*

Musharaka (from the Arabic *shirkah*) implies partnership in a venture, and can be defined as a form of partnership whereby two or more persons combine either their capital or labour together, to share the profits, enjoying similar rights and liabilities. It can take the form of a *mufawada*, meaning an unlimited, unrestricted and equal partnership in which the partners enjoy complete equality regarding the areas of capital, management and right of disposition. Each partner is both the agent and the guarantor of the other.

A more limited investment partnership is known as an *'inan* (*shirkah al'inan*). This type of partnership occurs when two or more parties contribute to a capital fund, either with money, contributions in kind or labour. Each partner is only the agent and not the guarantor of its partner. An *'inan Musharaka* is limited in scope to the specific undertaking. This version is the most common form of *Musharaka*.

For both versions of *Musharaka*, the partners share profits in an agreed manner and bear losses in proportion to their capital contributions.

Such contractual partnerships are considered proper because the parties concerned have willingly entered into a contractual agreement for joint investment and the sharing of profits and risks. As with *Mudaraba* (discussed in Chapter 5), the profits can be shared in any equitably agreed proportion. The bases for entitlement to the profits of a *Musharaka* are capital, active participation in the *Musharaka* business and responsibility.

Profits are to be distributed among the partners in the business on the basis of proportions agreed by them in advance. The profit share of every party must be determined as a proportion or percentage. Losses must, however, be shared in proportion to the capital contribution. On this point all Jurists are unanimous.

The word *Musharaka* means sharing, and is used to describe those joint business enterprises in which the partners share the profit or loss of the venture. Unlike an interest-based product, there is no guaranteed rate of return on the investment, because income is based on the profit earned by the joint venture, and may possibly result in losses.

This type of investment is seen as distributing the risks, and the profits, more equitably between the investors than a simple interest-based loan, in that the proportion of investment made by each investor determines the proportion of profit they receive from it. Thus rather than receiving a fixed rate of say, 20%, whether the profits on the enterprise are 2% or 300%, the investor will benefit in relation to the success of the venture. This type of financial product is therefore seen as favouring the ordinary depositors in a bank (unrestricted account holders) rather than giving all the benefits of the profit to the borrower.

Although there are many variants on the broad principle of the *Musharaka* structure, the most important subsets of the umbrella product are the previously mentioned *mufawada* and *'inan* forms of *Musharaka* financing. In a *mufawada* agreement, all participants rank equally in every respect – in other words, their initial contributions, their privileges and final profits will all be identical. In an *'inan* structure, different shareholders have different rights and are entitled to different profit shares reflecting the different contributions made by each participant; losses are shared on the same basis. However in practice, for all but the very smallest *Musharaka* deals, the second form (the *'inan*) is used.

The basic principles of *Musharaka* (as agreed by the majority of scholars) are as follows:

- Financing through *Musharaka* never implies lending money; rather it means active participation in the business.
- The investor or financier must share profits and losses incurred by the business, to the extent of their financing.
- Partners are at liberty to determine the ratio of profit allocated to each one of them. This may be different from the ratio of capital investment. However, the partner who excludes himself from the management of the business cannot claim more than the ratio of his capital investment.
- Losses suffered by each partner must be exactly in proportion to his capital contribution.

6.2 WHAT MAKES *MUSHARAKA SHARIA'A* COMPLIANT?

As with many of the Islamic modes of finance, it is necessary to turn to the *Ahadith* for confirmation of their *Sharia'a* compliance:

The legality of partnership is evident from the following quotes:

They share in a third.

An-Nisaa 12

Truly many are the partners (in business) who wrong each other:
Not so do those who believe, and work deeds of righteousness.

Saad 24

- It was reported in the *Hadith* from the Prophet:

> I am the third of the two partners, unless either of them betrays his friend, I withdraw from between them.

6.3 PRACTICALITIES OF IMPLEMENTING *MUSHARAKA*

In the early writings on Islamic banking, *Musharaka* was stressed as being the purest mode of finance among the models of interest-free banking. In contemporary Islamic banking, however, *Musharaka* is rare.

The reason for this is the complexity and the relatively higher degree of moral hazard involved. Under the *Sharia'a*, the *Musharaka* is a simple partnership, where two parties participate in a venture providing capital. Developing this partnership into a banking mode of finance is not easy. First, it has to be temporary, because a bank cannot engage in ownership and operation of joint stock companies. Second, it is difficult because *Musharaka* is the mixing of two sets of capital contributions. Whenever the Islamic bank gets into *Musharaka* by providing capital, it has to engage into an evaluation of the status of the other party. This is because profits at the end of *Musharaka* are the difference in the value of the *Musharaka* between the two points in time. This is an extremely complex calculation and is fraught with risk.

6.4 *SHARIA'A* RULES CONCERNING *MUSHARAKA*

The *Sharia'a* rules concerning *Musharaka* have been clearly set out by Usmani (1999):

1. It is a condition of *Musharaka* that the capital of the company is specific, existent and immediately available. It is invalid to establish a company on nonexistent funds or debt. The purpose of the company is to generate profit that can be disposed of and this cannot take effect in the event of the existence of debt or nonexistent capital.
2. It is not a condition that partners have equal shares in capital. Though variation in shares is permissible, it is subject to agreement.
3. It is a condition that the capital of the company is money and tangible assets. Some of the Jurists permit participating with tangible assets on condition that they are valued in the contract and the value agreed upon them becomes the capital of the company.
4. It is impermissible to impose conditions forbidding one of the partners from work, because each partner implicitly permits and gives power of attorney to the other partner to dispose of and work with the capital. It is permissible for one partner to work singly in the company with the mandate of the other partners.
5. A partner is a trustee of the funds received from the company and he provides guarantees only in cases of trespass or negligence. It is permissible to take a mortgage or a guarantee against trespass and negligence but it is impermissible to take security for profit or capital.
6. It is a condition that profit for each partner must be known in order to avoid uncertainty. It must be a pro rata ratio for all partners and must not be a lump sum because this contravenes the *Sharia'a* requirements relating to partnership.
7. In principle profit must be divided among partners in ratios proportionate to their shares in capital, but some of the Jurists permit variation in profit shares where it is determined by agreement. For example, one of the partners may have more business acumen than the others and so some variation in profit share may become necessary.

8. Each partner bears losses proportionate to his ratio of capital invested in the company and it is impermissible to impose conditions to the contrary.
9. In principle, partnership is a permissible and not a binding contract, and so it is admissible for any partner to rescind the contract whenever he wishes, provided that this occurs with the knowledge of the other partner or partners. Rescinding the contract without the knowledge of other partners prejudices their interests. Some Jurists are of the view that the partnership contract is binding up to the liquidation of capital or the accomplishment of the project accepted at the contract inception.

6.5 PRACTICAL EXAMPLES OF *MUSHARAKA*

Although a *Musharaka* partnership structure can be, and is, used for carrying on ordinary commercial activities, the basic concept of a *Musharaka* has also been used as a technique for Islamic financial institutions to provide finance to commercial enterprises. For example, the concept of *Musharaka* can be used to structure a working capital facility for a company, where that company has had a record of profitability.

A *Musharaka* working capital facility would operate much like a conventional working capital facility. The Islamic financial institution would provide the funds to its customer, usually by the deposit of the funds to the customer's account with the financial institution. The customer would access those funds in the ordinary course of its business. The difference, however, is that instead of debiting the customer's account with a predetermined rate of interest, the Islamic institution would periodically debit the customer's account with an amount equal to a predetermined rate of profit, subject to adjustment on a regular basis, usually quarterly.

At the end of the financial year, the profits are calculated. If the amount due to the Islamic financial institution exceeds the provisional profit already debited from the account, the amount not paid to the Islamic institution will be credited to a special reserve account that the company creates in its books. Conversely, if the amount due to the financial institution is less than the provisional profit already collected by the Islamic institution, the special reserve account will be reduced by the amount of the excess payment to the Islamic institution.

Upon the termination of the *Musharaka* financing, a final profit and loss account is prepared and, at that time, any balance in the special reserve account is shared by the financial institution and the customer in accordance with the ratio they have agreed upon at the inception of the contract.

If, during a financial year, the company generates losses, the special reserve account is reduced by the amount of those losses. If the balance of the special reserve account is insufficient to make good such losses, the customer may ask the Islamic financial institution for a refund (in whole or in part) of the provisional profits previously paid to the Islamic institution. The agreement between the financial institution and its customer lays down a time limit for this refund request.

6.5.1 Application of Diminishing *Musharaka*

Usmani (1999) has provided several examples of the applications of Diminishing *Musharaka*. According to this concept, a financier and his client participate either in the joint ownership of property or equipment, or in a joint commercial enterprise. The share of the financier is further divided into a number of units and it is understood that the client will purchase the units of the share of the financier, one by one, periodically. This process thereby increases the client's own share until all the units of the financier are purchased by him thereby making him the sole owner of the property, or the commercial enterprise, as the case may be. Diminishing *Musharaka*, based on the above concept, has taken different shapes in different transactions. Here are some examples:

- **House purchase.** Diminishing *Musharaka* has been used mostly in house financing. Say a client wants to purchase a house for which he does not have adequate funds. He approaches the financier who agrees to participate with him in purchasing the designated house. The client pays say a total of 20% of the price and the financier pays 80% of the price. Thus the financier owns 80% of the house while the client owns 20%. After purchasing the property jointly, the client uses the house for his residential requirements and pays rent to the financier for using his share in the property. At the same time the share of the financier is further divided into eight equal units, each unit representing a 10% ownership of the house.

  The client promises the financier that he will purchase one unit every three months. Accordingly, after the first term of three months, he purchases one unit of the share of the financier by paying a tenth of the price of the house. This reduces the share of the financier from 80% to 70%. Hence, the rent payable to the financier is also reduced to that extent. At the end of the second term, the client purchases another unit thereby increasing his share in the property to 40% and reducing the share of the financier to 60% and consequentially reducing the rent to that proportion. This process goes on in the same fashion until after the end of two years, the client purchases the whole share of the financier thereby reducing the share of the financier to zero and increasing his own share to 100%. This arrangement allows the financier to claim rent according to his proportion of ownership in the property and at the same time allows him a periodical return of a part of his principal through purchases of the units of his share.

- **Service sector applications.** 'A' wants to purchase a taxi for offering transport services to passengers and to earn the income through fares recovered from them, but he is short of funds. 'B' agrees to participate in the purchase of the taxi. Therefore, both of them purchase a taxi jointly. 'B' pays 80% of the price and 'A' pays 20% of the price. After the taxi is purchased, it is employed to provide taxi rides whereby the net income of say Rs. 1000 is earned on a daily basis. Since 'B' has an 80% share in the taxi it is agreed that 80% of the fare will be given to him and the rest of the 20% will be retained by 'A' who has 20% share in the taxi. This means that Rs. 800 is earned by 'B' and Rs. 200 by 'A' on a daily basis. At the same time the share of 'B' is further divided into eight units.

  Every three months 'A' purchases one unit from the share of 'B'. Consequently the share of 'B' is reduced to 70% and the share of 'A' is increased to 30% meaning that, as from that date, 'A' will be entitled to Rs. 300 from the daily income of the taxi and 'B' will earn Rs. 700. This process goes on until, after the expiry of two years, 'A' owns the whole taxi and 'B' has been repaid his original investment, along with the income earned by him.

- **Small business applications.** 'A' wishes to start the business of ready-made garments but lacks the required funds. 'B' agrees to participate with him for a specified period, say two years. 'A' contributes 40% of the investment and 'B' contributes 60%. Both start the business on the basis of Diminishing *Musharaka*. The proportion of the profit allocated for each one of them is expressly agreed upon. But at the same time 'B's share in the business is divided into six equal units and 'A' keeps purchasing these units on a gradual basis until after the end of the two years 'B' exits the business, leaving its exclusive ownership to 'A'. Apart from periodical profits earned by 'B', he is repaid the price of the units of his share which, in practical terms, repays him the original amount invested by him.

- *Commercial and real estate applications.* Diminishing *Musharaka* has been successfully applied by Jordan Islamic Bank mainly to finance real estate projects and the construction of commercial buildings and housing projects. The bank finances the projects, fully or partially, on the basis that the bank obtains a proportion of the net profits as a partner and receives another payment toward the final payment of the principal advanced. When the original amount is fully repaid, the ownership is fully transferred to the partner and the bank relinquishes its claim. Jordan Islamic Bank has financed the construction of a commercial market in Irbid, a community college in Jerash and a hospital in Zerqa, using this method of financing.

6.5.2 Application of *Musharaka* in Domestic Trade

Al Baraka Islamic Bank of Sudan uses the technique of *Musharaka* to finance the sale and purchase of goods in the local (Sudanese) market. *Musharaka* financing of domestic trade operates in the following manner.

The bank enters into a partnership agreement with the client for the sale and purchase of local goods whose specifications are given by the client. The total cost of the goods is divided between the parties and both parties agree to contribute their shares of the cost of the goods. A special *Musharaka* account is opened at the bank immediately after signing the contract. This specifies all the transactions pertaining to this account. It is the responsibility of the partners to arrange the purchase and sale of the goods in question.

Profits are distributed as follows: an agreed percentage of the net profits are given to the client with the remainder distributed among the partners of the *Musharaka* agreement in the same proportion as their capital contribution. In the case of a loss, the partners bear the loss exactly in proportion to their capital contribution.

6.5.3 Application of *Musharaka* for the Import of Goods

Al Baraka Islamic Bank of Sudan also employs the *Musharaka* technique to finance the import of goods. The contract is essentially the same as the one discussed above in terms of the sale and purchase of domestic goods, but differs in some details.

Under this technique, the importer requests the bank to participate in the import and sale of certain goods. The total cost of importing the goods is declared and each party specifies the capital contribution. The cost of the whole transaction is designated in the appropriate foreign currency. The importer pays a part of his contribution immediately after the contract has been signed and pays the rest after receiving the invoices. A special *Musharaka* account is opened at the bank. The bank then opens a letter of credit in favour of the importer and pays the full amount to the exporter after receiving the shipment documents. The cost of insurance is charged to the transaction account. The importer is responsible for the import, clearance and final sale of the goods in question. The net profits are distributed among the partners in the agreed proportion and any loss is shared in the same proportion as the actual capital contributions.

6.5.4 Letters of Credit on a *Musharaka* Basis

Bank Islam Malaysia issues Letters of Credit (L/C) under the principle of *Musharaka*.

Using this technique, the customer is required to inform the bank of his L/C requirements and negotiate the terms of reference for *Musharaka* financing. The customer places a deposit for his share of the cost of goods imported with the bank, which the bank accepts under the principle of *Wadia* (that is, as keeper and trustee of the funds). The bank then issues the L/C and pays the proceeds to the negotiating bank using the customer's deposit as well as its own finances, and subsequently releases the documents to the customer. The customer takes possession of the goods and disposes of them in the manner stipulated in the agreement. Profits derived from this operation are shared as agreed.

Musharaka is also used for contingency financing (for commodity, goods and equipment) requirements of bank corporate customers of different business sectors, for different maturities and multiple purposes including, in addition to working capital, the purchase of fixed assets. The bank usually extends to customers special *Musharaka* credit facilities each of which is determined based on the type of business and the purpose of finance. Each customer is assigned a certain credit line either in the form of *Musharaka* contract or contracts that are used for one time, or in the form of revolving *Musharaka* usable more than once during the terms of the facility.

6.5.5 Application of *Musharaka* in Agriculture

Islamic banks in Sudan and particularly the Sudanese Islamic Bank have developed yet another application of *Musharaka*. The Sudanese Islamic Bank has, on an experimental basis, been providing finance to farmers by means of a *Musharaka* agreement.

Under this technique, the Sudanese Islamic Bank and the farmer enter into a *Musharaka* contract under which the bank provides the farmer with certain fixed assets, such as ploughs, tractors, irrigation pumps, sprayers and so forth and some working capital, such as fuel, oil, seeds, pesticides and fertilisers. The farmer's equity is confined to providing land, labour and management. Since it is a partnership contract, there is no need for collateral or guarantees other than personal guarantees. Profits are shared between the farmer and the bank in such a way that the farmer is first paid 30% of the net profit as compensation for his management, and then the remaining 70% is shared between the bank and the farmer on a pro rata basis based on each partner's respective share in the equity.

6.5.6 Securitisation of *Musharaka*: *Musharaka Sukuk*

See Box 6.1 for an explanation of *Musharaka* certificates.

Box 6.1 *Musharaka* **certificates (*Sukuk*)**

Musharaka is a mode of financing that can be securitised easily, especially in the case of large projects where huge amounts are required and to which a limited number of people cannot afford to subscribe. Every subscriber can be given a *Musharaka* certificate that represents his proportionate ownership in the assets of the *Musharaka*. After the project is started these *Musharaka* certificates can be treated as negotiable instruments and can be bought and sold in the secondary market.

Trading in these certificates, however, is not allowed when all the assets of the *Musharaka* are still in liquid form (in the shape of cash or receivables or advances due from others).

It is important to emphasise that subscribing to a *Musharaka* is different from advancing a loan, in the form of buying a conventional bond. A bond issued to evidence a loan has nothing to do with the actual business undertaken with the borrowed money. The bond stands for a loan repayable to the holder mostly with interest. The *Musharaka* certificate, on the contrary, represents the direct pro rata ownership of the holder in the assets of the project.

6.6 PROBLEMS ASSOCIATED WITH *MUSHARAKA*

Usmani (1999) identifies and comments on some of the complications with *Musharaka* financing, which revolve around the following issues:

- confidence of depositors;
- dishonesty;
- secrecy of the business.

6.6.1 Confidence of Depositors

One concern is the risk that the active partner in a *Musharaka* is likely to pass on losses of the business to the financing bank or institution. The financing bank or institution will then pass on the loss to depositors. The depositors fearing the risk of loss will not want to deposit their money in the banks and financial institutions offering this mode of finance and thus their savings will either remain idle or be used in transactions outside the Islamic banking channels.

If this argument were correct, which it may be, it would assume that banks do not undertake the normal due diligence exercise. Before financing on the basis of *Musharaka*, the banks and financial institutions would certainly study the feasibility of the proposed business for which funds are needed. Even in the conventional system of interest-based loans, banks do not advance loans to each and every applicant. They study the potential of the business and if they perceive that the business is not profitable, they refuse to advance a loan. In the case of *Musharaka*, Islamic banks will have to carry out this due diligence with more depth and precaution.

In practice no bank or financial institution will restrict itself to a single *Musharaka*. They will always have a diversified portfolio of *Musharaka*. In defence of the *Musharaka* mode of finance, if a bank has financed 100 of its clients on the basis of *Musharaka*, after studying the feasibility of the proposal of each one of them, it is unlikely that all these *Musharaka* or the majority of them will result in a loss. After taking proper measures and due care, what can happen, at the most, is that some of them make a loss. On the other hand, the profitable *Musharaka* are expected to give more return than the interest-based loans, because the actual profit is supposed to be distributed between the client and the bank. The effect is that the *Musharaka* portfolio, as a whole and under normal circumstances, is not expected to suffer an excessive loss.

6.6.2 Dishonesty: Asymmetric Risk

Another fear regarding *Musharaka* financing is that dishonest clients may exploit the instrument of *Musharaka* by not paying any return to the financiers. They can always show that the business did not earn any profit. Indeed, at one extreme, they can claim that they have suffered a substantial loss, in which case not only the profit but also the principal amount will be jeopardized. The problem of dishonesty certainly needs to be addressed. A well designed system of auditing needs to be implemented whereby the accounts of all the clients are fully maintained and properly controlled. If any misconduct, dishonesty or negligence is established against a client, he must be subject to punitive steps.

It should be said, however, that Islamic banks are not just commercial institutions. They have been established to introduce a new system of banking that has its own philosophy. They are duty bound, to some extent, to promote this new system, even if they apprehend that it would reduce the size of their profits. This means that they are advised to use the instrument of *Musharaka* on a selective basis. One would expect that each bank has a number of clients whose integrity is beyond all doubts. It is advisable that Islamic banks finance these clients on the basis of *Musharaka*.

Moreover, there are some sectors of financing where *Musharaka* can be used relatively easily. For example, the use of *Musharaka* instruments in financing exports has little room for dishonesty. For example, the exporter has the specific order from abroad; the prices are agreed; the costs are not difficult to determine; payments are normally secured by a letter of credit; and the payments are made through the bank itself. There is no reason, in such cases, why the *Musharaka* arrangement should not be considered.

6.6.3 Secrecy of the Business

Another cause for concern with *Musharaka* is that, by making the financier a partner in the business of the client, it may result in the disclosure of inside information, regarding the business, to the financier, and through him to other business competitors.

The solution to this problem is straightforward. The client, while entering into the *Musharaka*, may impose a condition that the financier will not interfere with the management affairs, and that he will not disclose any information about the business to any person without prior permission of the client.

6.7 COMPARISON OF *MUSHARAKA* WITH THE CONVENTIONAL BANKING EQUIVALENT

One way of illustrating the difference is to compare the working mechanics of a conventional bank and its relationship with depositors and borrowers and compare this arrangement with *Musharaka* finance in an Islamic bank (see Figure 6.1). Although profit-sharing and interest-based lending may seem alike, the differences are clearly more than semantic ones. The yield is not guaranteed in the profit-sharing mode. In addition, in interest-based lending the loan is not contingent on the profit or loss outcome, and is usually secured, so that the debtor has to repay the borrowed capital plus the fixed (or predetermined) interest amount. Thus, with interest-based lending, the financial losses fall most directly upon the borrower.

6.7.1 Profit and Loss Share (PLS) Contracts

A PLS contract means that the outcome is sharing based and cannot be predetermined. Shareholders are only repaid if profits are made and if no profits are made then no payouts take place. There are two types of PLS contracts, described below.

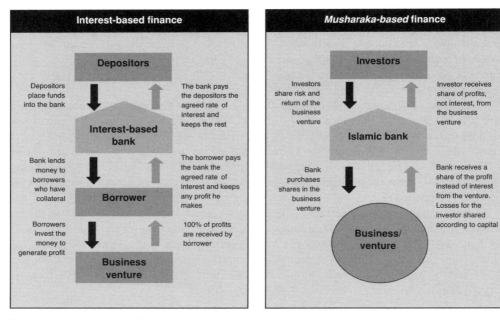

Figure 6.1   Conventional interest-based finance as compared with *Musharaka*

6.7.1.1   *Musharaka PLS Contracts*

The *Musharaka* PLS contract is an equity participation contract. The bank is not the sole provider of funds to finance a project. Two or more partners contribute to the joint capital of an investment. Profits are shared between the parties in a proportion agreed in advance. Losses are shared strictly in relation to the respective capital contributions. Figure 6.2 illustrates these modes of finance.

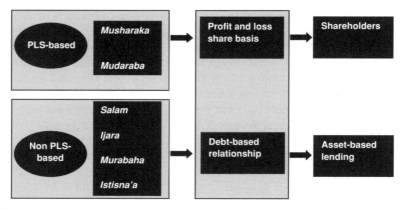

Figure 6.2   Islamic modes of finance

6.7.1.2   *Mudaraba PLS Contracts*

The *Mudaraba* contract is a contract between two parties: an Islamic bank as an investor (*Rab ul Mall*) who provides a second party, the entrepreneur (*Mudarib*), with financial resources to finance a particular project. Profits are shared between the parties in a proportion agreed in advance. Losses are the liability of the Islamic bank and the *Mudarib* sacrifices only its efforts and expected share in the profits.

6.7.2 Islamically Permissible Deferred Sales Contracts

Jurists have ruled it valid to sell an object immediately, with a deferred price, possibly paid in instalments, greater than its cash price. All the major *Madhabs* (Schools of Islamic jurisprudence), *Shafiis, Hanafis, Malikis* and *Hanbalis* have agreed to this principle. The rationale is that the seller of an object for a price to be paid in instalments, in the future, is sacrificing a benefit in order to make the object available to the person who is buying it with a deferred payment.

This sacrifice is based on the fact that the seller gets paid at a later date. Thus the seller is making a sacrifice in that he is not able to get paid today and thereby purchase something else or simply have the cash today. Thus, the increase in the deferred price may be viewed as compensation to the seller. The Jurists ruled these sales valid as long as the contract is independently specified and contains no ignorance (*jahala*).

Islamically permissible deferred sales create deferred obligations using the concept of counter-values described in Chapter 3:

• *Murabaha*: sale with a known profit. The object of sale is delivered at the contract time but the price becomes due as debt.
• *Salam* sale. The price is paid at the time of contract but the object of sale becomes due as debt-in-kind.
• *Istisna'a* sale. The price is paid at the time of contract and the object of sale is to be manufactured and delivered later.
• *Ijara*. Sale of the rights to use assets where assets are delivered to the user, who in turn pays periodical rentals later.

6.8 SUMMARY

To further clarify *Musharaka*, please take a look at the flow chart in Figure 6.3. *Musharaka* is sometimes criticised as being a dated instrument that cannot be applied in the modern world. However, this criticism is somewhat unjustified. Islam has not prescribed a specific form or procedure for *Musharaka*; rather it has set some broad principles that can accommodate numerous forms and procedures. A new form or procedure in *Musharaka* that would make it suitable for modern financial needs cannot be rejected merely because it has no precedent in the past. In fact, every new form can be acceptable as long as it conforms to the principles laid down by the *Sharia'a*.

Even though *Musharaka* is considered to be the most authentic form of Islamic financing, the risk associated with sharing losses means that it is not as popular as the other modes. To make this type of finance more appealing to the customer, some financial institutions have started guaranteeing profits in *Musharaka*. By doing so, these institutions are contravening the basic principle of Islamic finance that requires linking rewards to risks. If profits are guaranteed, the

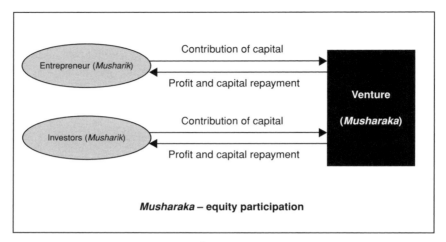

Figure 6.3 *Musharaka* flow chart

risk factor is eliminated, making the profit resemble interest and certainly being contrary to the *Sharia'a*.

Although these actions may help Islamic banks grow in the short run, the long-term costs (harm to reputation and authenticity and *Sharia'a*-compliance risk) will outweigh the benefits. Such moves also provide ammunition to the critics of the system, who are continually questioning whether the system is nothing more than an interest-based system operating under the guise of profit.

Although less popular than other Islamic financial instruments, *Musharaka* is still considered to be one of the most authentic forms of *Sharia'a*-approved financing. Recognising the problem that some financing instruments used by Islamic financial institution closely resemble interest-bearing instruments, Muslim scholars have voiced their opinion that more profit and loss sharing instruments should be developed and used. In recent times there have also been calls for Muslim countries to follow the lead of Iran and Pakistan, where their governments have strongly recommended the Islamic financial system as the only available finance option. It must be said that these endeavours have not met with universal success.

By relying on *Musharaka* for financing projects, Islamic financial institutions can erode any fears that Islamic financial institutions are essentially providing interest-bearing products under the guise of profit and mark-up. This principle is important for the survival and future growth of Islamic finance.

REFERENCE

Usmani, T.U. (1999). *An Introduction to Islamic Finance*. Idaratul-Ma'arif. Karachi, Pakistan.

7

Ijara as a Mode of Islamic Finance

Ijara is the transfer of ownership of a service for an agreed upon consideration. According to the Muslim Jurists (the *Fuqaha*), it has three major elements:

- a form, which includes an offer and consent;
- two parties: a lessor (the owner of the leased asset) and a lessee (the party who reaps the services of the leased asset);
- the object of the (*Ijara*) contract, which includes the rental amount and the service (transferred to the lessee).

Operating *Ijara* contracts are ones that do not end up with the transfer of ownership of leased assets to the lessee.

Ijara wa Iqtina are *Ijara* contracts that do end up with the transfer of ownership of leased assets to the lessee. *Ijara wa Iqtina* may take one of the following forms:

- *Ijara wa Iqtina* that transfers the ownership of leased assets to the lessee – if the lessee so desires – for a price represented by the rental payments made by the lessee over the lease term. At the end of the lease term, and after the last instalment is paid, legal title of the leased assets passes automatically to the lessee on the basis of a new contract.
- *Ijara wa Iqtina* that gives the lessee the right of ownership of leased assets at the end of the lease term on the basis of a new contract for a specified price, which may be a token price.
- *Ijara wa Iqtina* agreements that gives the lessee one of three options that he may exercise at the end of the lease term:
  - purchasing the leased asset for a price that is determined based on rental payments made by the lessee;
  - renewal of *Ijara* for another term;
  - returning the leased asset to the lessor (owner).

Source: Accounting and Auditing Organisation for Islamic Financial Institutions (AAOIFI)

7.1 DEFINITION OF *IJARA*

Ijara is a term of Islamic *Fiqh* (Islamic jurisprudence). Lexically, it means to give something for rent. In Islamic jurisprudence, the term *Ijara* is used for two different situations.

The first and most common type of *Ijara* relates to the usage (usufruct) of assets and properties. *Ijara* in this sense means to transfer the usufruct of a particular property to another person in exchange for a rent claimed from him. In this case, the term *Ijara* is analogous to the English term 'leasing'. To use the Arabic terminology the lessor is called *mujir*, the lessee is called *mustajir* and the rent payable to the lessor is called *ujrah*.

The second meaning of *Ijara* is to employ the services of a person for wages paid to him as a consideration for his hired services. In other words it refers to the services of human beings. In this case the employer is called *mustajir* and the employee is called *ajir*.

For example; if 'A' employs 'B' in his office as a manager on a monthly salary, 'A' is a *mustajir* and 'B' is an *ajir*. Similarly, if 'A' hires the services of a taxi to take his baggage to the airport, 'A' is a *mustajir* while the taxi-driver is an *ajir*. In both cases the transaction between the parties is termed an *Ijara*. This type of *Ijara* includes every transaction where the services of a person are hired by someone else. This person may be a doctor, lawyer, teacher, accountant or any person who can render some services with a market value.

7.1.1 Definition of Usufruct

This term is used throughout all discussions regarding *Ijara*. Usufruct is the right of enjoying a thing, the property of which is vested in another, and to draw from the same all the profit, utility and advantage that it may produce, provided it be without altering the substance of the thing.

7.1.2 *Ijara* and *Ijara wa Iqtina*

Ijara and *Ijara wa Iqtina* (also sometimes known as *Ijara Muntahia Bittamleek* and defined in detail below) are unanimously considered by the Islamic scholars as permissible modes of finance under the *Sharia'a*, applying the leasing mode of finance.

The Islamic Development Bank (IDB), the largest trade financing institution in the Islamic world, defines leasing as a 'medium-term mode of financing, which involves purchasing, and subsequently transferring, the right of use of equipment and machinery to the beneficiary for a specific period of time, during which time the IDB retains the ownership of the asset'.

Under the *Ijara* mode of financing, the bank would buy the equipment or machinery and lease it out to its clients who may opt to buy the items eventually. In the latter case the monthly payments will consist of two components: first, rental for the use of the equipment and second, instalments towards the purchase price. The original amount of the rent for the leased assets should be fixed in advance. However, benchmarking against the London Inter-Bank Offered Rate (LIBOR) is permitted.

The Western counterparts for these Islamic instruments would be 'operating leases' and 'financial leases'. An *Ijara*, or operating lease, is based on a contract between the lessor and lessee for the use of a specific asset. The lessor retains the ownership of the asset and the lessee has possession and use of the asset on payment of specified rentals over a specified period. The rentals are insufficient to enable the lessor to recover fully the initial capital outlay. The residual value is later recovered through disposal or re-leasing the equipment to other users.

An *Ijara wa Iqtina* on the other hand is more like a conventional financial lease. The rentals during the term of the lease are sufficient to amortise the leasing company's investment and provide an element of profit. The profit element in an *Ijara wa Iqtina* is permissible, despite its similarity to an interest charge.

Under the *Ijara* scheme of financing, the bank purchases a real asset (the bank may purchase the asset as per the specifications provided by the prospective client) and leases it to the client. The period of lease, which may be from three months to five years or more, is determined by mutual agreement, according to the nature of the asset.

During the period of lease, the asset remains under the ownership of the bank but the physical possession of the asset and the right of use is transferred to the lessee, hence the term 'usufruct'. After the leasing period expires, the asset reverts to the lessor. The bank and the lessee agree upon a lease payment schedule based on the amount and terms of financing.

7.1.3 Definition of *Ijara wa Iqtina*

Ijara wa Iqtina is a form of leasing where an asset (building or physical equipment) is leased by the lessor to the lessee in a way that, at the end of an agreed lease period, the lessee becomes the owner of the asset by purchasing it from the lessor during or at the end of the lease period at an agreed sale price.

Given the client's promise to lease from the bank, the bank will purchase, for the client and in the bank's name, an asset specified in the client's promise and then lease it to the client on similar terms to a conventional financial lease. The lease rental is structured in such a way that at the end of the lease period, the purchasing cost and profit is recovered and the bank transfers the ownership of the asset to the client for a nominal sale price, or as a gift by a separate sale or gift contract at the end of the lease period.

7.1.4 Leasing as a Mode of Financing

Like *Murabaha* (discussed in Chapter 4), leasing was not originally a mode of financing. It was simply a transaction meant to transfer the usufruct of an asset from one person to another for an agreed period against an agreed consideration. However, many Islamic financial institutions have adopted leasing as a mode of financing instead of long-term lending on the basis of charging interest. This kind of lease is generally known as a financial lease, as to be distinguished from the operating lease, and many basic features of actual leasing transaction have been dispensed with therein.

7.2 WHAT MAKES *IJARA SHARIA'A* COMPLIANT?

The *Sharia'a* allows a fixed charge relating to tangible assets as opposed to financial assets because, by converting financial capital into tangible assets, the financier has assumed risks for which compensation is permissible. This is one of the key elements making a transaction Islamically acceptable.

Since the distinguishing feature of *Ijara* is that the assets remain the property of the Islamic bank, it has to put them up for rent every time the lease period expires so as not to have them remain unused for long periods of time. Under this mode of finance the bank bears the risk of an economic recession or reduced demand for the assets.

In addition, leasing has been justified on the grounds that by retaining ownership the bank runs the risk of premature obsolescence. The rental equipment is often used in a transient manner and the lessor is charged with the responsibility for maintenance. In the case of rental the lessor is also charged with the responsibility for coping with the product's obsolescence, so that it may be regarded as a service-oriented business. This element of risk is a key component in making *Ijara* acceptable within the *Sharia'a*.

7.3 PRACTICALITIES OF IMPLEMENTING *IJARA*

The following points describe how to implement *Ijara* in practice:

1. The contract of *Ijara* financing can be used by an Islamic bank to provide customers with short to medium-term financing to lease items. These items may include

- equipment;
- machinery;
- consumer goods;
- computers;
- motor vehicles;
- other suitable and acceptable assets.

2. The usage of the asset to be leased by the customer and to be financed by the bank must not be *haram* (forbidden) such as the lease of a machine for processing alcoholic intoxicants.
3. In the process of extending *Ijara* financing to the customer, the following factors are to be considered:
   - used industrial equipment market;
   - second hand value;
   - capital allowances.
4. Repossession will be instituted by the lessor if the lessee defaults. Examples of default are
   - default in payment;
   - failure to observe or perform any of the provisions of the lease;
   - a winding-up petition filed against the lessee;
   - lessee gives notice of its intention to redeem.
5. All costs incurred in the repossession process shall be borne by the lessee.
6. *Guarantees*: the concept of guarantee in Islam is known as *Al Kafalah*. Under *Ijara* the provision of guarantees is allowable. Examples of guarantees are:
   - personal or individual guarantee;
   - corporate guarantee.
7. *Security*: funds supplied by depositors and investors are used for financing and investment activities, and therefore the bank has a prime responsibility to protect its interest and normally extend financing on a secured basis in order to reduce the credit risks involved. In Islam, the concept of security is known as *Al-Rahn*
   The land and building or other property acceptable by the bank can be accepted as collateral for a financing facility under *Ijara*. Land and buildings can be secured by way of a legal charge. A first legal charge is the best mode of security and this is usually insisted upon in most cases. The bank may accept a second charge in very special cases.

An illustration of the calculation of lease rentals is given in Table 7.1 (on the opposite page).

7.4 *SHARIA'A* RULES *CONCERNING IJARA*

As with the other Islamic modes of finance, the evidence of legality comes from the *Ahadith*:

- Allah says:

    ... and if they suckle your (offspring) give them their recompense.

    (*Al-Talaq* 6)

    Said one of the (damsels): 'O my (dear father! Engage Him on wages: truly the best of men for thee to employ is the (man) who is strong and trusty'.

    Al-Qasas 26

- Abu Said Al-Khudari related that the Messenger of Allah said, 'He who hires a worker must inform him of his wage'.

Related by Albyhaghi through Abu Huraira and the Hadith 'Give the worker his wage before his sweat dries'.

Ibn Maja

• There is consensus among the *Ummah* for the *Sharia'a* compliance of *Ijara*, from the time of *Sahaba*, the Companions of the Prophet, up to modern times, given that physical assets are needed in order to generate business activities.

Table 7.1   Calculation of monthly lease rental and total lease rentals

1)	Formula		
	a)	Total lease rentals (TLR) =	$CF + (CF \times i \times n)$
		where CF =	Cost of financing
		i =	Rate of return per annum (flat)
		n =	Period of financing in years
	b)	Monthly lease rental =	$\dfrac{\text{TLR}}{N \times 12}$
2)	An example		
		Cost of financing or purchase price =	$30,000
		Rate of profit =	8% flat per annum
		Period of lease =	5 years (60 months)
	a)	Total lease rentals =	$30,000 + ($30,000 \times 8\% \times 5)$
		=	$42,000
	b)	Monthly lease rental =	$\dfrac{\$42,000}{60}$
		=	$700
	c)	Amount of profit =	$42,000 – $30,000
		=	$12,000

7.5 BASIC RULES OF ISLAMIC LEASING

The basic rules of Islamic leasing are set out by Usmani (1999):

1. Leasing is a contract whereby the owner of something transfers its usufruct to another person for an agreed period, at an agreed consideration.
2. The subject of the lease must have a valuable use. Therefore items having no usufruct at all cannot be leased
3. It is necessary, for a valid contract of lease, that the corpus of the leased property remains under the ownership of the seller, and only its usufruct is transferred to the lessee. Thus, anything which cannot be used without being consumed cannot be leased out. Therefore, the lease cannot be effected in respect of money, eatables, fuel, ammunition and so on, because their use is not possible unless they are consumed.

   If anything of this latter nature is leased out, it will be deemed to be a loan and all the rules concerning a loan transaction shall accordingly apply. Any rent charged on this invalid lease will be deemed to be interest charged on a loan (*riba*).
4. As the corpus of the leased property remains under the ownership of the lessor, all the liabilities emerging from the ownership of the lessor must be borne by the lessor. The liabilities relevant to the direct use of the property, however, shall be borne by the lessee.
5. The period of the lease must be determined in clear terms.

6. The lessee cannot use the leased asset for any purpose other than the purpose specified in the lease agreement. If no such purpose is specified in the agreement, the lessee can use it for whatever purpose it is used for in the normal course of the business. However, if the lessee wishes to use it for what may be categorised as an abnormal purpose, he cannot do so unless the lessor allows him to do so in express terms.
7. The lessee is liable to compensate the lessor for any damage to the leased asset caused by any misuse or negligence on the part of the lessee.
8. The leased asset shall remain at the risk of the lessor throughout the lease period in the sense that any harm or loss, caused by factors beyond the control of the lessee, shall be borne by the lessor.
9. A property jointly owned by two or more persons can be leased out, and the rental should be distributed between all the joint owners according to the proportion of their respective shares in the property.
10. A joint owner of a property can lease his proportionate share to his co-sharer only, and not to any other person.
11. It is necessary, for a valid lease, that the leased asset is fully identified by the parties.
12. The rental must be determined at the time of contract for the whole period of the lease; however, benchmarking against LIBOR is permitted (see Section 7.5.1).
13. The determination of rental on the basis of the aggregate cost incurred in the purchase of the asset by the lessor, as normally done in financial leases, is not against the rules of the *Sharia'a*, if both parties agree to it. This holds true provided that all the other conditions of a valid lease, prescribed by the *Sharia'a*, are fully adhered to.
14. The lessor cannot increase the rent unilaterally, and any agreement to this effect is void.
15. The rent or any other part thereof may be payable in advance before the delivery of the asset to the lessee, but the amount so collected by the lessor shall remain with him as an 'on account' payment and must be adjusted towards the rent after its being due.
16. The lease period commences from the date on which the leased asset has been delivered to the lessee, irrespective as to whether the lessee has started using it or not.
17. If the leased asset has totally lost the function for which it was leased, and no repair is possible, the lease must terminate on the day in which such loss has been caused. However, if the loss is caused by misuse or negligence on the part of the lessee, he will be liable to compensate the lessor for the depreciated value up to what it was before the damage took place.

7.5.1 Benchmarking Against LIBOR is Permitted with *Ijara*

A question is often raised as to why Islamic banks, more often than not, base the *Ijara* lease rent on fluctuating conventional benchmarks such as LIBOR. Why not, it is argued, pre-fix the lease rent at the outset for the entire lease term? There are two main reasons for benchmarking against LIBOR:

- The absence of an internationally acceptable Islamic profit benchmark, as compared to LIBOR in conventional banking.
- Apprehension in the customer's mind that he may end up paying a higher lease rent if it is fixed compared to the fluctuating benchmark-based interest rate charged by a conventional bank.

There are relatively few Islamic banks as against a very large number of conventional ones, and so it becomes important, on the part of Islamic banks, to remain competitive and, as such, adjust their profit earnings close to the market. By not adapting to market standards, they may not be able to achieve the purpose of adding value to the investments of their shareholders and depositors as *Mudarib* (fund manager).

Therefore, the *Ijara* agreements adopted by the Islamic banks provide that, for the sake of clarity and ease of understanding, the rental will be equal to a benchmark rate at the start of an *Ijara* period (such as three or six-month LIBOR) plus a spread, called a margin. The rent is readjusted for each *Ijara* period on the same basis in order for the Islamic banks to remain in line with the market.

The objection raised against this practice is that, by subjecting the rental payments as being equal to a rate of interest, the transaction may be rendered akin to an interest-based financing.

The reply to this argument is that so long as all the other *Sharia'a* parameters are fulfilled, the *Ijara* agreement may use any benchmark for merely determining the amount of periodical rental.

It is important to remember that the main difference between conventional financial leasing and *Ijara* is that in the latter the lessor assumes the full ownership risks of the corpus of the leased asset.

If the asset is destroyed during the lease period, without the lessee's negligence, the lessor will bear the full loss besides also losing the right to continue to earn rent. In addition, the lessor will be required to refund any prepaid rent to the lessee.

Mere use of the conventional benchmark does not render the contract invalid from a *Sharia'a* perspective because it is simply meant to determine the rent for the underlying asset. It is not interest on a loan since nothing is being lent by the bank.

Another question that has been raised is that future variations in the LIBOR rate being unknown, the rent thus tied to it may be uncertain (in this case there is an element of *gharar*). *Gharar* (uncertainty) is not allowed under the *Sharia'a* because all considerations in a contract must be clearly known and understood by the parties entering into it. It is true that the *Sharia'a* does not condone a contract with the element of uncertainty in it, primarily to avoid any dispute in future. However, this aspect is absent in an *Ijara*, which is based on a well defined benchmark, because both parties agree in writing that LIBOR will serve as the criterion for determining the rent. As such, whatever rental amount is ascertained by the lessor, based on this benchmark, will be acceptable to the lessee.

7.6 PRACTICAL EXAMPLES OF *IJARA*

Islamic leasing (*Ijara*) and lease purchase (*Ijara wa Iqtina*) are now widely accepted as financing instruments. Assets that can be leased range from vehicles and building machinery to equipment and even aircraft. But Ijara is considered particularly suitable for small- and medium-scale businesses and the fact that it helps growth in investment and capital formation within the economy.

Ijara wa Iqtina, as previously discussed, is a contract in which an Islamic bank purchases equipment, buildings or an entire project and rents them to the client. The client agrees to make payments into an Islamic investment account, which will eventually lead to the client's purchase of the equipment or the project from the bank. The profits that accumulate in the investment account are paid to the client.

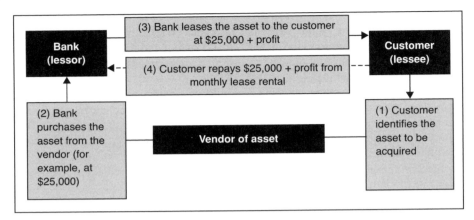

Figure 7.1 *Ijara* leasing operation

In 1990, the Dubai-based Emirates Airline asked the Al Rajhi Banking and Investment Corporation (ARBIC), which operates on Islamic principles, to raise US$60 million lease financing for an A310-300 Airbus. This was the first aircraft leasing deal to be handled by an Islamic bank and it attracted support from Islamic commercial banks.

In the same year, Gulf Air asked the Faisal Islamic Bank of Bahrain (FIBB) to raise US$365 million for the purchase of six Boeing 767s. The FIBB offered an Islamic lease maturing in 12 years, but this fell through owing to the Gulf crisis and, at the end of the war, the contract was given to conventional banks. The ARBIC mandate, however, proved that Islamic lease financing could compete strongly with conventional aircraft leasing. This method was used by The Albaraka International Bank in London to finance the purchase of a new minicab fleet for Pakistani taxi drivers in Sheffield. Figure 7.1 illustrates the steps involved in *Ijara*.

7.6.1 Lease Purchase Transactions

The basic idea behind lease purchase transactions (*Ijara wa Iqtina*) is that an asset is given to the client for lease at an agreed rental. At the same time, the lessee is allowed to purchase the asset at an agreed price. The technique is practised at Islamic banks in various forms, some of which are described below.

Al Baraka Investment Company uses the technique of *Ijara wa Iqtina* to finance the purchase of large capital items such as property, industrial plant and heavy machinery. It involves direct leasing where investors in the scheme receive regular monthly payments that represent an agreed rental. At the expiry of the lease, the lessee purchases the equipment.

Bank Islam Malaysia also uses lease purchase contracts. The procedure adopted is the same as that described above except that the client and the bank enter into an agreement, at the time of the lease, that the client will purchase the equipment at an agreed price with the provision that the lease rentals previously paid shall constitute part of the price.

Ijara wa Iqtina is also widely used by Islamic banks in Iran. They purchase the needed machinery, equipment or immovable property and lease it to firms. At the time of the contract, the firms guarantee to take possession of the leased assets if the terms of the contract are fulfilled. The terms of the lease cannot exceed the useful life of the asset, which is determined by the Central Bank of Iran. Banks in Iran are not allowed to lease those assets whose useful life is less than two years. Furthermore, Article 10 of the Law of Usury Free Banking of 1983 authorises banks, in coordination with the Ministry of Housing and Urban Development, to undertake the construction of low-priced residential units for sale on a lease purchase basis.

7.7 KEY DIFFERENCES BETWEEN AN *IJARA* CONTRACT AND A CONVENTIONAL LEASE

Sharia'a law does not object to payment for the use of an asset. The lessor acquires the asset and leases it to the client for an agreed sum, payable in instalments over a period of time. *Ijara* contracts may be entered into for the long-, medium- or short-term and may be adapted to fulfil the functions of either conventional finance or operating leases. Moreover, these contracts can be subject to English or New York law. *Sharia'a* compliance is a moral rather than a legal issue. There are, however, a few significant differences between a conventional Western lease and an *Ijara* lease. Four of the main differences, and some of the mechanisms for circumventing the *Sharia'a* complications, are discussed in the following sections.

7.7.1 Rental Payments Based on Interest

Where an asset is financed by way of floating-rate funds, the owner will usually pass the risk of rate fluctuations down to the lessee through the rentals payable by the lessee. This originally created a problem in the Islamic context where lease rentals could not be directly expressed by reference to interest rates, an issue discussed earlier.

This difficulty was, to a certain extent, surmountable. In leasing transactions the lessor is providing an asset, not funds, and so the return is in the form of rent, rather than principal and interest. The lessor is, in effect, using its funds productively to invest in an asset and is accepting the associated risk. In an *Ijara* lease the amount and timing of the lease payments should be agreed in advance, though the agreed schedule and amount of those payments need not be uniform.

In some leases the problem has been overcome by referring to the rental payable under the lease at the date of signing, but subject to adjustments by reference to provisions in other documents. In another lease variant, the rent can be adjusted by cross-reference to fluctuating rentals payable under a non-Islamic lease being signed at the same time and at the same rentals. Other transactions have included a rental adjustment letter linking rentals to LIBOR, as mentioned earlier.

7.7.2 Penalty Interest with a Default

Western conventional leases usually provide for default interest on late payment of amounts due. This is not possible in Islamic leases. In an *Ijara* lease the same effect can be achieved in different ways, for example by providing for some form of discount formula, where an agreed rate of discount is applied for each day that payment is made prior to a backstop date. The backstop date is chosen to reflect a commercial period in which funds might be expected, at the latest, to be paid. However, if payment is made after the backstop date, then the lessor cannot recover any additional amount. In other leases an alternative penalty is applied with late-payment fees replacing the conventional default rate of interest.

7.7.3 Insurance and Maintenance Issues

In contrast with most conventional leases, in an *Ijara* lease the responsibility for maintaining and insuring the leased asset remains that of the lessor throughout. Therefore, the owner or lessor will agree, in the lease, to ensure the maintenance and insurance of the asset.

The conventional position of the lessor relieving itself of these burdens can be achieved within the *Ijara* framework. In this case, the owner or lessor recovers the insurance costs by increasing the rental payments and the lessor appoints the lessee, or another third party, as its agent to obtain the required insurance, in return for a fee.

Maintenance obligations can be dealt with in a similar way, where the lessor agrees in the lease to perform all maintenance and repair obligations but appoints the lessee or another third party to perform such obligations on behalf of the lessor, in return for a fee. The extent to which maintenance responsibilities have been transferred is usually reflected in the lease payments due from the lessee.

7.7.4 *Sharia'a* Board Issues

One distinct feature of Islamic financial institutions is the role of the *Sharia'a* board, discussed in detail in Chapter 2, which forms an integral part of an Islamic financing institution. The role of the *Sharia'a* board, is to monitor the workings of the Islamic financing institution from a *Sharia'a* standpoint and to review every new transaction to make sure that it is *Sharia'a* compliant. The boards include some of the most respected contemporary scholars of *Sharia'a* law. Yet *Sharia'a* law is open to interpretation and these boards often have divergent views on key *Sharia'a* issues.

There is no fixed practical guide as to what constitutes an acceptable Islamic financial instrument, and the suggestions mentioned above, which are designed to achieve the same effect as conventional leases within an *Ijara* framework, need to be viewed in this light. A document or structure may be accepted by one *Sharia'a* board but rejected by another. It should also be said that many of the above mentioned techniques do not adhere to the spirit of the *Sharia'a*.

7.8 COMPARISON OF *IJARA* WITH THE CONVENTIONAL BANKING EQUIVALENT

This section looks at the mechanics of a conventional bank and its relationship with depositors and borrowers, and compares this arrangement with *Ijara* finance in an Islamic bank (see Figure 7.2).

Although profit-sharing and interest-based lending may seem alike, the differences are clearly more than semantic. The yield is not guaranteed in the profit-sharing mode. In addition in interest-based lending, the loan is not contingent on the profit or loss outcome, and is usually secured, so that the debtor has to repay the borrowed capital plus the fixed (or predetermined) interest amount regardless of the resulting yield of the capital. Thus, with interest-based lending, the financial losses fall most directly upon the borrower.

7.9 *IJARA*: DIFFERENCES FROM THE OTHER ISLAMIC FINANCING TECHNIQUES

There are several ways to classify Islamic finance modes of finance. In this context the contracts are broken down into two groups known as

- Islamically permissible deferred sales contracts;
- PLS contracts.

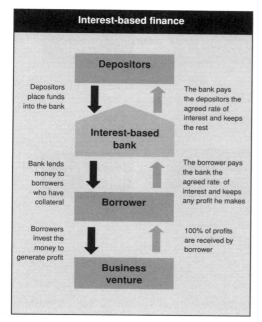
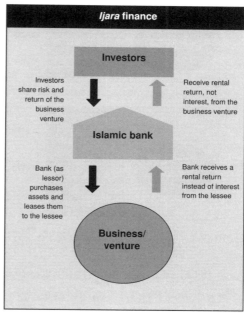

Figure 7.2   Conventional interest-based finance as compared with *Ijara*

7.9.1 Islamically Permissible Deferred Sales Contracts

Jurists have ruled it valid to sell an object immediately, with a deferred price, possibly paid in instalments, greater than its cash price. All the major *Madhabs* (Schools of Islamic jurisprudence), *Shafiis*, *Hanafis*, *Malikis* and *Hanbalis* have agreed to this principle. The reasoning is that the seller of an object for a price to be paid in instalments, in the future, is sacrificing a benefit in order to make the object available to the person who is buying it with a deferred payment.

This sacrifice is based on the fact that the seller gets paid at a later date. Thus the seller is making a sacrifice in that he is not able to get paid today and thereby purchase something else or simply have the cash today. Thus, the increase in the deferred price may be viewed as compensation to the seller. The Jurists ruled these sales valid as long as the contract is independently specified and contains no ignorance (*jahala*).

Islamically permissible deferred sales create deferred obligations using the concept of counter-values described in Chapter 3:

- *Ijara*. Sale of the rights to use assets where assets are delivered to the user, who in turn pays periodical rentals later.
- *Murabaha*: sale with a known profit. The object of sale is delivered at the contract time but the price becomes due as debt.
- *Salam* sale. The price is paid at the time of contract but the object of sale becomes due as debt-in-kind.
- *Istisna'a* sale. The price is paid at the time of contract and the object of sale is to be manufactured and delivered later.

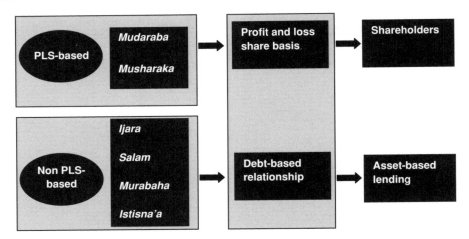

Figure 7.3   Islamic modes of finance

7.9.2 Profit and Loss Share (PLS) Contracts

A PLS contract means that the outcome is sharing based and cannot be predetermined. Shareholders are only repaid if profits are made and if no profits are made then no payouts take place. There two types of PLS contracts as discussed in the next two sections.

7.9.2.1 Mudaraba *PLS Contracts*

The *Mudaraba* contract is a contract between two parties: an Islamic bank as an investor (*Rab ul Mall*) who provides a second party, the entrepreneur (*Mudarib*), with financial resources to finance a particular project. Profits are shared between the parties in a proportion agreed in advance. Losses are the liability of the Islamic bank and the *Mudarib* sacrifices only its efforts and expected share in the profits.

7.9.2.2 Musharaka *PLS Contracts*

The *Musharaka* PLS contract is an equity participation contract. The bank is not the sole provider of funds to finance a project. Two or more partners contribute to the joint capital of an investment. Profits are shared between the parties in a proportion agreed in advance. Losses are shared strictly in relation to the respective capital contributions. Figure 7.3 illustrates these modes of finance.

7.10 SUMMARY

The flowcharts in Figures 7.4 and 7.5 help to clarify *Ijara* further. *Ijara* is an Islamic form of leasing: in fact, it is another form of mark-up structure, in which the bank buys capital equipment or property and leases it out under instalment plans to end users. As in conventional leasing there may be an option to buy the goods at the end of the *Ijara* built into the contracts, known as *Ijara wa Iqtina*. The instalments consist of rental for use and part repayment of capital.

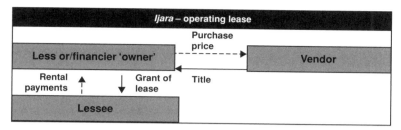

Figure 7.4   *Ijara* – operating lease

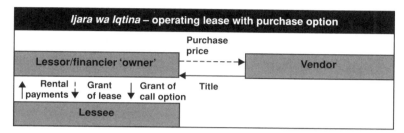

Figure 7.5   *Ijara wa Iqtina* – operating lease with purchase option

The customer selects the asset to be financed and the bank then purchases it from the supplier and leases it to the customer for an agreed period. Refinancing of assets owned by the client, in a sale and leaseback arrangement, is allowed under certain circumstances. As the owner of the asset, the bank is paid rent, fixed or variable as agreed by the parties. The rental amount is often linked to LIBOR.

The bank must exercise all the lessor's rights and obligations such as maintenance, insurance and repair. The lessee gets the use of the asset for the period of the lease subject to payment of rent. The lessee may assume the obligations such as maintenance for a reduced rent. The fact that there is a real tangible good to be financed means that this is the most *Sharia'a*-compliant of the mark-up products.

Although Islamic bankers have sought to avoid business risk, particularly through using *Murabaha*, the essential element of most such deals is the linking to a genuine identifiable trade transaction. Islamic finance seekers thus have to open themselves up to their banks even more than their Western counterparts and can only obtain finance for genuine needs. The profit and loss sharing contracts of *Musharaka* and *Mudaraba* are more difficult to obtain given the preference, in practice, for Islamic banks to prefer the less risky alternative modes of finance.

Ijara contracts may be entered into for the long, medium or short term and may be adapted to fulfil the functions of either conventional finance or operating leases. Moreover, these contracts can be subject to English or New York law in international transactions.

REFERENCE

Usmani, T.U. (1999). *An Introduction to Islamic Finance*. Idaratul-Ma'arif. Karachi, Pakistan.

8

Istisna'a as a Mode of Islamic Finance

Istisna'a is a sale contract whereby the purchaser asks the seller to manufacture a specifically defined product, using the seller's raw materials, at a given price.

Istisna'a is a sale contract between *al-mustasni* (the ultimate purchaser) and *al-musania'a* (the seller). In *Istisna'a*, the *al-musania'a* – based on an order from the *al-mustasni* – undertakes to have manufactured or otherwise acquire *al-masnoo* (the subject matter of the contract) according to specification and sell it to the *al-mustasni* for an agreed upon price and method of settlement. This may be, at the time of contracting, by instalments or deferred to a specific future time. It is a condition of the *Istisna'a* contract that *al-musania'a* should provide either the raw materials or the labour.

The contractual agreement of *Istisna'a* has a characteristic similar to that of *Salam* (discussed in Chapter 9) in that it provides for the sale of a product not available at the time of sale. It also has a characteristic similar to an ordinary sale of goods in that deferred payment is allowed. However, unlike *Salam*, the price in the *Istisna'a* contract is not paid when the deal is concluded. A third characteristic of the contractual agreement of *Istisna'a* is that it is similar to *Ijara* in that labour is required in both.

Parallel *Istisna'a*

If *al-mustasni* (the ultimate purchaser) does not stipulate in the contract that *al-musania'a* (the seller) should manufacture *al-masnoo* (the asset) by himself, then *al-musania'a* may enter into a second *Istisna'a* contract in order to fulfil his contractual obligations in the first contract. This second contract is called a Parallel *Istisna'a*.

Source: Accounting and Auditing Organisation for Islamic Financial Institutions (AAOIFI)

8.1 DEFINITION OF *ISTISNA'A*

The word *Istisna'a* is derived from the Arabic term *Sina'a*, meaning to manufacture a specific commodity. *Istisna'a* is an agreement whereby a customer requiring an item, equipment, a building or a project, which needs to be constructed, manufactured, fabricated or assembled, approaches the bank for financing. The bank offers to have the said item constructed, manufactured or assembled and then, after adding its profit margin, sells it to the customer. The buyer can pay the price later, either in a lump sum or in instalments.

Istisna'a is a financing method used for the production of specific goods. It is also a frequently applied model for construction finance. In essence, *Istisna'a* is an agreement whereby one party pays for goods to be manufactured or pays for something to be constructed. As a general rule the ultimate user will make periodic instalments according to the actual progress in construction or manufacturing. For example, a ferry company wanting to buy a new ferry would make periodic instalment payments to the shipbuilder as the assembly process moves forward.

In theory the contract could be made directly between the end user and the manufacturer, but typically it is a three-party contract, whereby the bank acts as an intermediary. In this case, a parallel or back-to-back *Istisna'a* structure is used that consists of two *Istisna'a* contracts, and this constitutes the basis of such an arrangement. Under the first agreement the bank agrees to let the client pay back on a longer-term schedule, whereas under the second contract the bank, in the function of a purchaser, makes progress instalment payments to the producer over a shorter period of time.

Normally, the bank makes profits by adding a mark-up. Hence the bank's compensation is the differential between the values of payments under the two contracts. Clearly, there is a considerable resemblance with commissioned purchase through *Murabaha* (see Chapter 4*)*.

8.1.1 *Istisna'a* and Parallel *Istisna'a*

In *Istisna'a* the bank simultaneously enters into two parallel agreements as follows:

- *First agreement*, which is between the bank and the customer. The customer provides to the bank complete and detailed specifications for the asset (item, equipment, building or project) to be acquired including its layout, design and materials to be used, as well as the desired quality and performance standards, and the time of completion. The specifications may also identify the contractors, manufacturers and the suppliers of the raw materials. The customer may also provide an estimate of the costs involved, or the bank may obtain the quotations from the contractors, manufacturers or suppliers specified by the customer. The bank then adds, to the costs provided, its profit margin and quotes a price to the customer. On approval and acceptance by the customer, they enter into an agreement, which includes, among other things, the mode of payment to the bank. This could be in the form of a lump sum, or in instalments.
- *Second agreement*, which is between the bank and the contractors, manufacturers or suppliers. Along with the first agreement, the bank simultaneously enters into an agreement with the contractors, manufacturers or suppliers for the assembly, fabrication, manufacture or construction of the asset, by the given date, as per the specifications. The bank pays all the costs directly to them. On completion of the asset, the bank hands it over to the customer. The customer then pays the price either in lump sum or in instalments as agreed.

Box 8.1 provides details of *Istisna'a* terminology and Figure 8.1 provides a summary of the parties concerned.

Box 8.1 *Istisna'a* **terminology**

- *Al-mustasni*: (the buyer, entrepreneur).
- *Al-musania'a*: (the seller, manufacturer) – provides labour and raw materials.
- *Al-masnoo*: (the asset to be built, made, manufactured) – must be known and be specific as to
  - specificity;
  - quality;
  - quantity.

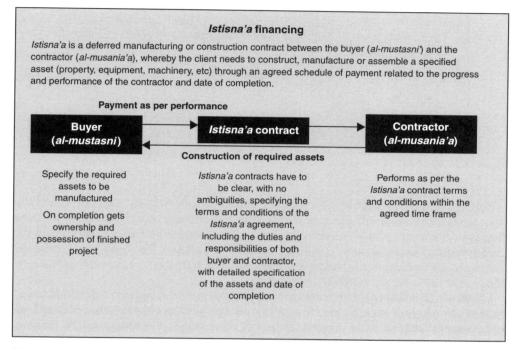

Figure 8.1   Summary of parties involved in *Istisna'a* financing

8.2 WHAT MAKES *ISTISNA'A SHARIA'A* COMPLIANT?

Similarly to *Murabaha* and *Ijara*, no direct support for the principle of *Istisna'a* can be found by studying the major sources of *Sharia'a* law. In fact, the majority of religious schools argue that *Istisna'a* is inconsistent with *Sharia'a* law. Only the Hanafi School accepts the *Istisna'a* contract and then merely because there is a need within society and customary practice (*urf*) to have an Islamically acceptable form of project finance. Notwithstanding the lack of juristic support for *Istisna'a*, it is still a widely employed method among Islamic banks.

As regards the legal effect of the agreement within the *Sharia'a*, the majority of its supporters say that the *Istisna'a* contract is not binding on any party until the construction is ready and approved by the buyer or until the goods are made and accepted by the final purchaser.

8.3 PRACTICALITIES OF IMPLEMENTING *ISTISNA'A*

The deal usually starts with the client approaching a bank to finance, say, a new building. Rather than extending a loan, the bank may suggest using *Istisna'a* to construct an interest-free transaction. The client is asked to present to the bank his ready-made blueprints and plans and any government required permits. He also advises on his preferred contractor for possible consideration by the bank. After concluding a credit evaluation of the client, the contractor (usually the one recommended by the client) provides the bank with an estimate, which is usually valid for a few months.

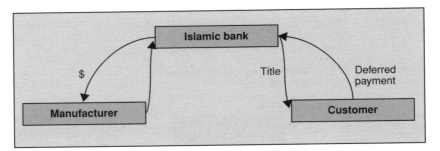

Figure 8.2   Parties to an *Istisna'a*

During this time the bank signs a contract with the client, whereby the latter is actually buying, on deferred payment, the specified asset that is to be constructed by the bank. The bank then signs a contract with the contractor to construct the specified asset using exactly the same specifications and contract conditions agreed with the client. The bank's payment to the contractor is in cash, while the bank receives the sale price from the client through instalments. This is Islamic financial intermediation in action.

The bank's profits are the difference between the cash payments made to the contractor and the deferred payment made by the client. Profit can be calculated in any which way, as long as the amount is known to the client at the time of contracting. The profit cannot be variable, and cannot be increased if instalments are not paid on time. Figure 8.2 illustrates the parties to an *Istisna'a*.

8.4 *SHARIA'A* RULES CONCERNING *ISTISNA'A*

The fundamental starting point is that an *Istisna'a* agreement is not a construction contract, although elements of it will likely deal with construction issues. It is a subset of *Sharia'a* approved sale contracts.

Usmani (1999) sets out the fundamental factors for a valid sale contract under the *Sharia'a* as follows:

- the asset must exist and be owned by the seller when the sale is made;
- the seller must also actually possess the asset, which can be in person or through an agent (for example, constructive ownership).

If both these factors are not present, the sale is not valid under the *Sharia'a* unless it falls into one of two exceptions. The two exceptions are *Salam* (see Chapter 9) and *Istisna'a*, the exception being discussed here.

Sharia'a rulings for *Istisna'a* are as follows:

- *Istisna'a* is an exceptional mode of sale, at an agreed price, whereby the buyer places an order to manufacture, assemble or construct, or cause so to do something to be delivered at a future date.
- The commodity must be known and specified to the extent of removing any ambiguity regarding its specifications including kind, type, quality and quantity, in order to avoid *gharar* (uncertainty).

- The price of the goods to be manufactured must be fixed in absolute and unambiguous terms. The agreed price may be paid in lump sum or in instalments, as mutually agreed by the parties.
- The provision of the material required for the manufacture of the commodity is not the responsibility of the buyer.
- Unless otherwise mutually agreed, any party may cancel the contract unilaterally if the seller has not incurred any direct or indirect cost in relation thereto.
- If the goods manufactured conform to the specifications agreed between the parties, the orderer (purchaser) cannot decline to accept them unless there is an obvious defect in the goods. However, the agreement can stipulate that if the delivery is not made within the mutually agreed time period, then the buyer can refuse to accept the goods.
- The bank (the buyer in the *Istisna'a*) can enter into a Parallel *Istisna'a* contract without any condition or linkage with the original *Istisna'a* contract. In one of the contracts the bank will be the buyer and in the second contract the seller. Each of the two contracts shall be independent of the other. They cannot be tied up in such a manner that the rights and obligations of one contract are dependent on the rights and obligations of the parallel contract.
- In *Istisna'a* transactions the buyer shall not, before taking possession (actual or constructive) of the goods, sell or transfer ownership of the goods to any other person.
- If the seller fails to deliver the goods, within the stipulated period, the price of the commodity can be reduced by a specified amount per day as per the agreement.
- The agreement can provide for a penalty payment calculated at the agreed rate in percent per day or per annum: the penalty must be donated to charity. Any security or collateral provided can be sold by the bank (purchaser) without the intervention of a court.
- In the case of default by the client, the banks can also approach competent courts for an award of damages, at the discretion of the court. This must be determined on the basis of direct and indirect costs incurred, and must not be related to the time value of money and any opportunity cost.

8.5 PRACTICAL EXAMPLES OF *ISTISNA'A*

Istisna'a is an Islamic financing structure best suited to finance the construction of capital equipment such as aircraft, oil rigs and machinery. Unlike *Murabaha*, where the investor can only buy the goods after they have been manufactured, *Istisna'a* enables the Islamic investor to purchase, in advance, equipment under construction.

At the end of the construction period the equipment is totally owned by the investor. At that point, the Islamic investor (owner) can then sell the equipment spot, lease it or sell it on deferred basis to an end user.

Istisna'a is the same technique as *Salam* as used for the financing of agricultural produce. *Istisna'a* can also be used for providing financing in certain transactions, especially in the house finance sector.

If the client has his own land and seeks financing for the construction of a house, the financier may undertake to construct the house on the land, on the basis of *Istisna'a*. If the client has no land the financier may undertake to provide him with a constructed house on a specified piece of land.

With *Istisna'a*, it is not necessary that the price is paid in advance or that it is paid at the time of delivery (it may be deferred at any time according to the agreement of the parties), and therefore the time of payment may be fixed in whatever manner is mutually agreed.

On the other hand it is not necessary that the financier himself constructs the house. He can enter into a parallel contract of *Istisna'a* with a third party, or may hire the services of a contractor (other than the client). In both cases, he can calculate his cost and fix the price of *Istisna'a* with his client in a manner that gives him a reasonable profit over his cost. The client may start to pay instalments right from the day when the contract of *Istisna'a* is signed by the parties, and may continue during the construction of the house and after it is handed over to the client. In order to secure the payment of the instalments, the financier may keep the title deeds of the house or land, or any other property of the client as a security, until the last instalment is paid by the client. The financier, in this case, will be responsible for the construction of the house in full conformity with the specifications detailed in the agreement.

The UK-based ABC International Bank, a wholly-owned subsidiary of the Arab Banking Corporation (ABC) Group in Bahrain, has pioneered a Parallel Phased *Istisna'a* (PPI), which sets new standards for the provision of *Sharia'a*-compliant construction finance in the UK. One of the risks associated with *Istisna'a* financing for building contracts is that they can be expensive because of the drawn-out nature of construction activity and the possible delays that can very often occur. As such the financing naturally carries a cost of capital from the day it is disbursed.

ABC's PPI mitigates this scenario through the use of multiple phased *Istisna'a* contracts for specific parts of the construction cycle. In other words the construction project is broken up into several *Istisna'a*s, which allows for a staggered financing and the drawdown of the funds, which subsequently carry a lower cost of capital. ABC International Bank has financed the construction of an inner-city residential development in Gotts Island, Leeds, in the UK, consisting of 183 residential flats and 72 parking spaces.

ABC entered into a contract with its equity partners, primarily investors from the Gulf Co-operation Council countries, and also has a separate contractual relationship with the developer, which, in the case of Phase II of the Gotts Island Project, is the UK-based Mayfair International Limited.

The instrument of *Istisna'a* may also be used for project financing on similar lines. If a client wants to install, say, an air conditioning plant in his factory, and the plant needs to be manufactured, the financier may undertake to construct the plant using the contract of *Istisna'a* according to the aforesaid procedure. Similarly, the contract of *Istisna'a* can be used for building a bridge or a motorway.

The modern Buy, Operate and Transfer (BOT) agreements may also be formalised on the basis of *Istisna'a*. If a government wants to construct a motorway, it may enter into a contract of *Istisna'a* with a builder. In this case, the deal for the builder may be the right to operate the motorway and collect tolls for a specified period.

An illustration of the structure applied to finance a satellite-based telecom project is given in Figure 8.3. This structure combines both the *Istisna'a* and *Ijara* (see Chapter 7) modes of Islamic finance.

8.6 KEY ISSUES ASSOCIATED WITH *ISTISNA'A*

Apart from the credit risk of the bank's client, in *Istisna'a* the banks will carry performance risk. Since the bank's client has no recourse or any contractual relationship with the actual

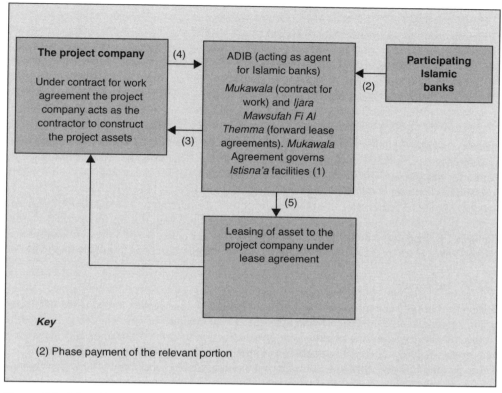

Figure 8.3   Financing of a satellite-based telecom project (*Istisna'a* or *Ijara wa Iqtina*)

manufacturer or contractor, the bank is always liable for any failure. This risk, however, can be reduced by taking a performance bond from the manufacturer or contractor.

Furthermore, the contract to manufacture or construct is based on the same blueprints and specifications provided by the client. The latter can also provide information concerning the best source of supply or reliable contractors. The bank has no incentive to choose a contractor or a manufacturer other than the one recommended by the client.

Many scholars permit the bank, once the goods are delivered, to be only a guarantor to the manufacturer or contractor. Hence the client can have a direct recourse to them whereas the bank bears the risks only if they fail to honour their commitment to the client.

8.6.1 Guarantees

The value of the goods or the asset to be constructed will be a debt receivable from the client. The bank can request any guarantees equal or in excess of this amount in a manner similar to conventional banking. Furthermore, the bank can request performance bonds from the contractors, and warranties after delivery. In all cases the two contracts (bank versus client and bank versus contractor or manufacturer) should always be separate.

8.6.2 Other Issues Relating to *Istisna'a*

Three other important issues relate to *Istisna'a*:

- delay in delivery;
- insurance;
- events of default.

8.6.2.1 Delay in Delivery

If there is a delay in delivery, the only permitted penalty under the *Sharia'a* is compensation by reference to a specific amount for each day of delay. This must be without prejudice to claims for damages arising from other losses if, for example, the delay goes beyond a cutoff date and the contract is then actually terminated.

If there is a delay in delivery, this then legally entitles the purchaser to terminate the *Istisna'a*. However, the purchaser can give the seller additional time and, during this period, charge damages for the delay. The purchaser can then give further notice to the seller demanding that delivery takes place by the new date. If that is not met, the purchaser can terminate the *Istisna'a*.

8.6.2.2 Insurance

During the period when the asset is being manufactured or constructed, arguably the purchaser is not interested in whether or not the asset under manufacture or construction is insured. If the asset is destroyed during manufacture or construction then the seller must take steps such that, by the delivery date, he has another asset that meets the purchaser's specifications.

The position may be different, however, if the purchaser pays instalments during the manufacture or construction period or if the asset is such that its destruction or damage means that there is no chance of a new asset being ready by the delivery date. If a building is destroyed or seriously damaged while under construction, this will almost certainly mean that a rebuild will not be ready by the contractual delivery date.

The same may also be the case with highly complex capital assets, such as aircraft. If instalments are paid during the manufacture or construction process, the purchaser might have a valid reason for having its interest noted on, for example, the contractor's insurance policy and may have it assigned in its favour. If during the construction period the asset under construction is destroyed or damaged to such extent that there is no possibility of delivery occurring on the delivery date, the purchaser may decide to treat this as a form of anticipatory breach, bringing the *Istisna'a* to an end.

In these circumstances, the benefit of insurance may assist in securing payments due to the purchaser from the seller (that is, the purchaser can claim the purchase instalments that it has paid and, possibly, additional damages).

From the seller's perspective, if delivery of the asset takes place and the purchaser owes instalments of the purchase price, it is acceptable for the seller to secure that obligation. Taking security over the property insurance taken out by the purchaser in its capacity as the owner of the completed asset is acceptable under the *Sharia'a*.

8.6.2.3 Events of Default

It is permissible under the *Sharia'a* to provide that, if various events occur, a party can terminate the *Istisna'a*. Such events, and the remedies and rights that they trigger, must be drafted in the context that *Istisna'a* is a sale contract. As such, events of default can be broken down into events that occur before delivery and those that occur after delivery. Furthermore, these events can, in turn, be broken down into whether they affect the seller or whether they affect the purchaser.

Default before delivery

If the events are caused by the *seller*, the purchaser can terminate the *Istisna'a*, demand the return of any purchase price instalments and claim damages arising out of the default of the seller. If the events are caused by the *purchaser*, the seller has a claim for damages arising out of the default by the purchaser. To the extent that the damages are less than any instalments paid by the purchaser, the seller must pay back the balance of the purchase instalments to the purchaser. If the damages are greater than the purchase instalments received, the seller has a claim for the excess.

Default after delivery

On the basis that possession and title to the asset will have passed to the purchaser, here are the two options depending on who caused the events:

- *Seller caused the event*: this will usually only arise due to the failure by the seller to finish any snag list items or to remedy defects. If the breach is such that the asset cannot be used for its intended purpose, the purchaser could terminate the *Istisna'a* and seek the recovery of the purchase price instalments that it has paid. If that were not sufficient to cover its loss, the purchaser would have a claim in damages for the excess.
- *Purchaser caused the event*: this will usually be the failure to pay the purchase price instalments as and when due. In this situation, given that title to the asset will have been transferred to the purchaser, the seller would not usually have the legal right to demand the return of the asset for failure to pay. The claim would be one for a debt that was due and payable. To cover this risk, the seller will usually seek security to cover the payment of the instalments (such as a mortgage or other security interest over the asset), which will enable it to recover amounts due through the enforcement of that security held.

8.7 COMPARISON OF *ISTISNA'A* WITH THE CONVENTIONAL BANKING EQUIVALENT

Figure 8.4 illustrates this issue by comparing the working mechanics of a conventional bank and its relationship with depositors and borrowers with *Istisna'a* finance in an Islamic bank.

8.8 *ISTISNA'A*: DIFFERENCES FROM THE OTHER ISLAMIC FINANCING TECHNIQUES

There are several ways to classify Islamic finance modes of finance. In this context the contracts are broken down into two groups:

- Islamically permissible deferred sales contracts;
- PLS contracts.

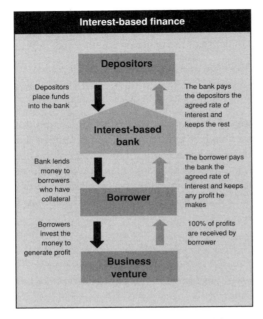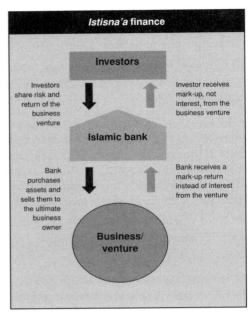

Figure 8.4   Conventional interest-based finance as compared with *Istisna'a*

8.8.1 Islamically Permissible Deferred Sales Contracts

Jurists have ruled it valid to sell an object immediately, with a deferred price, possibly paid in instalments, greater than its cash price. All the major *Madhabs* (Schools of Islamic jurisprudence), *Shafiis*, *Hanafis*, *Malikis* and *Hanbalis* have agreed to this principle. The rationale is that the seller of an object for a price to be paid in instalments, in the future, is sacrificing a benefit in order to make the object available to the person who is buying it with a deferred payment.

This sacrifice is based on the fact that the seller gets paid at a later date. Thus the seller is making a sacrifice in that he is not able to get paid today and thereby purchase something else or simply have the cash. Thus, the increase in the deferred price may be viewed as compensation to the seller. The Jurists ruled these sales valid as long as the contract is independently specified and contains no ignorance (*jahala*).

Islamically permissible deferred sales create deferred obligations using the concept of counter-values described in Chapter 3:

- *Istisna'a* sale. The price is paid at the time of contract and the object of sale is to be manufactured and delivered later.
- *Murabaha*: sale with a known profit. The object of sale is delivered at the contract time but the price becomes due as debt.
- *Salam* sale. The price is paid at the time of contract but the object of sale becomes due as debt-in-kind.
- *Ijara*. The sale of the rights to use assets where assets are delivered to the user, who in turn pays periodical rentals later.

8.8.2 Profit and Loss Share (PLS) Contracts

A PLS contract means that the outcome is sharing based and cannot be predetermined. Shareholders are only repaid if profits are made and if no profits are made then no payouts take place. There are two types of PLS contracts as described in the next two sections.

8.8.2.1 Mudaraba *PLS Contracts*

The *Mudaraba* contract is a contract between two parties: an Islamic bank as an investor (*Rab ul Mall*) who provides a second party, the entrepreneur (*mudarib*), with financial resources to finance a particular project. Profits are shared between the parties in a proportion agreed in advance. Losses are the liability of the Islamic bank and the *mudarib* sacrifices only its efforts and expected share in the profits.

8.8.2.2 Musharaka *PLS Contracts*

The *Musharaka* PLS contract is an equity participation contract. The bank is not the sole provider of funds to finance a project. Two or more partners contribute to the joint capital of an investment. Profits are shared between the parties in a proportion agreed in advance. Losses are shared strictly in relation to the respective capital contributions. Figure 8.5 illustrates these modes of finance.

8.8.3 Differences Between *Istisna'a* and *Salam*

The following list summarises some points of difference between *Istisna'a* and *Salam* (described in Chapter 9):

- The subject of *Istisna'a* is always an item that needs manufacturing, whereas Salam can be effected on any item, no matter whether it needs manufacturing or not.

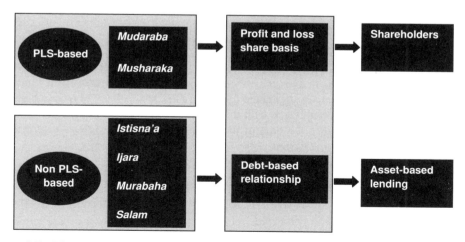

Figure 8.5 Islamic modes of finance

- The price must be paid in full in advance with a *Salam* contract. This is not necessary with *Istisna'a*.
- The contract of *Salam*, once effected, cannot be cancelled unilaterally, whereas the contract of *Istisna'a* can be cancelled before the manufacturer starts the work.
- The time of delivery is an essential part of the sale in *Salam* but the time of delivery does not have to be fixed in *Istisna'a*.

8.8.4 Differences between *Istisna'a* and *Ijara*

The manufacturer in *Istisna'a* undertakes to make the required goods with his own raw materials. This transaction therefore implies that the manufacturer should obtain the necessary material, if he does not already possess them, and undertake the work required for making the ordered goods with it. In this respect, *Istisna'a* differs from *Ijara*: otherwise the contract would amount to a hiring of the sellers wage labour as occurs under *Ijara*.

If the customer provides the material and the manufacturer is required to use his labour and skill only, the transaction is not *Istisna'a*. In this case it will be an *Ijara* transaction whereby the services of a person are hired for a specific fee paid to him.

According to the *Sharia'a* scholars, *Istisna'a* is a forward sale contract involving the acquisition of goods by specification or order, where the price is paid progressively in accordance with the progress of the job completion. This is practised, for example, when purchasing houses to be constructed where the payments made to the developer or builder are according to the stage of work completed.

In the case of another forward sale contract, *Salam*, the full payment, is made in advance to the seller before delivery of the goods. In Islamic financing, the applications of *Salam* and *Istisna'a* are purchasing mechanisms, whereas *Murabaha* and *Bai' Bithaman Ajil* (a sale with a deferred payment) are for financing sales.

Istisna'a is a kind of sale in which a commodity is transacted before it exists. If the manufacturer undertakes to construct the goods for the customer with the manufacturer's own materials, the transaction of *Istisna'a* comes into existence. But it is necessary, for the validity of *Istisna'a*, that the price is fixed with the consent of the parties and that the necessary specification of the commodity (intended to be manufactured) is fully agreed between them.

8.9 SUMMARY

To help clarify *Istisna'a*, take a look at the depiction in Figure 8.6. *Istisna'a* is the Islamic vehicle for financing construction or manufacturing projects such as apartment buildings, aircraft, shipbuilding and so on. A significant feature of *Istisna'a* is that it permits a financing transaction to take place in compliance with the *Sharia'a* even though the subject matter of the transaction does not exist at the time of the contract. Another important feature is that payments can be immediate or deferred.

The steps involved in an *Istisna'a* sale are as follows:

1. The client initiates the process by expressing, to the bank, his desire to manufacture or construct an asset at a specific cost. He gives detailed specifications of the item to be manufactured, constructed or fabricated.
2. The bank agrees to manufacture, construct or fabricate the asset, and to deliver it to the client in a specific time period.

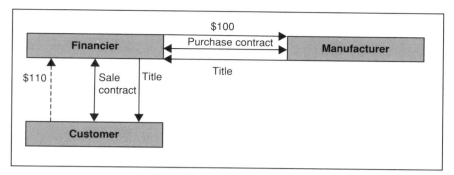

Figure 8.6   The *Istisna'a* mode of finance

3. The bank then enters into a contract with the manufacturer, contractor or fabricator, who agrees to manufacture, construct or fabricate the specified asset and deliver it in due time.
4. Final delivery of the asset is made either to the bank or to the client as agreed in the contract.
5. Customer payments can be immediate or deferred.
6. An Islamic bank can use *Istisna'a* in two ways:

   It is permissible for the bank to buy an asset under an *Istisna'a* contract and sell it either on receipt of a cash instalment or a deferred payment basis.

   It is also permissible for the bank to enter into a *Istisna'a* contract in the capacity of seller to a client who needs to purchase a particular asset and then draw a Parallel *Istisna'a* contract in the capacity of a buyer with another party to make (manufacture) the asset agreed upon in the first contract.

The first *Istisna'a* can be immediate or deferred (the payment). The payment terms in the second *Istisna'a* can also be cash or deferred. Contracts in the nature of Build, Operate and Transfer (BOT) can be categorised as *Istisna'a* transactions. For example, a government may enter into a contract with a builder to be repaid through a toll collection over a specified period. *Istisna'a* is also applied in the construction industry including apartment buildings, hospitals, schools and universities.

REFERENCE

Usmani, T.U. (1999). *An Introduction to Islamic Finance*. Idaratul-Ma'arif. Karachi, Pakistan

9

Salam as a Mode of Islamic Finance

> **Salam** is a contract involving the purchase of a commodity for deferred delivery in exchange for immediate payment according to specified conditions, or the sale of a commodity for deferred delivery in exchange for immediate payment.
>
> **Parallel _Salam_**
>
> A Parallel _Salam_ is a _Salam_ contract whereby the seller depends, for executing his obligation, on receiving what is due to him, in his capacity as the buyer, from a sale in a previous _Salam_ contract without making the execution of the second _Salam_ contract dependent on the execution of the first one.
>
> _Source_: Accounting and Auditing Organisation for Islamic Financial Institutions (AAOIFI)

9.1 DEFINITION OF _SALAM_

Salam is a sale whereby the seller undertakes to supply some specific goods to the buyer at a future date, in exchange for an advanced price fully paid at spot. Here the price received is in the form of cash, but the delivery of the purchased goods is deferred. In Arabic the buyer is called _muslam_, the seller _muslam ileihi_, the cash price paid _Ras ul Mall_ and the purchased commodity is termed _muslam fihi_.

Salam was allowed by the Prophet subject to certain conditions. The basic purpose of a _Salam_ sale was to meet the needs of small farmers who needed finance to grow their crops (particularly dates) and to feed their families up to the time of harvest. After the prohibition of _riba_ (interest), they could not take usurious loans. Therefore they were allowed to sell their agricultural products in advance of the harvest.

Similarly, the traders of Arabia used to export certain goods to other places and import some other goods to their homeland. They needed finance to undertake this type of business and yet could not borrow from the money lenders after the prohibition of _riba_. It was therefore made permissible that they could sell their goods in advance. After receiving their cash price, they could then more easily undertake their everyday business.

Not every commodity is suitable for a _Salam_ contract. It is usually applied only to fungible commodities (i.e. a commodity that is freely interchangeable with another in satisfying an obligation). Some basic rules governing the _Salam_ sale are given below:

- The price should be paid in full at the time of the contract.
- Goods whose quality or quantity cannot be determined by exact specification cannot be sold through the contract of _Salam_, for example, precious stones.
- Goods can be sold only by specifying the attributes the goods possess. The goods cannot be particularised to a given farm, field or tree.
- The exact date and place of delivery must also be specified.

Islamic banks can provide financing by way of a *Salam* contract by entering into two separate *Salam* contracts, or one *Salam* contract and an instalment sales contract. For example, the bank could buy a commodity by making an advance payment to the supplier and fixing the date of delivery at the client's desired date. It can then sell the commodity to a third party either on a *Salam* or sale by instalments basis. If the two were both *Salam* contracts, the second contract known as a Parallel *Salam* contract, would be for delivery of the same quantity and description as that constituting the subject matter of the first *Salam* contract. This second contract would be concluded after the first contract, because its price has to be paid immediately upon conclusion of the contract.

To be valid from the *Sharia'a* point of view, the second contract must be independent (or not linked to the delivery in the first contract). If the second contract consists of a sale by instalments, its date should be subsequent to the date on which the bank would receive the commodity.

9.2 WHAT MAKES *SALAM SHARIA'A* COMPLIANT?

To explain why *Salam* is *Sharia'a* compliant, it is necessary to refer to the *Ahadith* to explain the evidence of legality.

Salam is a kind of debt because the subject of the *Salam* contract is the liability of the seller up to the due date, and so its permissibility is subsumed in the following verse:

> O ye who believe! When ye deal with each other, in transactions involving future obligations in a fixed period of time, reduce them to writing.
>
> *Al-Baqara 282*

In addition, the Prophet said:

> He who sells on *Salam* must sell a specific volume and a specific weight to a specific due date.

All the Muslim jurists are unanimous regarding the principle that *Salam* will not be valid unless all the *Sharia'a* conditions are fully observed, because they are based on the express *Ahadith* of the Prophet. The most famous *Hadith* in this context is the one which the Prophet said

> Whoever wishes to enter into a contract of *Salam*, he must effect the *Salam* according to the specified measure and the specified weight and the specified date of delivery.

There is consensus among Muslims on the permissibility of *Salam* due to the practical need for it and because the commodity in the contract is a recompense for the price paid in advance. The commodity to be delivered is similar to the price in a credit sale and so it is considered to be an affirmed liability, and thereby acceptable under the *Sharia'a*.

9.3 PRACTICALITIES OF IMPLEMENTING *SALAM*

A *Salam* contract is a debt obligation, albeit in goods not money. It is normal, therefore, to support this obligation by guarantees and securities up to an amount equal to the value of the goods.

Guarantees and securities in a *Salam* contract are necessary to implement it. In order to ensure that the seller delivers the commodity on the agreed date, the bank can also ask him to furnish a security, which may be in the form of a guarantee or in the form of a mortgage or hypothecation. In the case of default in delivery, the guarantor may be asked to deliver the same commodity and if there is a mortgage, the buyer or financier can sell the mortgaged property and the sale proceeds can be used either to realise the required commodity by purchasing it from the market or to recover the price advanced by the bank.

9.4 *SHARIA'A* RULES CONCERNING *SALAM*

It is one of the basic conditions for the validity of any sale in *Sharia'a* that any commodity (intended to be sold) must be in the physical or constructive possession of the seller. This condition has three elements:

- The commodity must exist. This means that a commodity that does not exist at the time of sale cannot normally be sold.
- The seller should have acquired ownership of that commodity. This means that if the commodity exists but the seller does not own it, he cannot sell it to anybody.
- Mere ownership is not enough: it should have come into the possession of the seller, physically or constructively. If the seller owns a commodity, but he has not taken delivery either himself or through an agent, he cannot sell it.

There are only two exceptions to this general principle in the *Sharia'a*. One is *Salam*, discussed in this chapter, and the other is *Istisna'a* (see Chapter 8). Both are sales of a special nature.

Salam is beneficial to the seller because he receives the price in advance. It is beneficial to the buyer also, because the price in *Salam* is usually lower than the price in spot sales. The permissibility of *Salam* was an exception to the general rule that prohibits forward sales, and therefore, it was subjected to some strict conditions.

Usmani (1999) sets out the *Sharia'a* rules regarding *Salam* (that is, advance payment against deferred delivery sale), which are summarised as follows:

1. *Salam* means a kind of sale whereby the seller undertakes to supply specific goods to a buyer at a future date in consideration of a price being fully paid in advance at the time the contract of sale is made.
2. The buyer must pay the price in full to the seller at the time of effecting the sale. Otherwise it will be tantamount to a sale of debt against debt, which is expressly prohibited in the *Sharia'a*.
3. The specifications, quality and quantity of the commodity must be determined in order to avoid any ambiguity (*gharar*) that could become a cause of dispute.
4. The date and place of delivery must be agreed upon but can be changed with mutual consent of the parties.
5. *Salam* can be effected in respect of the Arabic term *Dhawatul-Amthal*, which classifies the acceptable *Salam* commodities as those that are homogenous in terms of characteristics and are traded by counting, measuring or weighing according to usage and the customs of trade. Items such as precious stones, farm animals and so on cannot be sold through the contract of *Salam* because every stone or individual animal is normally different from any other.
6. It is necessary that the commodity that is the subject of *Salam* contract should normally be expected to be available at the time of delivery.
7. *Salam* cannot be effected in respect of things that must be delivered on spot. Examples of spot transactions are exchange of gold with silver or wheat with barley where it is necessary, according to the *Sharia'a*, that the delivery of both be simultaneous.

8. *Salam* cannot be tied to the produce of a particular farm, field or tree.

9. In a *Salam* transaction, the buyer cannot contractually bind the seller to buy-back the commodity that will be delivered by the seller to the buyer. However, after the delivery is effected, the buyer and the seller can enter into a transaction of sale, independently and with free will.

10. In *Salam* transactions the buyer shall not, before taking possession (actual or constructive) of the goods, sell or transfer ownership in the goods to any person.

11. The bank (the buyer in *Salam*) can enter into a Parallel *Salam* contract without any condition or linkage with the original *Salam* contract. In one contract the bank will be the buyer and in the second contract the seller. Each one of the two contracts shall be independent of the other. They cannot be tied together in a manner that the rights and obligations of the original contract are dependent on the rights and obligations of the parallel contract.

12. In order to ensure that the seller delivers the commodity on the agreed date the bank can ask him to furnish security or guarantees.

13. In the case of multiple commodities, the quantity and period of delivery for each of them should be fixed separately.

14. A penalty can be agreed at the outset in the *Salam* contract for any delay in delivery of the concerned commodity by the client or the seller of the commodity. In that case, the client shall be liable to pay a penalty calculated at the agreed rate in percent per day or per annum. However, that penalty must be donated to charity. The banks can also approach competent courts for an award of damages, at the discretion of the courts. This must be determined on the basis of direct and indirect costs incurred, other than the time value of money or the opportunity cost. Also, security or collateral can be sold by the bank (purchaser) without the intervention of a court.

9.5 *SHARIA'A* RULES CONCERNING PARALLEL *SALAM*

Since Islamic banks and financial institutions are using the instrument of Parallel *Salam*, it is also important that the *Sharia'a* rules for the validity of this arrangement are observed, as follows:

- In a Parallel *Salam* contract, the bank enters two different contracts. In one of them, the bank is the buyer and in the second the bank is the seller. Each of these contracts must be independent of the other. They cannot be tied up in a manner such that the rights and obligations of one contact are dependent on the rights and obligations of the parallel contract. Each contract should have its own force and its performance should not be contingent on the other.

  For example, if 'A' purchases 1000 bags of wheat from 'B' by way of *Salam* to be delivered on 31 December, 'A' can contract a Parallel *Salam* with 'C' to deliver 1000 bags of wheat to him on 31 December. But while contracting Parallel *Salam* with 'C', the delivery of wheat to 'C' cannot be conditional upon taking delivery from 'B'. Therefore, even if 'B' does not deliver wheat on 31 December, 'A' is duty bound to deliver 1000 bags of wheat to 'C'. He can seek whatever recourse he has against 'B', but he cannot rid himself from his liability to deliver wheat to 'C'.

  Similarly, if 'B' delivers defective goods that do not conform to the agreed specifications, 'A' is still obligated to deliver the goods to 'C' according to the specifications agreed with him.

- Parallel *Salam* is allowed with a third party only. The seller in the first contract cannot be the purchaser in the Parallel *Salam*, because it will be a buy-back contract. This is not permissible in the *Sharia'a*.

  Even if the purchaser in the second contract is a separate legal entity, but is fully owned by the seller in the first contract, the arrangement is not allowed, because in practical terms it will amount to a buy-back arrangement.

  For example, assume that 'A' purchases 1000 bags of wheat by way of *Salam* from 'B', a joint stock company. 'B' has a subsidiary 'C', which is a separate legal entity but is fully owned by 'B'. 'A' cannot contract the Parallel *Salam* with 'C'. However, if 'C' is not wholly owned by 'B', 'A' can contract Parallel *Salam* with it, even if some shareholders are common between 'B' and 'C'.

9.6 PRACTICAL EXAMPLES OF *SALAM*

Salam is allowed under the *Sharia'a* in order to fulfil the needs of farmers and traders. Therefore, it is basically a mode of financing for small farmers and traders. This mode of financing can be used by banks and financial institutions, especially in financing the agricultural sector. The price in *Salam* may be fixed at a lower rate than the price of those commodities delivered at spot. In this way, the difference between the two prices may be a valid profit for the banks or financial institutions.

9.7 BENEFITS OF THE *SALAM* CONTRACT

Firstly, after purchasing a commodity by way of *Salam*, the financial institution may sell it through a Parallel *Salam* for the same date of delivery, as mentioned above. The period of *Salam* in the second (parallel) transaction being shorter, the price may be a little higher than the price of the first transaction and the difference between the two prices will be the profit earned by the bank. The shorter is the period of *Salam*, the higher the price and the greater the profit. In this way the banks may manage their short-term financing portfolios.

Secondly, if a Parallel *Salam* is not feasible for one reason or another, the financial institution can obtain a promise to purchase from a third party. This promise should be unilateral from the expected buyer. Being merely a promise, and not the actual sale, their buyers do not have to pay the price in advance. Therefore, a higher price may be fixed and as soon as the commodity is received by the institution it is sold to the third party at a pre-agreed price, according to the terms of the promise.

A third option is sometimes proposed that, at the date of delivery, the commodity is sold back to the seller at a higher price. However this suggestion is not in line with the dictates of the *Sharia'a*. It is never permitted under the *Sharia'a* that the purchased commodity is sold back to the seller before the buyer takes its delivery and, if it is done at a higher price, it will be tantamount to *riba*, which is totally prohibited. Even if it is sold back to the seller after taking delivery from him, it cannot be pre-arranged at the time of original sale. This proposal is not acceptable within the *Sharia'a*.

9.8 PROBLEMS ASSOCIATED WITH *SALAM*

In addition to the credit risk (sellers default), which is normal for any type of finance, the bank faces market risk. Although prices at the time of delivery may be higher than that of the *Salam* price, the market price may fluctuate in any direction. Unfortunately, not many strategies can be taken to mitigate this problem. Goods bought under a *Salam* contract cannot be sold before actual delivery and possession by the bank. The bank cannot simply sell the goods forward if prices are expected to fall before delivery.

One possibility of hedging may be adopted through Parallel *Salam*, discussed earlier. In this case the bank enters the market as a seller of goods of similar specification once the *Salam* contract is concluded. The term can be designed to fall at the same date of delivery. It is important to note here that the bank is not actually selling the same goods that were the subject of the first *Salam*. Hence there are two separate contracts, one in which the bank is the buyer, the other in which the bank is the seller.

9.9 COMPARISON OF *SALAM* WITH THE CONVENTIONAL BANKING EQUIVALENT

To help clarify this issue, Figure 9.1 compares the mechanics of a conventional bank, and its relationship with depositors and borrowers, to *Salam* finance in an Islamic bank.

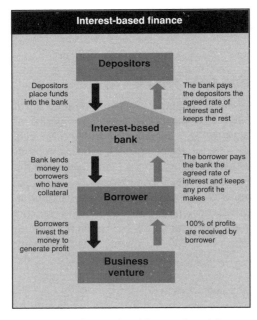
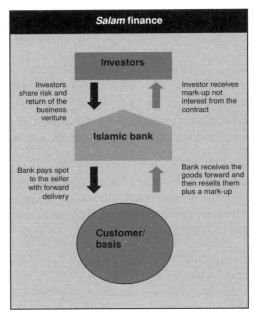

Figure 9.1   Conventional interest-based finance as compared with *Salam*

9.10 *SALAM*: DIFFERENCES FROM THE OTHER ISLAMIC FINANCING TECHNIQUES

There are several ways to classify Islamic finance modes of finance. In this context the contracts are broken down into two groups known as

• Islamically permissible deferred sales contracts;
• PLS contracts.

9.10.1 Islamically Permissible Deferred Sales Contracts

Jurists have ruled it valid to sell an object immediately, with a deferred price, possibly paid in instalments, greater than its cash price. All the major *Madhabs* (Schools of Islamic jurisprudence), *Shafiis*, *Hanafis*, *Malikis* and *Hanbalis* have agreed to this principle. The rationale is that the seller of an object for a price to be paid in instalments, in the future, is sacrificing a benefit in order to make the object available to the person who is buying it with a deferred payment.

This sacrifice is based on the fact that the seller gets paid at a later date. Thus the seller is making a sacrifice in that he is not able to get paid today and thereby purchase something else or simply have the cash. Thus, the increase in the deferred price may be viewed as compensation to the seller. The Jurists ruled these sales valid as long as the contract is independently specified and contains no ignorance (*jahala*).

Islamically permissible deferred sales create deferred obligations using the concept of counter-values described in Chapter 3:

- *Salam* sale. The price is paid at the time of contract but the object of sale becomes due as debt-in kind.
- *Murabaha*: sale with a known profit. The object of sale is delivered at the contract time but the price becomes due as debt.
- *Istisna'a* sale. The price is paid at the time of contract and the object of sale is to be manufactured and delivered later.
- *Ijara*. Sale of the rights to use assets where assets are delivered to the user, who in turn pays periodical rentals later.

9.10.2 Profit and Loss Share (PLS) Contracts

A PLS contract means that the outcome is sharing based and cannot be predetermined. Shareholders are only repaid if profits are made and if no profits are made then no payouts take place. There two types of PLS contracts.

9.10.2.1 Mudaraba *PLS Contracts*

The *Mudaraba* contract is a contract between two parties: an Islamic bank as an investor (*Rab ul Mall*) who provides a second party, the entrepreneur (*mudarib*), with financial resources to finance a particular project. Profits are shared between the parties in a proportion agreed in advance. Losses are the liability of the Islamic bank and the *mudarib* sacrifices only its efforts and expected share in the profits.

9.10.2.2 Musharaka *PLS Contracts*

The *Musharaka* PLS contract is an equity participation contract. The bank is not the sole provider of funds to finance a project. Two or more partners contribute to the joint capital of an investment. Profits are shared between the parties in a proportion agreed in advance. Losses are shared strictly in relation to the respective capital contributions. Figure 9.2 illustrates these modes of finance.

In the case of a forward sale contract, *Salam*, the full payment is made in advance to the seller before delivery of the goods. In Islamic financing, the applications of *Salam* and *Istisna'a*

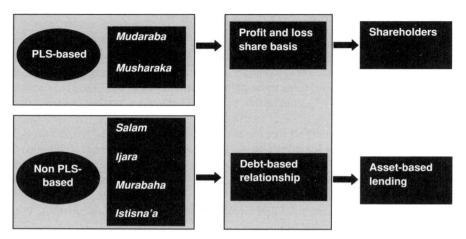

Figure 9.2 Islamic modes of finance

are as purchasing mechanisms, whereas *Murabaha* and *Bai' Bithaman Ajil* are for financing sales.

Salam is the second kind of sale (along with *Istisna'a*) in which a commodity, under the *Sharia'a* rules, can be transacted before it comes into existence.

9.10.3 Differences between *Salam* and *Istisna'a*

There are several points of difference between *Salam* and *Istisna'a*, and these are summarised below:

- The subject of *Istisna'a* is always an item that needs manufacturing, whereas *Salam* can be effected on any item, no matter whether it needs manufacturing or not.
- The price must be paid in full in advance with a *Salam* contract. This is not necessary in *Istisna'a*.
- The contract of *Salam*, once effected, cannot be cancelled unilaterally, whereas the contract of *Istisna'a* can be cancelled before the manufacturer starts the work.
- The time of delivery is an essential part of the sale in *Salam* whereas it is not necessary, with *Istisna'a*, for the time of delivery to be fixed.

9.11 SUMMARY

Salam is best be depicted by the flow chart in Figure 9.3. The Organisation of Islamic Conference Islamic Fiqh Academy in Jeddah has recognised *Salam* as a *Sharia'a*-compliant mode of Islamic banking.

Salam means a contract in which advance payment is made for goods to be delivered at a later date. The seller undertakes to supply some specific goods to the buyer at a future date in exchange for a price fully paid in advance at the time of contract. It is necessary that the quality of the commodity intended to be purchased is fully specified, leaving no ambiguity leading to dispute. The objects of this sale are goods and cannot be gold, silver or currencies. Barring

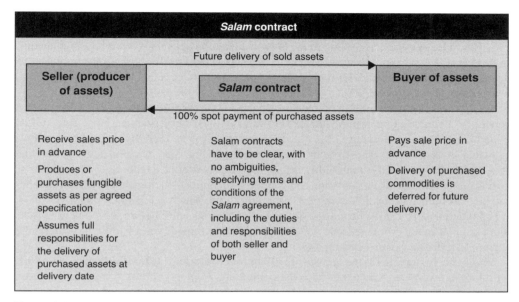

Figure 9.3   *Salam* flow chart

these cases, *Salam* covers almost anything, which is capable of being accurately described as to quantity, quality and workmanship.

For the validity of *Salam*, the buyer must pay the price in full to the seller at the time of effecting the sale. This is necessary because, in the absence of full payment by the buyer, it will be tantamount to a sale of debt against debt, which is expressly prohibited. Moreover, the basic wisdom behind the permissibility of *Salam* is to fulfil the instant needs of the seller. If the price is not paid to him in full the basic purpose of the transaction will be defeated.

As stated, *Salam* can be effected in only those commodities whose quality and quantity can be specified precisely. Items whose quality or quantity is not determined by the specification cannot be sold through the contract of *Salam*. For example, precious stones cannot be sold on the basis of *Salam*, because every precious stone is normally different from another in its quality or size or weight. Their exact specification is not generally possible.

Salam cannot be effected on a particular commodity or on a product of a particular field or farm. For example, if the seller undertakes to supply wheat of a particular field, or the fruit of a particular tree, the *Salam* will not be valid, because there is a possibility that produce of that particular field or the fruit of that tree is destroyed before the delivery and, given this possibility, the delivery remains uncertain. The same rule is applicable to every commodity whose supply is not certain. It is necessary that the quality of the commodity (intended to be purchased through *Salam*) be fully specified leaving no ambiguity that may lead to disputes. All possible details in this respect must be expressly mentioned.

It is also necessary that the quantity of the commodity be agreed upon in unequivocal terms. If the commodity is quantified by weight according to the usage of its traders, its weight must be determined, and if it is quantified through being measured, its exact measure should be known. What is normally weighed cannot be specified by measures and vice versa.

The exact date of delivery must be specified in the contract. *Salam* cannot be used in respect of those things that must be delivered at spot. For example, if gold is purchased in exchange for silver, it is necessary, according to the *Sharia'a*, that the delivery of both be simultaneous. In this case, *Salam* cannot be used. Similarly, if wheat is bartered for barley, the simultaneous delivery of both is necessary for the validity of sale. The effect is that the contract of *Salam*, in this case, is not allowed.

Salam sale is not permissible on existing commodities because damage and deterioration cannot be assured before delivery on the due date. Delivery may become impossible. *Salam* is permissible on a commodity of a specific locality if it is assured that it is almost always available in that locality and it rarely becomes unavailable. The place of delivery must be stated in the contract if the commodity necessitates transportation expenses.

It is permissible to take a mortgage and guarantor on *Salam* debt to guarantee that the seller satisfies his obligation by delivering the commodity sold, which is a liability on the due date. It is not permissible for the buyer of a *Salam* commodity to sell it before receiving it because that is similar to the prohibited sale of debt. The *Salam* commodity is a liability or debt on the seller and is not an existing commodity.

Salam sale is suitable for the finance of agricultural operations, where the bank can transact with farmers who are expected to have the commodity in plenty during harvest, either from their own crops or crops of others, which they can buy and deliver in case their crops fail. Thus the bank renders valuable services to the farmers in this way enabling them to achieve their production targets.

Salam sale is also used to finance commercial and industrial activities, especially for phases prior to the production and export of commodities. Banks apply *Salam* when financing artisans and small producers, by supplying them with inputs of production as *Salam* capital in exchange for some of their commodities to re-market. The scope of *Salam* is large enough to cover the needs of various groups such as farmers, industrialists, contractors or traders. It can provide finance for a variety of operational costs and capital goods.

REFERENCE

Usmani, T.U. (1999). *An Introduction to Islamic Finance*. Idaratul-Ma'arif. Karachi, Pakistan.

10
Takaful: Islamic Insurance

> Tie your camel first and then put your trust in Allah.
>
> This *Hadith* implies the need for Muslims to mitigate risk.

10.1 CASE FOR ISLAMIC INSURANCE

Islamic insurance is testament to the ability of Islamic finance to evolve and innovate. For years it had been an article of faith that conventional insurance was not compatible with Islam because it contained elements of *gharar* (uncertainty), *maisir* (gambling) and *riba* (interest). Since conventional insurance was all about uncertainty and chance occurrences, in the eyes of Muslims insurance looked like a catalogue of prohibited practices: inequality between premiums paid and benefits collected (or not collected) from the insurance company; premiums placed in interest bearing instruments; late payment of premiums resulting in interest and late fees; uncertainty over subject matter and duration of contracts and so on. In recent years, however, Islamic doctrine has come to terms with most forms of insurance.

10.2 ISLAMIC ISSUES WITH CONVENTIONAL INSURANCE

Both conventional insurance operating under common law and *Takaful* operating under the *Sharia'a* principles, share the common goals of providing a reasonable financial security against unpredicted catastrophe, disaster or risk befalling one's life or property. Although both conventional insurance and *Takaful* strive for a common ideal based on contractual principles, there are some key differences between both systems.

10.2.1 Issues in Conventional Insurance

Conventional insurance contains elements contradictory to Islamic *Sharia'a*, particularly *gharar*, *maisir* and *riba*. The conventional insurance contract contains uncertainty, it is argued, as regards whether the premium will be paid as promised and the fact that the exact amount of the premium and the exact time it will be paid in the future are also not known. Any form of contract that is lopsided in favour of one party at the expense and potential unjust loss to the other is classified as *gharar*.

In addition, if a claim is not made, the conventional insurance company may simply keep the premiums and the participant fails to obtain any financial profit whatsoever. Also the loss of premiums on cancellation of a life insurance policy by the policyholder is considered unjust. The double standard condition of charging a customer for a short period in general insurance, while only a proportional refund is made if the insurance company terminates the cover, is also considered unjust Islamically.

Conventional insurance also involves gambling, it is argued, because the participant contributes a small amount of premium in the hope of gaining a large sum if the insured loss actually takes place. In addition, the participant simply loses the money paid for the premium if the insured event does not occur.

Apart from the above, conventional insurance also involves interest, because an element of interest exists in conventional life insurance products. Payments to the beneficiaries of life insurance usually receive income from annuities based on investing in interest bearing instruments. This element of *riba* is strictly forbidden in Islam.

10.3 DEFINITION AND CONCEPT OF *TAKAFUL*

Insurance as a concept does not contradict the practices and requirements of the *Sharia'a* – in essence, insurance is synonymous with a system of mutual help – but 'security/insurance' itself is not a valid object of sale under the *Sharia'a*. Despite the acknowledged need for mutual help, Muslim Jurists are of the opinion that the operation of conventional insurance does not conform to the rules and requirements of *Sharia'a* because, as stated above, it involves the elements of *gharar*, *maisir* and *riba* in its investment activities.

Takaful is an Arabic word meaning guaranteeing each other or joint guarantee. The main core of the *Takaful* system – the aspect that makes it free from uncertainty and gambling – is *Tabarru'*, which means donation, gift or contribution. Each participant who needs protection must be motivated by the sincere intention to donate to other participants faced with difficulties. Islamic insurance is the system whereby each participant contributes into a fund that is used to support the other participants, with each participant contributing sufficient amounts to cover expected claims. *Takaful* emphasises unity and cooperation among participants. The objective of *Takaful* is to pay a defined loss from a defined fund. So *Takaful* is insurance practised under *Sharia'a* principles.

Takaful is not a new concept – it had been practised by the *Muhajirin* of Mecca and the *Ansar* of Medina following the *Hijra* of the Prophet over 1400 years ago.

10.3.1 How *Tabarru'* Eliminates the Problems of Conventional Insurance

Tabarru' is the agreement by a participant to relinquish, as a donation, a certain proportion of the *Takaful* contribution that he agrees or undertakes to pay, thereby enabling him to fulfil his obligation of mutual help and joint guarantee, should any of his fellow participants suffer a defined loss.

The concept of *Tabarru'* eliminates the element of uncertainty (*gharar*) in the *Takaful* contract. The reasoning behind this is that *gharar* does not exist in the *Tabarru'* relationship, according to the *Maliki* School of Islamic jurisprudence. The sharing of profit or surplus that may emerge from the operations of *Takaful* is made only after the obligation of assisting the fellow participants has been fulfilled. Thus, the operation of *Takaful* may be envisaged as a profit-sharing business venture between the *Takaful* operator and the individual members of a group of participants.

Insurance can only have a place in the *Sharia'a* if it is approved by the *Sharia'a* board, meaning that it has to be practised based on shared responsibility, mutual cooperation and solidarity, designed to safeguard against a defined risk.

10.3.2 Derivation of the Term *Takaful*

The term *Takaful* is an infinitive noun (*masdar*) derived from the root word *kafl*, which means guarantee or responsibility. Meanwhile *Takaful* – whose chief characteristic is *Musharaka* (see Chapter 6) – means sharing. Thus, the word *Takaful* means shared responsibility, shared guarantee, collective assurance and mutual undertakings. Technically *Takaful*, from the economic point of view, means a mutual guarantee or assurance based on the principles of *al-aqd* (contract) provided by a group of people living in the same society, against a defined risk or catastrophe befalling life, property or any form of valuable asset. Hence *Takaful* is sometimes known as cooperative insurance with mutual agreement.

Muslim Jurists have concluded that insurance in Islam should be based on the principles of mutuality and cooperation. Such insurance encompasses the elements of shared responsibility, joint indemnity, common interest and solidarity.

10.4 ISLAMIC ORIGINS OF *TAKAFUL*

According to a *Hadith*, one day the Prophet saw a Bedouin leaving a camel in the desert and he asked the Bedouin, 'Why don't you tie down your camel?'

> The Bedouin answered, 'I put my trust in Allah'.
> The Prophet said, 'Tie your camel first, then put your trust in Allah'.

What the Prophet did here was to encourage the Bedouin to reduce the risk of losing his camel. Similarly, in many other actions of the Prophet, it is well documented that he took steps to reduce risks.

One example was his actions during the *Hijra*, the migration of Mohammed and his followers to Medina in AD 622. Fearing danger, he hid in a cave instead of going straight to Medina. He commanded his Companions to migrate to Medina in batches instead of in one large group. Again this was to reduce risks. When he went to war, he put on his armour instead of wearing light clothes.

Islamic insurance was established in the early second century of the Islamic era when Muslim Arabs expanding trade into Asia mutually agreed to contribute to a fund to cover anyone in the group who incurred mishaps or robberies during the numerous sea voyages.

10.5 WHERE INSURANCE FITS WITHIN ISLAM

Muslims believe that everything that happens in this world is by the will (*Qadha* and *Qadar*) of Allah. Similarly any accident or misfortune that befalls anyone that results in the loss of life or belongings is by the will of Allah. If that is the case, one might ask, why bother with *Takaful*? Should Muslims not leave it to Allah and accept whatever accident, misfortune or catastrophe befalls them? Although this may be a valid point of view, Muslims are also taught to avoid or reduce the possibility of any misfortune by taking positive steps wherever possible.

Muslim Jurists acknowledge that the basis of shared responsibility in the system of *Aquila*, the payment of blood money, as practised between the Muslims of Mecca and Medina, laid the foundation of mutual insurance. In the modern world, one of the ways to reduce the risk of loss due to accident or misfortune is through insurance.

10.6 DEFINITION OF THE PARTIES TO A *TAKAFUL*

In *Takaful*, there are usually four parties involved:

- the participants;
- the *Takaful* operators;
- the insured;
- the beneficiaries.

The nature of *Takaful* is that anyone in society who has the legal capacity may contribute a sum of money to a mutual cooperative fund with a view to ensuring material security against a defined risk.

Those who contribute to the mutual fund are known as participants, while those who among the participants face the risk and are assisted by the fund are known as the insured. Those who actually benefit from the fund are known as the beneficiaries from the cooperative fund. The monetary contribution made by the participants to the fund is known as a mutual contribution. The fund, managed by a registered or licensed body or corporation, is known as a *Takaful* operator, which binds itself bilaterally to manage the fund according to *Sharia'a* principles and also to provide financial security.

The participant's contribution is normally put into two funds; one of them is an investment fund managed according to the principles of *Mudaraba* (profit and loss sharing – see Chapter 5) while the other is treated as a charity according to the principles of *Tabarru'*. This division of responsibilities is why the *Takaful* company is usually called a *Takaful* operator rather than an insurance company.

10.7 *TAKAFUL* IN PRACTICE

Theoretically, *Takaful* is perceived as 'cooperative insurance', where members contribute a certain sum of money to a common pool. The purpose of this system is not to earn profits but to uphold the principle of 'bear ye one another's burden'. The policyholders are in fact the managers of the fund and the ones in ultimate control. However, the commercialisation of *Takaful* has produced several variants of Islamic insurance, each reflecting a different experience, environment and perhaps a different school of thought.

10.8 *TAKAFUL* AND CONVENTIONAL INSURANCE

It is important to understand the technical differences between contractual formalities under *Takaful* and those under conventional insurance. Table 10.1 illustrates the contractual issues while Table 10.2 describes the key differences between *Takaful* and conventional insurance.

10.9 ALTERNATIVE MODELS OF *TAKAFUL*

The central concept for all *Takaful* models is the segregation between participants' and shareholders' funds, because the operator role is only to manage participants' funds on their behalf. There are, however, several alternative business models that can govern the relationship between the policyholder and the *Takaful* operator. There are at least four models, discussed in the next few sections.

10.9.1 *Ta'awun* Model

Under the *Ta'awun* model, *Takaful* operators usually employ the concept of *Mudaraba* in their daily transactions. In this concept, the *Takaful* operator and the policyholder only share the direct investment income. The policyholder is entitled to a 100% of the surplus with no deduction made prior to the distribution. This model is applicable to life *Takaful* because the fund is entirely distributed to the participants.

Table 10.1 Contractual issues affecting *Takaful* and conventional insurance

Under *Takaful*	Under conventional insurance
1 The governing rules relating to the formalities in a Takaful contract are based on the principles of *al- 'aqd*.	1 The governing principles relating to the formalities of insurance contract are based on the relevant Common Law principles.
2 A contract of *Takaful* is enforceable against both contracting parties as soon as the proposal is accepted by the *Takaful* operator.	2 The policy is normally enforceable only after the first premium is paid.
3 The contract of *Takaful* is bilateral in nature. This binds both contracting parties in the light of the *Qur'anic* sanction at *Surah al-Ma'idah ayat 1*.	3 The contract of insurance is a unilateral in nature. This binds only the insurer who is under an obligation to meet a reasonable claim made by the insured.
4 A cover note can be issued as a temporary document for an unlimited period of time.	4 A cover note is issued for a limited period of time with only a temporary effect.
5 A premium cannot be forfeited in any situation. It is treated as capital in Mudaraba financing and also as a *Tabarru'*.	5 The premium may be forfeited on the grounds of breach of utmost good faith.
6 Lapse of premium payment contribution does not mean the policy becomes invalid.	6 Lapse of a premium payment (including the grace period) means the policy is no longer valid.

10.9.2 Nonprofit Model

The nonprofit model is applied by social-governmental owned enterprises and programmes operated on a nonprofit basis. This model uses a contribution that is 100% *Tabarru'* (donation) from participants who willingly give to the less fortunate members of their community.

Table 10.2 Key differences between *Takaful* and conventional insurance

Takaful	Conventional insurance
1 *Takaful* is based on cooperation and is void of interest (*riba*) and other prohibitions.	1 Conventional insurance includes interest, uncertainty (*gharar*) and other prohibitions.
2 The presence of a legal control authority (*Sharia'a* board) to ensure that all the activities are done according to *Sharia'a* and void of any prohibitions.	2 The presence of a technical committee only.
3 The original premium payment goes back to the insured after deducting its share of the indemnities and expenses.	3 Neither the original premium nor any part of it goes back to the insured.
4 The profits of investing premiums belong to the insured after deducting the operator's share as a *Mudarib*.	4 The profits of investing premiums and assets belong to the commercial insurance company only.
5 The operator aims mainly at achieving cooperation among community members and developing the *Ummah* (the nation of Islam).	5 The company aims at achieving the highest profit possible for its owners.
6 The operator's profits are the result of investing its money, its share as a *Mudarib* and the fees for running insurance operations.	6 The company's profits are the result of investing its money in addition to the commercial profits resulting from the entire insurance operations.
7 The operator has a fixed capital that belongs to the participants and 'variable' capital that belongs to the policyholders.	7 The company has one source of capital that belongs to the commercial company only.

10.9.3 *Mudaraba* Model

Under the *Mudaraba* model, any surplus is shared between the policyholders and the *Takaful* operator. The sharing of such profit (surplus) may be in a ratio of 50:50, 60:40, 70:30 or whatever is mutually agreed between the contracting parties. Generally, these risk sharing arrangements allow the *Takaful* operator to share in the underwriting profits from operations as well as any favourable performance returns on invested premiums.

10.9.4 *Wakala* Model

Under the *Wakala* model, the cooperative risk sharing occurs among participants with a *Takaful* operator who earns a fee for services (as would a lawyer (*Wakeel*) or agent) and does not participate or share in any underwriting profits, because these belong to the participants. Under the *Wakala* model the operator may also charge a fund management fee and a performance incentive fee.

10.9.5 Applying the Relevant Model

A mixed model of *Wakala* and *Mudaraba* is the dominant model in the Middle East market and it is widely practised by *Takaful* operators worldwide. Under this model the *Wakala* structure is adopted for underwriting activities while the *Mudaraba* contract is adopted for investment activities. Consequently the *Takaful* operator has two funds, one for the shareholders and the other for participants (policyholders). With regard to underwriting activities, the shareholders act as the *Wakeel* (agent) on behalf of participants when managing their funds, whereby the *Takaful* operator (shareholders) receives contributions, pays claims, and arranges Re*Takaful* (see page 136–137) and all other necessary actions related to *Takaful* business.

In exchange for performing these tasks, the operator charges each participant a fee known as the *Wakala* fee, which is usually a percentage of the contribution paid by each participant. On the investment side, the operator invests the surplus contributions in different Islamic instruments based on the *Mudaraba* contract, whereby the operator acts as *Mudarib* on behalf of participants, the *Rab ul Mall* and capital provider(s). In order to satisfy the *Sharia'a* requirements, the profit-sharing ratio is fixed and agreed upon between the two parties at the inception of the contract.

10.10 *SHARIA'A* LAW AS APPLIED BY *TAKAFUL* OPERATORS

This section describes how *Sharia'a* law is applied by *Takaful* operators. The text gives particular attention to the appropriate *Sharia'a* principle and, where relevant, its basis in Islam.

10.10.1 Principles of Contract

An insurance policy binds the parties unilaterally by an offer and an acceptance based on the principles of contract. The fundamentals required in an insurance policy are the parties to the contract, legal capacities of the parties, offer and acceptance, consideration, subject matter, insurable interest and good faith. These concepts are found in most forms of contract law.

10.10.1.1   Basis in Islam

A contract is a promise by an offer and an acceptance, which must be fulfilled as Allah has commanded to the effect:

O ye who believe! Fulfil your obligations.

Surah al-Ma'idah, 5:1

With regards to the legal capacity as to age of the parties to the contract of insurance, a minor, that is below the age of 15 (the age of *rushd*, majority or puberty), is not able to buy a policy unless the guardian holds full supervision over the policy; also, the policy should be for the benefit of the minor.

The *Takaful Siswa* allows an infant between the age of the majority and the 15th day of birth to hold a *Takaful* policy for education, under the supervision of the respective guardian.

This operational method is justified by the following *Qur'anic* sanction:

> Make trial of orphans until they reach the age of marriage; if then you find sound judgement in them, release their property to them; but consume it not wastefully.

Surah an-Nisa, (4): 6

The requirement of minimum age of the parties in an insurance policy is the same as required in general contracts. Hence the above principles and other relevant principles relating to contract are basically applied to the formation of all insurance contracts.

10.10.2 Principles of Liability

An insurance policy covers losses arising from the death, accident, disaster and other losses to human life, property or business. The insurer (insurance company) undertakes in the policy to compensate against the losses to the agreed subject matter. Such undertaking is considered as vicarious liability. For instance, in the case of *Aquila* practised in the ancient Arab tribes and approved by the Prophet, if a person was killed by another from a different tribe, either mistakenly or negligently, this would bring a liability to the members of his tribe to pay blood money to the heirs of the slain.

Moreover, the rights and obligations in an insurance policy mainly arise from the law of contract and tort. For example, in the case of a motor accident, the operator (insurance company) is liable on behalf of the person who causes that accident (the insured), to compensate the victim. Here, the operator is bound by the terms stipulated in the proposal to pay that compensation under the principles of vicarious liability under the law of tort.

10.10.3 Principle of Utmost Good Faith

In an insurance contract, for the enforcement of the policy, the parties involved in it should have good faith. Therefore, nondisclosure of material facts, involvement of a fraudulent act, misrepresentations or false statements are all elements that could invalidate a policy of insurance.

10.10.3.1 Basis in Islam

Allah says:

> . . . Do not misappropriate your property among yourselves in vanities but let there be amongst you traffic and trade by mutual good will . . .

Surah an-Nisa, 4:29

10.10.4 Principles of *Mirath* and *Wasiyah*

In a life policy, the assured (in this case a Muslim) appoints a nominee who cannot be the absolute beneficiary. A nominee in a life insurance policy of a Muslim is a mere trustee who receives benefits from the policy and distributes them among the heirs of the deceased, in accordance with the principles of *Mirath* (the law of succession, inheritance) and *Wasiyah* (the disposal of property, bequest).

In this instance a nominee receives the policy monies payable on the death of the policy owner as an executor and not solely as a beneficiary, and any payment to the nominee forms part of the estate of the deceased policy owner and is subject to his debts. The licensed insurer is discharged from liability in respect of the policy monies paid. In the light of this provision the nominee in a policy nominated by a Muslim policyholder should be treated as a mere executor and not as an absolute beneficiary of the policy.

10.10.5 Principles of *Wakala* (Agency)

The appointment of the agent by the insurer and the broker by the insured is of utmost importance. In fact such appointments are widely practised for the purpose of making the transaction and dealings between the insurer and the insured more effective.

10.10.6 Principles of *Dhaman* (Guarantee)

In an insurance policy the insurer undertakes to provide material security for the insured against unexpected future loss, damage or risk. The idea of such a guarantee is justified by the principles of *Dhaman* (guarantee) under Islamic law, and in Islamic *Fiqh*, insurance can only be classed under *Dhaman*. This is governed by some essential *Sharia'a* conditions, including that the guarantor can only take upon himself a liability that has fallen, or may possibly fall, upon a person or property. Thus the *Dhaman* or guarantee may only be payable to the victim or, if the victim dies, to his legal heirs, according to their respective shares in the inheritance.

10.10.7 Principles of *Mudaraba* and *Musharaka*

The operation of an insurance policy under the *Sharia'a* is based on the principles of *Mudaraba* financing (discussed in detail in Chapter 5). This Islamic mode of finance is an alternative to the conventional interest-based transaction. A *Sharia'a*-based insurance policy is a transaction wherein both parties agree that the participant pays regular contributions and the operator invests the accumulated contributions in a lawful business. Both the insured and the operator share the profits in an agreed portion.

At the same time, the insurer also undertakes to provide the insured with compensation (in consideration of the paid-contribution) against an unexpected future loss or damage occurring to the subject matter of the policy. This is how the principles of *Mudaraba* financing in an insurance policy work. The insurance policy also operates on the basis of the principle of *Musharaka* (see Chapter 6) because both the operator and the participants are partners in the policy run by the *Takaful* operator.

10.10.8 Principles of Rights and Obligations

An insurance policy is based on the principles of rights and obligations arising from concerns for humanity and nature. It is logical and natural for every person in society to feel obliged to provide material security and protection as a right for themselves, their property and family, the poor and helpless, widows and children, faced with unexpected perils and dangers.

10.10.8.1 Basis in Islam

The Prophet also emphasised the importance of providing material security for widows and poor dependents in the following *Hadith*:

> Narrated by Safwan bin Salim, the Prophet said: 'The one who looks after and works for a widow and a poor person, is like a warrior fighting for Allah's cause or like a person who fasts during the day and prays all the night . . .'.

10.10.9 Principles of Humanitarian Law

One of the purposes of humanitarian law is to inculcate mutual understanding in the community, to protect against unexpected loss, damage or other forms of risks or hardships. Hence, an insurance policy contributes towards alleviating hardships for a person arising from unexpected material risks, which is of course within the scope of the principles of humanitarian law.

10.10.9.1 Basis in Islam

This aspect has been justified in the following *Hadith* of the Prophet, which reads:

> Narrated by Abu Huraira . . . the Holy Prophet said . . . 'whosoever removes a worldly grief from a believer, Allah will remove from him one of the griefs of the Day of Judgment. Whosoever alleviates a needy person, Allah will alleviate from him in this world and the next . . .'.

10.10.10 Principles of Mutual Cooperation

In a *Takaful* policy, both the operator and the participant mutually agree to lawful cooperation in which the participant provides capital (through the payments of contributions) to the operator (insurance company), enabling the insurer to invest the accumulated contributions in a lawful business (on the basis of *Mudaraba*). Meanwhile, the insurer, in return for the payments of the contributions, mutually agrees to compensate the insured in the event of an unexpected loss or damage or risk to the subject matter.

10.10.10.1 Basis in Islam

Such mutual cooperation among the parties in an insurance policy has been justified by the Divine principles of mutual cooperation, solidarity and brotherhood. Allah commanded:

> Help one another in righteousness and piety, but do not help one another in sin and transgression.
>
> *Surah al-Ma'idah, 5:2*

10.11 *TAKAFUL* OPERATORS

Table 10.3 gives six examples of the best known pioneering Islamic *Takaful* operators, along with date of establishment and country of origin.

Table 10.3   Pioneering Islamic *Takaful* operators

Pioneering Islamic *Takaful* operators
1   The Sudanese Islamic Insurance Co. was the first Islamic Insurance company, founded in 1979 (1399 AH) in Khartoum, by the Faisal Islamic Bank of Sudan.
2   The National Company for Cooperative insurance was founded in Riyadh, Kingdom of Saudi Arabia, in 1981 (1401 AH), by a Royal decree. It is a totally government owned company.
3   The Arab Islamic Insurance Co. (AIIC) was established in 1979 (1399 AH), in Dubai, by the Dubai Islamic Bank.
4   The Islamic Company for Insurance and Reinsurance was founded in 1985 (1405 AH) in Bahrain.
5   The International Islamic Insurance Company was founded in 1992 (1412 AH), in Bahrain. Bahrain Bank had an important role in its foundation and in the investment of its funds.
6   Islamic Insurance Limited was founded in 1995 (1416 AH), in Jordan by the Jordanian Islamic Bank.

10.12 DEFINITION OF RE*TAKAFUL* (REINSURANCE)

Reinsurance is a financial indemnity contract, according to which the conventional company or *Takaful* operator pays to the reinsurance company a portion, agreed upon from prescribed premiums, in return for the commitment of the insurance company to cover its portion of the risks of the direct insurance company. Reinsurance is best thought of as insurance for insurance companies.

10.13 RE*TAKAFUL*

Re*Takaful* (Islamic reinsurance) is a risk hedging method in which the *Takaful* operator resorts to either a conventional reinsurer or a Re*Takaful* operator to reinsure original insured risks against an undesirable future situation if the risk insured were above the normal underwriting claim. Thus, a *Takaful* operator may, based on limited financial resources, hedge against possible incapability to meet all *Takaful* insurance protection from a financially capable reinsurer.

As Figure 10.1 shows, the *Takaful* holders are individuals or companies that buy the *Takaful* products (either General *Takaful* or Family *Takaful* products) and pay an agreed-upon premium to the *Takaful* operator to protect them from unforeseen risk and also extraordinary losses. The *Takaful* operator will take a portion of money from the *Takaful* fund and pay a premium to the Re*Takaful* operator to get reinsurance protection to spread its risks. Reinsurance contracts may cover a specific risk or a broad class of business.

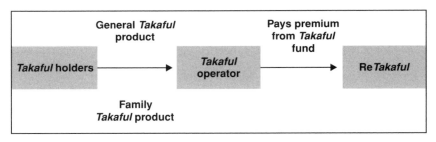

Figure 10.1   Re*Takaful process*

Table 10.4 Similarities between conventional and *Takaful* reinsurance

1	Reinsurance in conventional insurance companies and *Takaful* operators is between two parties: the reinsurance company and the insurance company/*Takaful* operator.
2	The reason for resorting to reinsurance by conventional companies and *Takaful* operators is the inability of the insurance companies to insure high-risk projects. They both wish to get coverage from the reinsurance company enabling them to handle the huge risks where financial indemnities could exceed the capabilities of the insurance companies themselves.
3	With regard to the payment of indemnities, in cases of the risks insured in the reinsurance contract, the relationship is established between the reinsurance company and the conventional or *Takaful* operator only. The insured does not have any rights with the reinsurance company, because his relationship is restricted to his insurer.
4	According to the reinsurance contract, the reinsurance company is committed to paying the financial indemnities to the conventional insurance company or *Takaful* operator, according to the conditions agreed upon between the two parties.
5	The reinsurance company provides the conventional company and the *Takaful* operator with financial statements: reinsurance commission and reinsurance profit commission.

Re*Takaful* does not, in principle, differ from *Takaful* operations. The *Sharia'a* principles applying to *Takaful* also apply to Re*Takaful* operations. The difference, if any, is that in the Re*Takaful* operations the participants are *Takaful* operators instead of individual participants. It is argued that the current practice of conventional insurance business has shown that a *Takaful* operator cannot efficiently operate without a Re*Takaful* facility. Therefore, there is a need for *Takaful* operators to share risks by way of establishing Re*Takaful* operators. In doing so, they share their risks with Re*Takaful* operators. The Re*Takaful* operator, on the other hand, assumes the responsibility of managing and investing the premiums of *Takaful* operators on the basis of profit and loss sharing.

It is useful to see all the similarities and differences between conventional and *Takaful* reinsurance. Table 10.4 illustrates the similarities and Table 10.5 the differences.

Table 10.5 Differences between conventional and *Takaful* reinsurance

1	Conventional insurance companies do not take into consideration, when practising reinsurance, the Islamic legitimacy of the transaction because they practice insurance regardless of whether it is or is not prohibited by the *Sharia'a*. But for *Takaful* operators this legitimacy is the basic core of all its transactions, including reinsurance. When practising reinsurance, the *Takaful* operator is committed to the legal instructions of the legal supervisory authorities and to the jurisprudence opinions and instructions. They must practise reinsurance according to Islamically-lawful criteria.
2	Conventional reinsurance companies keep reserves and invest them in interest-based financial assets. For *Takaful* reinsurance operators, the reserves are invested in Islamically-lawful ways.
3	The amounts paid by the reinsurance companies as indemnities for damage, reinsurance commission and reinsurance profit commission, are not subject to *Sharia'a* judgment in conventional companies whereas Takaful insurance operators are subject to the opinion of the supervisory *Sharia'a* board.

10.14 ROLE OF THE *SHARIA'A* BOARD IN *TAKAFUL*

Takaful operators are not just financial institutions that aim at making profits: they take the *Sharia'a* as their source and methodology. They innovate new products that abide by the regulations, principles and general purposes of *Sharia'a*.

10.14.1 Legal Basis for Assigning the *Sharia'a* Board

The basic legal system in each of the *Takaful* operators stipulates the necessity of assigning a *Sharia'a* board to ensure that the activities of the company do not contradict the regulations of the *Sharia'a*. The board also ensures that the *Takaful* operator is committed to the regulation and principles of *Sharia'a* in its practice of insurance activities.

10.14.2 Nature of the *Sharia'a* Board's Decisions

To achieve the goals and objectives of the *Sharia'a* board, its decisions and counsel must be binding on the *Takaful* operators:

- The administration of each company must adhere to the instructions, decisions and counsel issued by its *Sharia'*a board.
- If the counselling and instructions of the *Sharia'a* board contradict with the provisions of the law regulating the work of these operators, the *Sharia'a* board is to be followed, not the company law. However, the decisions of the Sharia'a board are restricted to that *Takaful* operator only.

10.14.3 *Sharia'a* Board's General Duties

The *Sharia'a* board's duties include: follow up, examination and analysis of all the operator's activities to ensure that they are undertaken according to the rules, regulations and purposes of the *Sharia'a*. This involves checking contracts, agreements and investments, identifying any mistakes and ensuring that they are corrected immediately.

10.14.4 *Sharia'a* Board's Detailed Duties

The *Sharia'a* board's detailed duties are as listed below:

- Check the legitimacy of the insurance policies practised by the company as follows:
  - It is not insuring Islamically-prohibited activities such as importing containers of alcoholic drinks.
  - It is not insuring institutions carrying out Islamically-prohibited activities; for example, conventional banks using interest-bearing products.
- Ensure that reinsurance agreements issued by the company comply with the instructions of the *Sharia'a* board.
- Check the legality of company investments so that they all comply with the regulations of the *Sharia'a* as follows:
  - Investments are void of any prohibited interest (on borrowings and deposits).
  - No shares are purchased in companies that practise Islamically-prohibited activities.
- Answer, advise and provide lawful solutions for any inquiries from the company's administration regarding any issues resulting from the practical application of insurance operations.
- Ensure that those who deal with the *Takaful* operator, regarding the operations and activities practised by the operator, are acting lawfully.
- Provide advice and guidance to the company's administration in everything that may lead to its advancement and prosperity, especially employees' commitment to the lawful regulations that must be followed in the field of Islamic insurance.

- Set up the required measures to correct the company's path according to the regulations of *Sharia'a* law in the event that any corrections are needed.
- Expand the knowledge of Islamic insurance through conducting research.
- Prepare and submit an annual report to the company's administration showing the legality of reinsurance polices, agreements and the company's investments, and ensuring that they are void of any violations of the regulations of the *Sharia'a*

Appendix 1
Comparative Features of Islamic Financing Techniques

This appendix provides a useful discussion, in one place, of all the issues that distinguish the different Islamic modes of finance. It enables one to see easily the differences and similarities between the *Sharia'a* contracts. The following classification criteria will be applied:

- nature of financing;
- role of the finance provider (*Rab ul Mall*) in the management of funds;
- extent of risk bearing by the finance provider;
- certainty/uncertainty of the rate of return on capital for the finance provider;
- cost of capital for the finance provider;
- relationship between the cost of capital and the rate of return on capital.

A.1 NATURE OF THE FINANCING

Islamic financing techniques can be distinguished from the point of view of the nature of financing involved in each technique. *Salam* and *Murabaha*-based modes can be regarded as debt-creating modes of financing because financing in these two modes is in the nature of debt. Here the finance user stands obliged to pay back the entire financing (or the commodity as agreed in *Salam*). The repayment by the finance user is, in fact, predetermined in advance and hence becomes a sort of debt from the finance user's point of view. On the other hand, *Mudaraba* and *Musharaka* are nondebt-creating modes in the sense that the finance user is not obliged to pay back the total amount of financing. To some extent *Ijara* can also be regarded as a nondebt-creating mode of financing. In *Mudaraba* and *Musharaka* the finance user pays the cost of capital according to the profits and losses that he makes from the use of the financing whereas in *Ijara* only the rent is paid, which may be a small part for any particular user of the total value of the asset.

The debt-creating modes involve a debt burden on the user irrespective of how much he benefits from the funds. Nondebt-creating modes do not carry a debt burden: the user pays according to the benefit he gets from the financing.

A.2 ROLE OF THE FINANCE PROVIDER IN THE MANAGEMENT/USE OF FUNDS

In *Salam*, the finance providers have no role in the management of the funds by the finance user. Once the finances have been handed over the finance user is free to use the funds as he thinks best. In a sense *Mudaraba* can also fall into this category because the finance provider is not allowed to interfere in the management of the enterprise in which his funds are being used.

On the other hand, *Musharaka* gives an opportunity for the finance provider to have a role in the management of the funds. In the case of *Murabaha* financing and *Ijara* financing the finance provider has full control over the use of the fund because funds are deployed by him.

A.3 RISK BEARING BY THE FINANCE PROVIDER

In both *Mudaraba* and *Musharaka* the entire capital invested by the finance provider is at risk. The finance provider in *Mudaraba* is responsible for bearing the financial loss of the enterprise in which the finances were used. His entire finances are, thus, at risk until the project is completed and the finances have been recovered.

In the case of *Musharaka* the finance user bears the financial loss in proportion to his capital invested in the total investment of the enterprise. In this case too, the entire capital of the finance provider remains at risk until the project is completed and the finances have been recovered.

Almost similar is the case with *Ijara*, where the entire amount of capital remains at stake because the capital owner is responsible for all the risks attached to the life of the asset. The capital will be under risk until the asset successfully completes its anticipated productive life.

The risk bearing in *Salam* arises due to the uncertainty of the future prices of the commodities involved in the contract.

In all of these four cases, *Mudaraba*, *Musharaka*, *Ijara* and *Salam*, the finance provider has at risk the entire amount of his capital as well as the opportunity cost of capital for the entire period until the capital is received back.

In *Murabaha* financing risk bearing takes place but is less than that involved in the above mentioned four techniques.

The risk bearing in *Murabaha* is only up to the stage when the goods are handed over to the buyer and not until receiving back the capital as in the above mentioned techniques. Once the goods are handed over to the finance user, all risk lies with him and the finance provider shares no risk till the recovery of the finance.

Other things remaining the same, the *Murabaha*-based financing involves minimum risk for the finance provider compared to other techniques for the following reasons:

- The finance provider does not bear risk for the entire period of the contract. The risk is only for that period in which a spot sale is made and until the goods are handed over to the client. For the remaining period of the contract, the amount of financing plus the agreed mark-up is in the nature of debt and is risk-free, given that collateral is usually provided. All the other financing techniques carry the risk throughout the period of the contract.
- *Murabaha*-based financing requires knowledge only of the current prices of the goods involved in determining the financing and a return on it. In the other techniques, some anticipation or forecasting has to be made about the values of various variables involved in financing. This introduces an element of risk to the extent that the forecasts may not come true: *Salam* requires forecasting future market prices; *Ijara* requires forecasting the productive life of the asset; and *Mudaraba* and *Musharaka* require forecasting the profitability of the enterprise/activity in which investment is to be made.

A.4 UNCERTAINTY OF THE RATE OF RETURN ON CAPITAL FOR THE FINANCE PROVIDER

All Islamic financing techniques require risk bearing by the finance provider. He has to bear the risk of loss of capital if he allows the use of money in any of these modes. This means that any return that he may expect, *ex-ante*, has some element of uncertainty. It is a common mistake to regard the trading-based and leasing-based financing techniques as fixed-return techniques. The misunderstanding arises for various reasons:

- *Murabaha*: Since the mark-up is fixed and predetermined as a percentage of the capital amount, this technique is considered to have a fixed rate of return. The mark-up itself is considered the fixed rate of return.
- *Ijara*: Since rent is fixed and predetermined, it is considered to imply a fixed rate of return because renting equipment worth, say, US$100,000 at an annual rent of US$10,000 means a 10% fixed rate of return on capital.
- *Salam*: Since the quantity and price of the goods to be purchased from the finance user are known and fixed in advance, the finance provider is assumed to have fixed the rate of return in advance.

In all these cases the amount charged to the finance user is usually assumed also to be the rate of return on capital. This is actually not the case. There are risks of losses involved for the finance provider in all these techniques.

In *Murabaha*-based financing a financier faces all risks normally involved in a trading activity such as goods getting damaged during transportation, storage and so on. Furthermore, the finance provider also runs the risk that the goods purchased for the finance user may not be finally accepted by the finance user on account of quality or any other pretext. These risks thus keep the rate of return uncertain until the goods have been finally handed over to the finance user.

In *Salam* financing, although the price, quality and quantity of the goods to be delivered to the financier are predetermined, the actual rate of return remains unknown until the goods in question are delivered to the buyer and he is able to dispose of them in the market. The actual rate of return will depend on the actual prices at the time of disposing of the goods compared with the prices paid for the goods and on the cost incurred in disposing of the goods.

The rent on an asset cannot be treated as a rate of return on capital invested in the asset for the following reasons:

- The owner of the asset is uncertain about the total life of the asset. The asset can bring earning only during its productive life. Also, the owner is not aware what price the asset will fetch if he decides to dispose of the asset at any time during its productive life.
- The owner of the asset is also uncertain about the extent to which the asset will remain on lease during its productive life. On expiry of the contract with the first lessee, the owner is uncertain about the time it will take him to find the next lessee and the rent that will be agreed upon with him. Even if the first lease continued it is quite possible that at some point of time the lessee may demand revision in the rent due to some unforeseen defect that may adversely affect the productivity of the asset or the service for which it was rented.

Mudaraba and *Musharaka* generate risks primarily at the end of the finance use. When it is a matter of financing only, the finance owner has little role in the case of *Mudaraba* and may have only a secondary role, in the case of *Musharaka*, in attempting to control the risk of loss.

On the other hand, *Ijara*, *Murabaha* and *Salam*-based financing involves a risk that is not generated at the end of the finance use. In *Ijara* the risk is associated with the anticipated life of the asset and its continuous employment on rent. In *Murabaha*-based financing the risk is involved during the purchase of the required goods and their handing over to the client. In *Salam* the risk occurs during the receipt of goods from the client and their disposal in the market. In all these three modes the finance user has no connection with the risk being faced by the finance owner.

A.5 COST OF CAPITAL FOR THE FINANCE USER

The amount that the finance user ends up paying to the finance owner over and above the original finance obtained is referred to here as the 'cost of capital'.

The cost of capital in the case of *Mudaraba*, *Musharaka* and *Salam* remains uncertain until the completion of the contract. The cost of capital in the case of *Ijara* and *Murabaha*-based financing is predetermined and fixed.

Thus, whereas the rate of return on capital is always supposed to be variable and uncertain, it is possible for the cost of capital to be fixed and predetermined if *Ijara* and *Murabaha* modes are used.

A.6 RELATIONSHIP BETWEEN THE COST OF CAPITAL AND THE RATE OF RETURN ON CAPITAL

In the case of *Mudaraba* and *Musharaka*, the cost of capital and the rate of return are explicitly the same. In the case of *Ijara*, *Murabaha* and *Salam*-based financing, however, the cost of capital and the rate of return on capital are divergent.

The case of *Ijara* and *Murabaha* is straightforward. The finance user pays a fixed and predetermined cost. In the case of *Salam*, the rate of return for the finance owner (being dependent on the price that he is able to get in the market minus the cost of marketing) may be different and unrelated to the cost that the finance user is obliged to pay.

Appendix 2

Top 500 Islamic Institutions 1–73

Ranking Latest	Ranking Previous	Country	Date of result	Institution	Type of institution	S: Full Islamic banks, W: Islamic windows	Sharia-compliant assets $m	% change	Total assets $m	% of sharia-compliant assets to total assets	Pre-tax profits $m	% change	Return on assets (%)	Year started service
1	1	Iran	20-Mar-09	Bank Melli Iran, Tehran	Government-owned bank	S	57,003.4	2.79	57,003.4	100	266.1	−30.10	0.47	n/a
2	2	Saudi Arabia	31-Dec-09	Al Rajhi Bank	Commercial and investment bank	S	45,527.9	3.52	45,527.9	100	1804.6	3.72	4.03	1987
3	4	Iran	10-Mar-10	Bank Mellat, Tehran	Government-owned bank	S	43,109.0	3.50	43,109.0	100	n/a	n/a	n/a	1980
4	3	Iran	20-Mar-09	Bank Saderat Iran, Tehran	Government-owned bank	S	41,981.0	−2.52	41,981.0	100	319.0	76.24	0.75	n/a
5	5	Kuwait	31-Mar-10	Kuwait Finance House	Commercial bank	S	40,317.6	7.88	40,317.6	100	105.9	−51.66	0.27	1977
6	6	Iran	20-Mar-09	Bank Tejarat, Tehran	Government-owned bank	S	34,545.8	16.76	34,545.8	100	396.0	24.66	1.24	1980
7	8	UAE	30-Jun-10	Dubai Islamic Bank, Dubai	Commercial and retail bank	S	22,834.8	−4.62	22,834.8	100	136.9	−39.41	0.59	1975
8	7	Iran	20-Mar-09	Bank Sepah, Tehran	Government-owned bank	S	22,502.0	−14.69	22,502.0	100	388.0	193.94	1.59	1925
9	9	Iran	19-Mar-09	Parsian Bank	Commercial bank	S	19,783.0	7.99	19,783.0	100	405.2	9.51	2.13	2002
10	15	Iran	20-Mar-09	Bank Maskan Iran (Housing Bank), Tehran	Government-owned bank	S	19,311.0	47.69	19,311.0	100	284.0	n/a	1.75	1938
11	13	UAE	30-Jun-10	Abu Dhabi Islamic Bank	Commercial and retail bank	S	18,619.0	17.60	18,619.0	100	162.1	28.84	0.94	May-97
12	10	Iran	20-Mar-09	Bank Keshavarzi (Agricultural Bank), Tehran	Government-owned bank	S	18,444.0	10.61	18,444.0	100	4.0	−69.23	0.02	1933
13	12	Saudi Arabia	31-Dec-09	National Commercial Bank, Jeddah	Commercial bank	W	17,112.5	6.06	68,653.9	24.93	1099.0	95.59	1.72	1991
14	11	UK	30-Sep-10	HSBC Amanah (Global)	Commercial and retail bank	S	16,699.0	0.98	2,418,454.0	0.69	n/a	n/a	n/a	1998
15	14	Malaysia	31-Dec-09	Bank Rakyat	Commercial bank	S	14,784.7	21.35	14,784.7	100	452.6	25.57	3.36	2003
16	17	Bahrain	30-Jun-10	Al Baraka Banking Group	Wholesale bank	S	13,623.2	18.35	13,623.2	100	124.8	2.19	0.99	2002
17	19	Malaysia	31-Mar-10	Maybank Islamic Berhad	Commercial bank	S	12,402.0	19.29	12,402.0	100	116.5	−19.86	1.02	Jan-08

		Country	Date	Bank	Type	S/W								
18	29	Iran	20-Mar-10	Pasargad Bank	Commercial bank	S	12,250.0	93.03	12,250.0	100	354.0	89.30	3.81	n/a
19	18	Saudi Arabia	31-Dec-09	Riyad Bank	Retail and commercial bank	W	11,912.5	10.21	47,039.8	25.32	808.1	14.85	1.80	Feb 2001
20	16	Saudi Arabia	30-Jun-10	Saudi British Bank (SABB)	Commercial bank	W	11,198.0	-8.87	32,082.0	34.90	n/a	n/a	n/a	1978
21	21	Qatar	31-Dec-09	Qatar Islamic Bank	Commercial and investment bank	S	10,789.2	17.08	10,789.2	100	492.9	9.27	4.93	1982
22	20	Iran	20-Mar-09	Eghtesad Novin Bank	Commercial bank	S	10,237.9	0.00	10,237.9	100	200.1	0.00	1.95	Aug-01
23	24	Malaysia	30-Jun-10	BIMB Holdings (Bank Islam Malaysia Berhad)	Commercial bank	S	9268.3	17.53	9268.3	100	23.4	-55.20	0.27	n/a
24	22	Saudi Arabia	31-Dec-09	Arab National Bank	Commercial bank	W	8506.7	-4.78	29,412.6	28.92	632.0	-4.67	2.05	1980
25	27	Saudi Arabia	31-Dec-09	Banque Saudi Fransi	Commercial bank	W	8124.8	14.40	32,152.7	25.27	658.1	-11.99	2.00	2005
26	25	Saudi Arabia	31-Dec-09	Bank Al Jazira	Commercial bank	S	7993.8	8.93	7993.8	100	7.3	-85.42	0.10	1975
27	32	Malaysia	31-Dec-09	CIMB Islamic Bank Berhad	Commercial and retail Islamic bank	S	7979.6	46.51	7979.6	100	49.8	74.69	0.74	Nov-04
28	30	Turkey	31-Dec-09	Asya Finans Kurumu (Bank Asya)	Commercial bank	S	7873.6	27.98	7873.6	100	206.5	507.03	2.94	1996
29	23	UAE	31-Dec-09	Emirates NBD	Commercial bank	W	7302.5	-13.41	76723.8	9.52	910.8	-9.20	1.19	1995
30	33	Iran	20-Mar-08	Bank Refah	Government-owned bank	S	7069.3	18.74	7069.3	100	52.1	302.91	0.80	1961
31	26	UAE	31-Dec-09	Emirates Islamic Bank	Commercial and retail bank	S	6890.9	-4.21	6890.9	100	35.6	-67.35	0.51	2004
32	36	Malaysia	31-Dec-09	Public Bank Islamic Berhad	Retail bank	S	6674.2	37.63	6674.2	100	136.9	37.35	2.38	Nov-08
33	43	Saudi Arabia	30-Jun-10	Alinma Bank	Commercial bank	S	6652.7	50.17	6652.7	100	-19.1	n/a	-0.35	May-08
34	41	Qatar	31-Dec-09	Masraf Al Rayan/Al Rayan Bank	Commercial and investment bank	S	6627.4	43.86	6627.4	100	241.9	-3.97	4.31	Oct-06
35	28	Saudi Arabia	31-Dec-09	Samba Financial Group	Commercial bank	W	6151.7	-3.14	49,471.5	12.43	1214.2	2.49	2.50	1980
36	55	Qatar	31-Dec-09	Qatar National Bank Al Islami	Commercial bank	W	6037.4	69.10	49,266.2	12.25	1151.5	503.87	2.53	2006
37	31	UAE	31-Dec-08	Noor Islamic Bank	Commercial and investment bank	S	5933.0	0.0	5933.0	100	188.2	0.00	3.17	2007

Ranking Latest	Previous	Country	Date of result	Institution	Type of institution	S: Full Islamic banks, W: Islamic windows	Sharia-compliant assets $m	% change	Total assets $m	% of sharia-compliant assets to total assets	Pre-tax profits $m	% change	Return on assets (%)	Year started service
38	40	Turkey	31-Dec-09	Türkiye Finans Katılım Bankası	Commercial and retail bank	S	5821.0	22.17	5821.0	100	166.1	20.05	3.14	1991
39	35	Bahrain	30-Jun-10	Ithmaar Bank BSC	Commercial and retail bank	S	5719.0	6.29	5719.0	100	8.3	−91.17	0.15	1984
40	34	Iran	20-Mar-09	Bank Sanat Va Maadan (Bank of Industry and Mines), Tehran	Government-owned bank	S	5399.0	−1.04	5399.0	100	95.0	28.38	1.75	1997
41	49	Malaysia	31-Mar-10	AMMB Holdings	Commercial bank	W	5274.8	22.14	29,477.6	17.89	420.6	13.06	1.48	Apr-06
42	50	Malaysia	31-Mar-10	AmIslamic Bank Berhad	Commercial bank	S	5259.2	22.11	5259.2	100	109.0	67.16	2.28	May-06
43	44	Egypt	31-Dec-09	Faisal Islamic Bank of Egypt, Cairo	Commercial bank	S	5086.6	16.19	5086.6	100	22.8	45.22	0.48	1977
44	69	Iran	21-Mar-09	Saman Bank	Commercial bank	S	4975.2	75.45	4975.2	100	80.0	184.68	2.05	n/a
45	42	Malaysia	31-Dec-09	Bank Muamalat Malaysia Berhad	Commercial bank	S	4881.8	15.99	4881.8	100	41.1	231.80	0.90	n/a
46	38	UAE	31-Dec-09	Dubai Bank (Masref Dubai)	Commercial bank	S	4739.8	−05.94	4739.8	100	−79.2	n/a	−1.62	2007
47	46	Saudi Arabia	31-Dec-09	Bank Albilad	Commercial bank	S	4643.0	8.47	4643.0	100	−66.2	n/a	−1.48	Nov-04
48	51	Turkey	31-Dec-09	Kuwait Turket Evcaf Finance House	Commercial bank	S	4564.3	19.00	4564.3	100	112.0	43.35	2.67	1983
49	57	Qatar	31-Dec-09	Qatar International Islamic Bank, Doha	Commercial and investment bank	S	4547.0	28.88	4547.0	100	140.5	2.03	3.48	1990
50	37	Bahrain	31-Dec-09	Arcapita Bank	Investment bank	S	4372.3	−14.89	4372.3	100	158.4	−55.65	3.33	1997
51	47	UAE	31-Dec-09	Sharjah Islamic Bank	Commercial bank	S	4352.7	2.96	4352.7	100	70.9	12.33	1.65	2002
52	62	Syria	31-Dec-09	Syrian International Islamic Bank	Commercial and retail Islamic bank	S	4325.5	35.28	4325.5	100	23.2	25.07	0.62	Sep-07
53	63	Turkey	31-Dec-09	Albarakah Tur (Albarakah Turkish Finance House)	Commercial bank	S	4302.4	33.95	4302.4	100	79.2	−13.38	2.11	1984

Rank		Country	Date	Name	Type									
54	39	Kuwait	31-Dec-08	Investment Dar	Investment bank	S	4287.6	-6.37	4287.6	100	-280.7	n/a	-6.33	1994
55	48	Malaysia	31-Dec-09	Cagamas Berhad	Commercial bank	W	4138.4	5.73	9604.2	43.09	163.3	-0.91	1.66	n/a
56	58	Bangladesh	31-Dec-09	Islami Bank Bangladesh Limited (IBBL)	Commercial bank	S	4017.8	20.54	4017.8	100	94.1	2.68	2.56	Aug-05
57	45	UAE	30-Sep-09	Amlak Finance	Credit and finance	S	3996.3	-7.45	3996.3	100	-49.4	n/a	-1.19	2006
58	52	Kuwait	31-Dec-09	Kuwait International Bank	Commercial and retail bank	S	3973.3	5.31	3973.3	100	-28.7	n/a	0.74	Jul-07
59	54	Iran	20-Mar-09	Export Development Bank of Iran (EDBI)	Government-owned bank	S	3837.0	0.81	3837.0	100	51.0	-53.21	1.33	1991
60	56	Iran	20-Mar-10	Karafarin Bank	Commercial bank	S	3765.0	-99.99	3765.0	100	152.0	-99.99	0.00	1999
61	59	Bahrain	30-Jun-10	Kuwait Finance House (Bahrain)	Commercial bank	S	3703.8	12.30	3703.8	100	43.6	-56.86	1.25	Jan-02
62	66	Malaysia	31-Dec-09	Kuwait Finance House (Malaysia) Berhad	Commercial and investment bank	S	3379.9	20.25	3379.9	100	-8.8	n/a	0.28	Feb-06
63	64	Kuwait	31-Dec-09	Bank Boubyan	Commercial bank	S	3361.6	14.79	3361.6	100	-180.1	n/a	-5.73	2004
64	61	Brunei	31-Dec-09	Bank Islam Brunei Darussalam Berhad	Commercial bank	S	3314.7	0.88	3314.7	100	84.9	22.32	2.57	2006
65	70	Malaysia	31-Dec-09	RHB Islamic Bank Berhad	Commercial bank	S	3271.7	0.2	3271.7	100	25.3	761.46	0.86	2005
66	60	UAE	31-Dec-09	Tamweel	Credit and finance	S	3169.1	-2.05	3169.1	100	-14.8	n/a	-0.46	Mar-04
67	91	Iran	20-Mar-10	Sarmayeh (Capital) Bank	Commercial bank	S	3132.3	160.80	3132.3	100	77.6	66.09	3.58	n/a
68	65	Jordan	31-Dec-09	Jordan Islamic Bank for Finance and Investment	Commercial bank	S	3074.7	0.60	3074.7	100	54.8	-22.32	1.79	1978
69	67	Saudi Arabia	31-Dec-09	Saudi Hollandi Bank	Commercial bank	W	3052.3	2.34	15,762.6	19.36	22.9	-92.98	0.14	1926
70	68	Sudan	31-Dec-08	Omdurman National Bank	Commercial bank	S	2868.7	0.00	2868.7	100	30.3	0.00	1.06	1993
71	n/a	Iran	20-Mar-09	Sina Bank	Commercial and retail bank	S	2834.4	16.51	2834.4	100	57.9	93.60	2.20	Mar-09
72	73	Malaysia	31-Dec-09	Hong Leong Islamic Bank Berhad	Commercial bank	S	2669.2	12.57	2669.2	100	29.2	14.27	1.16	n/a
73	165	Saudi Arabia	31-Dec-09	Saudi Investment Bank	Commercial bank	W	2520.3	656.69	13,372.8	18.85	143.7	1.65	1.04	1976

Glossary

This glossary provides the key terms used in Islamic banking and finance. (A bold/italic term in a definition indicates that the word is defined elsewhere in the Glossary.)

Amanah: This refers to deposits held in trust. A person can hold a property in trust for another, sometimes by express contract and sometimes by implication of a contract. *Amanah* entails an absence of liability for loss except in the breach of duty. Current accounts are regarded as *Amanah* (trust). If the bank gets authority to use current accounts funds in its business, *Amanah* transforms into a loan. As every loan has to be repaid, banks are liable to repay the full amount of the current accounts.

Arbun: Down payment. A non-refundable deposit paid by a buyer retaining a right to confirm or cancel the sale.

Bai' Muajjal: Literally this means a credit sale. Technically, it is a financing technique adopted by Islamic banks that takes the form of **Murabaha** *Muajjal*. It is a contract in which the seller earns a profit margin on his purchase price and allows the buyer to pay the price of the commodity at a future date in a lump sum or in instalments. He has to mention expressly the cost of the commodity and the margin of profit is mutually agreed upon.

Bai' al-'Inah: A contract that involves the sale and buy-back transaction of assets by a seller. A seller sells the asset to a buyer on a cash basis. The seller later buys back the same asset on a deferred payment basis where the price is higher than the cash price.

Bai' al-Istijrar: A contract between the client and the supplier, whereby the supplier agrees to supply a particular produce on an ongoing basis, for example monthly, at an agreed price and on the basis of an agreed mode of payment.

Bai' al-Dayn: A transaction that involves the sale and purchase of securities or debt certificates that complies with the **Sharia'a**. Securities or debt certificates will be issued by a debtor to a creditor as evidence of indebtedness.

Bai' al-Muzayadah: An action by a person to sell an asset in the open market, which is accompanied by the process of bidding among potential buyers. The asset for sale will be awarded to the person who has offered the highest price.

Bai' bil Wafa: Sale with a right of the seller enabling him to repurchase (redeem) the property by refunding the purchase price. According to the majority of *Fuqaha* this is not permissible.

Bai' Bithaman Ajil (BBA): A contract that refers to the sale and purchase transactions for the financing of assets on a deferred and an instalment basis with a pre-agreed payment period. The sale price will include a profit margin.

Dayn (debt): A *Dayn* comes into existence as a result of a contract or credit transaction. It is incurred by way of rent, sale, purchase or in any other way that leaves it as a debt to another. *Duyun* (debts) should be repaid without any profit to the lender because they are advanced to help the needy and meet their demands and, therefore, the lender should not impose on the borrower more than he was given on credit.

Dhaman: Contract of guarantee, security or collateral.

Family Takaful: This arrangement provides members, or their beneficiaries, with financial protection they will be provided with monetary benefits if they suffer a tragedy. Members can also enjoy long-term investment returns from the savings portion based on a pre-agreed ratio.

Fiqh: Islamic law. The science of the *Sharia'a*. Practical jurisprudence or human articulations of divine rules encompassing both law and ethics. *Fiqh* may be understood as the Jurists' understanding of the *Sharia'a,* or Jurists' law. *Fiqh al-Muamalat* is Islamic commercial jurisprudence, or the rules for transacting in a *Sharia'a*-compliant manner. This is an important source of Islamic banking and economics.

Gharar: Any element of absolute or excessive uncertainty in any business or contract. *Gharar* potentially leads to undue loss to a party and unjustified enrichment of another. This is prohibited under the *Sharia'a*.

Al Ghunm bil Ghurm: This provides the rationale and the principle of profit sharing in *Shirkah* arrangements. Earning profit is legitimised only by engaging in an economic venture involving risk sharing that ultimately contributes to economic development.

Halal: Anything permitted by the *Sharia'a*.

Haram: Anything prohibited by the *Sharia'a*.

Hawalah: Literally, this means transfer. Legally, it is an agreement by which a debtor is freed from a debt by another party becoming responsible for it or by the transfer of a claim of a debt shifting the responsibility from one person to another. It also refers to the document by which the transfer takes place.

Hibah: Gift.

Ijara: Leasing. This is the sale of a definite usufruct of any asset in exchange for definite reward. It refers to a contract under which Islamic banks lease equipment, buildings or other facilities to a client, against an agreed rental.

Ijara wa Iqtina: A mode of financing, by way of hire purchase, adopted by Islamic banks. It is a contract under which an Islamic bank finances equipment, buildings or other facilities for the client against an agreed rental together with a unilateral undertaking by the bank or the client that, at the end of the lease period, the ownership in the asset will be transferred to the lessee. The undertaking, or the promise, does not become an integral part of the lease contract in order to make it conditional. The rental, as well as the purchase price, is fixed in such a manner that the bank gets back its principal sum along with some profit. This is usually determined in advance.

Ijtihad: An endeavour of a qualified Jurist to derive or formulate a rule of law to determine the true ruling of the divine law in a matter on which the revelation is not explicit or certain. This would be on the basis of *Nass* (evidence) found in the *Qur'an* and the *Sunnah*.

Ijma: Consensus of all or a majority of the leading qualified Jurists on a certain *Sharia'a* matter at a certain moment in time.

'Inah: A double sale by which the borrower and the lender sell and then resell an object between them, once for cash and once for a higher price on credit, with the net result being a loan with interest.

'Inan (type of **Sharikah**): A form of partnership in which each partner contributes capital and has a right to work for the business, not necessarily equally.

Istihsan: A doctrine of Islamic law that allows exceptions to strict legal reasoning, or guiding choice among possible legal outcomes, when considerations of human welfare so demand.

Istisna'a: A contractual agreement for manufacturing goods and commodities, allowing cash payment in advance and future delivery or a future payment and future delivery. A manufacturer or builder agrees to produce or build a well described good or building at a given price on a given date in the future. The price can be paid in instalments, step by step as agreed between the parties. *Istisna'a* can be used for financing the manufacture or construction of houses, plant, projects and the building of bridges, roads and power stations.

Iwad: An equivalent counter-value or recompense. This is an important principle of Islamic finance. Contracts without *iwad* are not Islamically acceptable.

Jahala: Ignorance, lack of knowledge; indefiniteness in a contract, sometimes leading to **gharar**.

Jua'alah: Literally, *Jua'alah* constitutes wages, pay, stipend or reward. Legally, it is a contract for performing a given task against a prescribed fee in a given period. *Ujrah* is a similar contract in which any work is done against a stipulated wage or fee.

Kafalah: (suretyship)Literally, *Kafalah* means responsibility, or suretyship. Legally in *Kafalah* a third party becomes a surety for the payment of debt. It is a pledge given to a creditor that the debtor will pay the debt or fine. Suretyship in Islamic law is the creation of an additional liability with regard to the claim, not to the debt itself.

Khiyar: Option or a power to annul or cancel a contract.

Maisir: An ancient Arabian game of chance played with arrows without heads and feathers, for stakes of slaughtered and quartered camels. It came to be identified with all types of gambling.

al-masnoo: The subject matter of an **Istisna'a** contract.

al-musania'a: The seller/manufacturer in an **Istisna'a** contract.

al-muslam: The buyer in a **Salam** contract.

al-muslam fihi: The commodity to be delivered in a **Salam** contract.

al-muslam ileihi: The seller in a **Salam** contract.

al-mustasni: The ultimate buyer in an **Istisna'a** contract.

Mithli: (fungible goods) Goods that can be returned in kind, that is gold for gold, silver for silver, US$ for US$, wheat for wheat and so on.

Mujtahid: Legal expert, or a Jurist who expends great effort in deriving a legal opinion interpreting the sources of *Sharia'a* law.

Mudaraba: (trust financing) An agreement made between two parties one of whom provides 100% of the capital for the project and who has no control over the management of the project, and another party know as a **Mudarib**, who manages the project using his entrepreneurial skills. Profits arising from the project are distributed according to a predetermined ratio. Losses are borne by the provider of capital.

Mudarib: The managing partner in a **Mudaraba** contract.

Mujir: The lessor – a person or institution who provides an asset with an **Ijara** (lease).

Murabaha (cost plus financing): A contract sale between the bank and its client for the sale of goods at a price that includes a profit margin agreed by both parties. As a financing technique it involves the purchase of goods by the bank as requested by its client. The goods are sold to the client with an agreed mark-up.

Musawamah: A general kind of sale in which the price of the commodity to be traded is arrived at by bargaining between the seller and the purchaser without any reference to the price paid or cost incurred by the former.

Musharaka (joint venture financing): This Islamic financing technique involves a joint venture between two parties who both provide capital for the financing of a project. Both parties share profits on a pre-agreed ratio, but losses are shared on the basis of equity participation. Management of the project may be carried out by both the parties or by just one party. This is a very flexible arrangement where the sharing of the profits and management can be negotiated and pre-agreed by all parties.

Musharik: Professional who manages the transactions under the **Musharaka** mode of financing

Mustajir: The lessee – a person (or institution) to whom an asset with an **Ijara** (lease) is provided.

Mutajara: Deposits made by banks in Saudi Arabia to SAMA, the central bank.

Muwakkil: The person who appoints the **Wakil** in a **Wakala** contract.

Qard (loan of fungible objects): Legally, *Qard* means to give something of value without expecting any return. *Qard* can provide help, charity or money needed for a specific occasion (death, wedding and so on). No monetary return is expected although the finance must be repaid. The Prophet is reported to have said '. . . every loan must be paid. . .'. But if a debtor is in difficulty, the creditor is expected to extend time or even voluntarily remit the whole or a part of the principal. The literal meaning of *Qard* is to cut. It is so called because the property is really cut off when it is given to the borrower.

Qimar: Gambling. Technically, it is an arrangement in which possession of something of value is contingent upon the happening of an uncertain event. By implication it applies to a situation in which there is a loss for one party and a gain for the other without specifying which party will lose and which will gain.

Qiyas: Literally, this means measure, example, comparison or analogy. Technically, it means a derivation of the law on the analogy of an existing law if the basis (*'ilaih*) of the two is the same. It is one of the sources of **Sharia'a** law.

Rab ul Mall: Capital investor/finance provider.

Rahn: (pledge or collateral). Legally, *Rahn* means to pledge or lodge a real or corporeal property of material value, in accordance with the law, as security, for a debt or pecuniary obligation so as to make it possible for the creditor to recover the debt or some portion of the goods or property. In the pre-Islamic contracts, *Rahn* implied a type of 'earnest money', which was lodged as a guarantee and material evidence or proof of a contract, especially when there was no scribe available to confirm this in writing.

Ras ul Mall: Capital (cost) paid (in cash, kind or benefit) in both **Salam** and **Istisna'a** contracts; i.e., the price paid.

Riba: An excess or increase. Technically, it means an increase over principal in a loan transaction or in exchange for a commodity accrued to the owner (lender) without giving an equivalent counter-value or recompense (*'iwad*), in return, to the other party. *Riba* means an increase that is without an *'iwad* or equal counter-value.

Riba Al-Fadl: '*Riba* in excess': the quality premium when exchanging low quality with better quality goods, for example, dates for dates, wheat for wheat and so on. In other words, an excess in the exchange of *Ribawi* goods within a single genus. The concept of *Riba Al-Fadl* refers to sale transactions while **Riba Al-Nasiah** refers to loan transactions.

Riba Al-Nasiah: '*Riba* of delay' is due to an exchange not being immediate with or without excess in one of the counter-values. It is an increment on the principal of a loan or debt payable, and refers to the practice of lending money for any length of time on the understanding that the borrower will return to the lender, at the end of the period, the amount originally lent together with an increase on it, in consideration of the lender having granted him time to pay. Interest, in all modern conventional banking transactions, falls under the purview of *Riba Al-Nasiah*. As money in the present banking system is exchanged for money with excess and delay, it falls under the definition of *riba*. There is a general accord reached among scholars that *riba* is prohibited under **Sharia'a** law.

Sadaqah: Deeds of giving, charitable donations, alms and so on.

Sahib-ul-Mal: Under the **Mudaraba Takaful** model, the entrepreneur (or **Mudarib** – the **Takaful** operator) accepts payment of the **Takaful** instalments or **Takaful** contributions premium (termed the **Ras ul Mall**) from investors or providers of capital or fund (**Takaful** participants) acting as *Sahib-ul-Mal*.

Salaf: (loan/debt): Literally, a loan that draws forth no profit for the creditor. In a wider sense this includes loans for specified periods; that is, for short, intermediate and long term loans. *Salaf* is another name for **Salam** wherein the price of the commodity is paid in advance while the commodity or the counter-value is supplied in the future. Thus the contract creates a liability for the seller.

Salam: A contract in which advance payment is made for goods to be delivered later. The seller undertakes to supply some specific goods to the buyer at a future date in exchange for a price fully paid in advance at the time of contract. According to the normal rules of the **Sharia'a**, no sale can be affected unless the goods are in existence at the time of the contract. However *Salam* forms an exception, given by the Prophet, to the general rule provided the goods are defined and the date of delivery is fixed. It is necessary that the quality of the commodity intended to be purchased is fully specified leaving no ambiguity potentially leading to a dispute. The objects of the *Salam* sale are goods and cannot be gold, silver or currencies. The latter are regarded as monetary values, the exchange of which is covered under rules of **Sarf**, that is mutual exchange should be hand to hand (spot) without delay. With this latter exception, *Salam* covers almost everything capable of being definitively described as to quantity, quality and workmanship.

Sarf: Basically, in pre-Islamic times this was the exchange of gold for gold, silver for silver and gold for silver or vice versa. In **Sharia'a** law such exchange is regarded as sale of price for price (*Bai al Thaman bil Thaman*), and each price is consideration of the other. *Sarf* also means the sale of monetary value for monetary value, meaning foreign exchange transactions.

Sharia'a: The term *Sharia'a* has two meanings: Islamic Law and the totality of divine categorisations of human acts (Islam). *Sharia'a* rules do not always function as rules of law in the Western sense, because they include obligations, duties and moral considerations not generally thought of as 'law'. *Sharia'a* rules, therefore, admitting of both a legal and moral dimension, have as their purpose the fostering of obedience to Allah the Almighty. In the legal terminology, *Sharia'a* means the law as extracted by the **Mujtahid** from the sources of law.

Shirkah: A contract between two or more persons who launch a business or financial enterprise to make profits. In the conventional books of **Fiqh**, the partnership business may include both **Musharaka** and **Mudaraba**.

Sukuk: Islamic bonds, similar to asset-backed bonds.

Sunnah: Custom, habit or way of life. Technically, this refers to the utterances of the Prophet Mohammed other than the *Qur'an*, being known as the *Hadith*, or his personal acts, or sayings of others, tacitly approved by the Prophet.

Tabarru': A donation or gift, the purpose of which is not commercial but is given in seeking the pleasure of Allah. Any benefit that is given by one person to another without getting something in exchange is called *Tabarru'*.

Takaful: A *Sharia'a*-compliant system of insurance in which the participants donate part of, or all of their contributions, which are used to pay claims for damages suffered by some of the participants. The *Takaful* operator's role is restricted to managing the insurance operations and investing the insurance contributions.

Tamlik: Complete and exclusive personal possession. The act of giving, in a *zakat* sense, is only complete, from an Islamic perspective, if there is a full transfer of ownership of the *zakat* donation.

Tapir: Spending wastefully on objects that have been explicitly prohibited by the ***Sharia'a***, irrespective of the amount of expenditure.

Wadia: System in which an Islamic bank acts as keeper and trustee of depositor funds.

Wakala: A contract of agency in which one person appoints someone else to perform a certain task on his behalf, usually against a certain fee.

Wakil: The agent appointed by the ***Muwakkil*** in a ***Wakala*** contract.

Waqf: An Islamic endowment in which a particular property is set aside, in perpetuity, for a particular charity.

Zakat: Literally, this means blessing, purification, increase or cultivation of good deeds. It is a religious obligation of alms-giving, on a Muslim, to pay 2.5% of certain kinds of wealth annually to one of the eight categories of needy Muslims.

Bibliography

This text draws on a wide variety of references. In order to appreciate the central elements that lie at the heart of Islamic banking, readers are strongly urged to consult the following *Sura* from the *Qur'an*. The key references to *riba* can be found in

- Sura 2: 275–280
- Sura 3: 130
- Sura 4: 161
- Sura 30: 39

BOOKS

Ahmad, Ausaf and Khan, Tariqullah (1997). *Islamic Financial Instruments for Public Sector Resource Mobilization*, Jeddah, Saudi Arabia: IDB, IRTI.

Ahmad, Ausaf and Khan, Tariqullah (eds) (1998). *Islamic Financial Instruments for Public Sector Resource Mobilization*, Jeddah, Saudi Arabia: IRTI.

Ahmad, Khurshid (ed.) (1976). *Studies in Islamic Economics*, Leicester, UK: The Islamic Foundation.

Al-Harran, Saad Abdul Sattar (1993). *Islamic Finance: Partnership Financing*, Selangor, Malaysia: Pelanduk Publications.

Al-Harran, Saad Abdul Sattar (1995). *Leading Issues in Islamic Banking and Finance*, Selangor, Malaysia: Pelanduk Publications.

Ali, Syed Ameer (1978). *The Spirit of Islam: A History of the Evolution and Ideals of Islam, with a Life of the Prophet*, London, UK: Chatto & Windus.

Ali, S. Nazim and Ali, Naseem N. (1994). *Information Sources on Islamic Banking and Economics, 1980–1990*, Kegan Paul International.

al-Misri, Ahmad ibn Naqid (1988). *Reliance of the Traveller: A Classical Manual of Islamic Sacred Law*, Translation by Nuh Ha Mim Keller: Amana Publications.

Al-Omar, Fouad and Abdel Haq, Mohammed (1996). *Islamic Banking, Theory, Practice and Challenges*, London, UK: Oxford University.

al-Qaradawi, Yusuf (1985). *The Lawful and the Prohibited in Islam*, Kuala Lumpur, Malaysia: Islamic Book Trust.

Archer, Simon and Karim, Rifaat Abdel (2002). *Islamic Finance: Innovation and Growth*, London, UK: Euromoney Books and AAOIFI.

Ariff, Mohammad and Mannan, M.A. (1990). *Developing a System of Islamic Financial Instruments*, Jeddah, Saudi Arabia: IDB, IRTI.

Armstrong, Karen (2002). *Islam: A Short History*, New York, USA: Modern Library (revised edn).

Ayub, Mohammad (2002). *Islamic Banking and Finance: Theory and Practice*, Karachi, Pakistan: State Bank Printing Press.

BenDjilali, Boualem and Khan, Tariqullah (1995). *Economics of Diminishing Musharakah*, Jeddah, Saudi Arabia: IRTI.

Bowker, John (1999). *What Muslims Believe*, Oxford, UK: OneWorld.

Burton, John (1990). *The Sources of Islamic Law: Islamic Theories of Abrogation*, Edinburgh, UK: Edinburgh University Press.

Burton, John (1994). *An Introduction to the Hadith*, Edinburgh, UK: Edinburgh University Press.

Chapra, M.U. (1985). *Towards a Just Monetary System*, Leicester, UK: The Islamic Foundation.

Chapra, M.U. (1992). *Islam and the Economic Challenge*, Leicester, UK: The Islamic Foundation.

Chapra, M.U. (2000). *The Future of Islamic Economics*, Leicester, UK: The Islamic Foundation.

Cook, Michael (2000). *The Koran: A Very Short Introduction*, Oxford, UK: Oxford University Press.

Cooter, Robert and Thomas Ulen (2000). *Law and Economics*, 3rd edition, Reading, MA, USA: Addison-Wesley.

Coulson, N.J. (1994). *A History of Islamic Law*, Edinburgh, UK: Edinburgh University Press.

De Lorenzo, Yusuf Talal (eds) (1997). *A Compendium of Legal Opinions on the Operations of Islamic Banks: Murabahah, Mudarabah and Musharakah*, London, UK: Institute of Islamic Banking and Insurance.

El-Gamal, M.A. (2003). *A Basic Guide to Contemporary Islamic Banking and Finance*, elgamal@rice.edu http://www.ruf.rice.edu/~elgamal

El-Gamal, M.A. (2003). *Financial Transactions in Islamic Jurisprudence*, Vols 1 and 2, Translation by Dr Al-Zuhayli: Kitaabun.com

Esposito, John L. (1995). *The Oxford Encyclopedia of the Modern Islamic World*, 4 vols, Oxford, UK: Oxford University Press.

Farouqui, Mahmood (ed.) (1997). *Islamic Banking and Investment: Challenge and Opportunity*, Kegan Paul International.

Garrett, R. and Graham, A. (eds) (1998). *Islamic Law and Finance*, Introduction by William Ballantyne, London, UK: Graham & Trotman.

Hallaq, Wael B. (ed.) (2003). *The Formation of Islamic Law*, Aldershot, UK: Ashgate.

Haron, Sudin (1997). *Islamic Banking: Rules and Regulations*, Selangor, Malaysia: Pelanduk Publications.

Haron, Sudin and Bala Shanmugam (1997). *Islamic Banking System: Concepts and Applications*, Selangor, Malaysia: Pelanduk Publications.

Henry, C.M. and Rodney Wilson (eds) (2004). *Politics of Islamic Finance*, Edinburgh, UK: Edinburgh University Press.

Homoud, Sami Hassan (1985). *Islamic Banking*, London, UK: Arabian Information.

Homoud, S. (1985). *Islamic Banking*, London, UK: Graham & Trotman.

Institute of Islamic Banking and Insurance (1996). *Islamic Banking: An Overview*, London, UK: Institute of Islamic Banking and Insurance.

Institute of Islamic Banking and Insurance (2000). *International Directory of Islamic Banks and Institutions*, London, UK: Institute of Islamic Banking and Insurance.

International Association of Islamic Banks (1997). *Directory of Islamic Banks and Financial Institutions*, Jeddah, Saudi Arabia: International Association of Islamic Banks.

Iqbal, M. (ed.) (2002). *Islamic Banking and Finance*, Leicester, UK: The Islamic Foundation.

Iqbal, M. and Khan, Tariqullah (2005). *Financial Engineering and Islamic Contracts*, Basingstoke, UK: Palgrave-Macmillan.

Iqbal, M. and Molyneux, Philip (2005). *Thirty Years of Islamic Banking: History and Performance*, Basingstoke, UK: Palgrave-Macmillan.

Iqbal, Munawar and Llewellyn, David T. (2002). *Islamic Banking and Finance: New Perspectives in Profit Sharing and Risk*, London, UK: Edward Elgar Publishers.

Jaffer, S. (ed.) (2004). *Islamic Asset Management: Forming the Future for Sharia-Compliant Investment Strategies*, London, UK: Euromoney.

Kahf, Monzer and Khan, Tariqullah (1992). *Principles of Islamic Financing*, Jeddah, Saudi Arabia: IRTI.

Kamal, H. (2001). *Islamic Commercial Law: An Analysis of Futures and Options*, Cambridge, UK: Islamic Text Society.

Kamali, Mohammad Hashim (2000). *Principles of Islamic Jurisprudence*, Cambridge, UK: The Islamic Texts Society, revised edn.

Kettell, B. (1999). *Fed-watching: The impact of the Fed on the World's Financial Markets*, Financial Times-Prentice Hall.

Kettell, B. (1999). *What Drives Financial Markets?* Financial Times-Prentice Hall.

Kettell, B. (2000). *What drives the Currency Markets?* Financial Times-Prentice Hall.

Kettell, B. (2001). *Economics for Financial Market*, Butterworth's-Heinemann.

Kettell, B. (2001). *Financial Economics*, Financial Times-Prentice Hall.

Kettell, B. (2002). *Islamic Banking in the Kingdom of Bahrain*, Bahrain Monetary Agency (BMA).

Kettell, B. (2006). *Sukuk: a definitive guide to Islamic Structured Finance*, Thompson Hine.

Khan, M. Fahim (1996). *Islamic Futures and their Markets*, Jeddah, Saudi Arabia: IRTI.

Khan, Shahrukh Rafi (1988). *Profit and Loss Sharing: An Islamic Experiment in Finance and Banking*, Oxford, UK: Oxford University Press.

Khan, W.M. (1985). *Towards an Interest-Free Islamic Economic System*, Leicester, UK: The Islamic Foundation.

Lewis, Mervyn K. and Latifa M. Algaoud (2001). *Islamic Banking*, Cheltenham, UK: Edward Elgar.

Mehdi, Rubya (1994). *The Islamization of the Law in Pakistan*, Richmond, Surrey: Curzon Press.

Mills, Paul S. and John R. Presley (1999). *Islamic Finance: Theory and Practice*, London, UK: Macmillan.

Moore, Philip (1997). *Islamic Finance: A Partnership for Growth*, London, UK: Euromoney.

Rahman, Yahia Abdul (1994). *Interest Free Islamic Banking – Lariba Bank*, Kuala Lumpur, Malaysia: Al-Hilal Publishing.

Rosly, S.A. (2005). *Critical Issues in Islamic Banking and Financial Markets*, Bloomington, IN, USA: AuthorHouse.

Roy, O. (2004). *Globalised Islam, The Search for a New Ummah*, Huot & Co.

Saeed, Abdullah (1997). *Islamic Banking and Interest: A Study of the Prohibition of Ribā and Its Contemporary Interpretation*, 2nd edition, Leiden, The Netherlands: E.J. Brill.

Saleh, Nabil A. (1992). *Unlawful Gain and Legitimate Profit in Islamic Law*, 2nd edition, London, UK: Graham and Trotman.

Shirazi (1990). *Islamic Banking Contracts*, London, UK: Butterworth-Heinemann.

Siddiqi, M.N. (1983). *Issues in Islamic Banking*, Leicester, UK: The Islamic Foundation.

Siddiqi, M.N. (1985). *Partnership and Profit Sharing*, Leicester, UK: The Islamic Foundation.

Siddiqi, M.N. (1988). *Banking Without Interest*, Leicester, UK: The Islamic Foundation.

Udovitch, Abraham L. (1970) *Partnership and Profit in Medieval Islam*, Princeton, NJ, USA: Princeton University Press.

Usmani, M.T. (1998). *An Introduction to Islamic Finance*, Karachi, Pakistan: Idaratul-Ma'arif.

Usmani, M.T. (2000). *The Historic Judgment on Interest*, Karachi, Pakistan: Idaratul-Ma'arif.

Vogal, Frank E. and Samuel L. Hayes (1988). *Islamic Law and Finance: Religion, Risk and Return*, The Hague, The Netherlands: Kluwer Law International.

Warde, I. (2000). *Islamic Finance in the Global Economy*, Edinburgh, UK: Edinburgh University Press.

Zineldin, Mosad (1990), *The Economics of Money and Banking: A Theoretical and Empirical Study of Islamic Interest-Free Banking*, Stockholm, Sweden: Almqvist & Wiksell International.

AAOIFI PUBLICATIONS

AAOIFI (1999). *Statement on the Purpose and Calculation of the Capital Adequacy Ratio for Islamic Banks*, Manama, Bahrain: The Accounting & Auditing Organization for Islamic Financial Institutions.

AAOIFI (2002). *Accounting, Auditing and Governance Standards*, Manama, Bahrain: The Accounting & Auditing Organization for Islamic Financial Institutions.

AAOIFI (2002). *Investment Sukuk (Shari'ah Standard No.18)*, Manama, Bahrain: The Accounting & Auditing Organization for Islamic Financial Institutions.

AAOIFI (2003). *Shari'ah Standards*, Manama, Bahrain: The Accounting & Auditing Organization for Islamic Financial Institutions.

AAOIFI (2004). *Guiding Principles of Risk Management for Institutions* (Insurance companies offering only Islamic Financial Services), Manama, Bahrain: The Accounting & Auditing Organization for Islamic Financial Institutions.

AAOIFI (2004). *Capital Adequacy Standard for Institutions* (offering only Islamic Financial Services), Manama, Bahrain: The Accounting & Auditing Organization for Islamic Financial Institutions.

ARTICLES AND PAPERS

Abdallah, A. (1987). 'Islamic Banking', *Journal of Islamic Banking and Finance*, Jan–Mar, 4(1): 31–56.
Abdul, Majid and Abdul, Rais (2003). 'Development of Liquidity Management Instruments: Challenges and Opportunities', paper presented to the *International Conference on Islamic Banking: Risk Management, Regulation and Supervision*, held in Jakarta, Indonesia, 30 September–2 October 2003, organised by IRTI, Bank Indonesia and Ministry of Finance: Indonesia.
Abdul-Rahman, Yahla and Abdulah, S. Tug (1999). 'Towards a LARIBA (Islamic) Mortgage in the United States: Providing an Alternative to the Traditional Mortgages', *International Journal of Islamic Financial Services*, 1(2), Jul–Sep.
Aftab, M. (1986). 'Pakistan moves to Islamic banking', *The Banker*, June: 57–60.
Aggarwal, R.K. and Yousef, T. (2000). 'Islamic Banks and Investment Financing', *Journal of Money, Credit and Banking*, 32, 93–120.
Ahmad, Dr. Abdel Rahman Yousri (2001). 'Riba, its Economic Rationale and Implications', *New Horizon*, 109, May–June.
Ahmad, Ziauddin (1995). 'Islamic Banking: State of the Art', *IDB Prize Lecture*, Jeddah, Saudi Arabia: Islamic Research and Training Institute, Islamic Development Bank.
Alam, M.A. (2000). 'Islamic Banking in Bangladesh: A Case Study of IBBL', *International Journal of Islamic Financial Services*, 1(4), Jan–Mar.
Al-Bashir, M. and Muhammed al-Amine (2001). 'The Islamic Bonds Market: Possibilities and Challenges', *International Journal of Islamic Financial Services*, 3(1), Apr–Jun.
Al-Jarhi, Mabid Ali and Iqbal, Munawar (2001). 'Islamic Banking: FAQs', Occasional Paper #4, Jeddah, Saudi Arabia: Islamic Research and Training Institute.
Al-Suwailem, Sami (2000). 'Decision Under Uncertainty, An Islamic Perspective', in Islamic Finance: Challenges and Opportunities in the Twenty-First Century (Conference Papers). Loughborough: *Fourth International Conference on Islamic Economics and Banking*.
Anouar, H. (2002). 'Profitability of Islamic Banks', *International Journal of Islamic Financial Services*, 4(2), Jul–Sep.
Archer, S., Karim, R. Abdel and Al-Deehani, T. (1998). 'Financial Contracting, Governance Structures and the Accounting Regulation of Islamic Banks: An Analysis in Terms of Agency Theory and Transaction Cost Economics', *Journal of Management and Governance*, 2, 149–170.
Ariff, M. (1982). 'Monetary Policy in an Interest-Free Islamic Economy – Nature and Scope' in Ariff, M. (ed.). *Monetary and Fiscal Economics of Islam*, Jeddah, Saudi Arabia: International Centre for Research in Islamic Economics.
Ayub, Muhammad (1995). 'Meaning of Riba', *Journal of Islamic Banking and Finance*, 12(2).
Babikir, Osman Ahmed (2001). Islamic Financial Instruments to Manage Short-term Excess Liquidity, Research Paper No.41, 2nd edn, Jeddah, Saudi Arabia: Islamic Research and Training Institute.
Bacha, O.I. (1999). 'Financial Derivatives: Some Thoughts for Reconsideration', *International Journal of Islamic Financial Services*, 1(1), Apr–Jun.
Baldwin, K. (2002). 'Risk Management in Islamic Banks', in Karim, R. Abdel and Archer, S. (eds). *Islamic Finance: Innovation and Growth*, Euromoney Books and AAOIFI, pp. 176–197.
Basel Committee on Banking Supervision (BCBS) (2003). Consultative Document – Overview of the New Basel Capital Accord, Bank for International Settlements, April.
Bashir, A. (1996). 'Profit-sharing Contracts and Investment under Asymmetric Information', *Research in Middle East Economics*, 1, 173–186.
Buckmaster, Daphne (ed.) (1996). 'Central Bank Supervision: The Need for Unity', in *Islamic Banking: An Overview*, London: Institute of Islamic Banking and Insurance, pp. 143–145.
Buckmaster, Daphne, (ed.) (1996). 'Alternative Tools of Supervision by Central Banks', in *Islamic Banking: An Overview*, London: Institute of Islamic Banking and Insurance, pp. 146–150.
Chapra, M. Umer (1982). 'Money and Banking in an Islamic Economy', in Ariff, M. (ed.) *Monetary and Fiscal Economics of Islam*, Jeddah, Saudi Arabia: International Centre for Research in Islamic Economics.

Chapra, M. Umer (2000). 'Why has Islam Prohibited Interest?: Rationale Behind the Prohibition of Interest', *Review of Islamic Economics*, 9.

Chapra, M. Umer and Habib Ahmed (2002). Corporate Governance in Islamic Financial Institutions, Occasional Paper No. 6, Jeddah, Saudi Arabia: Islamic Research and Training Institute.

Chapra, M. Umer and Tariqullah Khan (2000). 'Regulation and Supervision of Islamic Banks', Occasional Paper No.3, Jeddah, Saudi Arabia: Islamic Development Bank – Islamic Research and Training Institute.

Cunningham, A. (2001). 'Culture of Accounting: What are the Real Constraints for Islamic Finance in a Riba-Based Global Economy?' London, UK: Moody's Investor Services.

Dale, Richard (2000). 'Comparative Models of Banking Supervision', paper presented to the *Conference on Islamic Banking Supervision*, Bahrain: AAOIFI, February.

Dar, H.A. and Presley, J.R. (1999). 'Islamic Finance: A Western Perspective', *International Journal of Islamic Financial Services*, 1(1), Apr–June.

Dar, H.A. and Presley, J.R. (2000). 'Lack of Profit Sharing in Islamic Banking: Management and Control Imbalances', *International Journal of Islamic Financial Services*, 2(2), Jul–Sep.

El-Din, A.K. (1986). 'Ten Years of Islamic Banking', *Journal of Islamic Banking and Finance*, Jul–Sep, 3(3): 49–66.

El-Gamal, Mahmoud (2000). 'An Economic Explication of the Prohibition of Gharar in Classical Islamic Jurisprudence', in Islamic Finance: Challenges and Opportunities in the Twenty First Century (Conference Papers). Loughborough: *Fourth International Conference on Islamic Economics and Banking*.

Elgari, M. Ali (1997). 'Short Term Financial Instruments Based on Salam Contracts', in Ausaf Ahmad and Tariqullah Khan (eds.). *Islamic Financial Instruments for Public Sector Resource Mobilization*, Jeddah, Saudi Arabia: Islamic Research and Training Institute, pp. 249–66.

El-Karanshawy, Hatem (1998). 'CAMEL Ratings and their Relevance for Islamic Banks', paper presented to a Seminar on Islamic Banking Supervision, organised by the Arab Monetary Fund: Abu Dhabi.

El Sheikkh, Fath El Rahman (2000). 'The Regulation of Islamic Banks by Central Banks', *The Journal of International Banking Regulation*, Fall, 43–49.

Errico, Luca, and Mitra Farahbaksh (1998). 'Islamic Banking: Issues in Prudential Regulations and Supervision', IMF Working Paper 98/30, Washington: International Monetary Fund.

Fadeel, Mahmoud (2002). 'Legal Aspects of Islamic Finance', in Archer, Simon and Karim, Rifaat Abdel (eds). *Islamic Finance: Growth and Innovation*, London, UK: Euromoney Books.

Gafoor, A.L.M. Abdul (2001). 'Mudaraba-based Investment and Finance', *New Horizon*, 110, July.

Gafoor, A.L.M. Abdul (2001). 'Riba-free Commercial Banking', *New Horizon*, 112, September.

Grais, W. and Kantur, Z. (2003). 'The Changing Financial Landscape: Opportunities and Challenges for the Middle East and North Africa', *World Bank Policy Research Working Paper* 3050, May 2003.

Haque, Nadeemul and Abbas Mirakhor (1999). 'The Design of Instruments for Government Finance in an Islamic Economy', *Islamic Economic Studies*, 6(2): 27–43.

Haron, S. and Norafifah Ahmad (2000). 'The Effects of Conventional Interest Rates on Funds Deposited with Islamic Banking System in Malaysia', *International Journal of Islamic Financial Services*, 1(4), Jan–Mar.

Hassan, Sabir Mohammad (2000). 'Capital Adequacy and Basel Guidelines: On Risk Weights of Assets for Islamic Banks', paper presented at the Conference on the Regulation of Islamic Banks, in Bahrain, February.

Hoque, M.Z. and Masdul Alam Choudhury (2003). 'Islamic Finance: A Western Perspective Revisited', *International Journal of Islamic Financial Services*, 4(4), Apr–June.

Ibrahim, Tag El-Din S. (1991). 'Risk Aversion, Moral Hazard and Financial Islamization Policy', *Review of Islamic Economics*, 1(1).

Iqbal, Zamir and Abbas Mirakhor (2002). 'Development of Islamic Financial Institutions and Challenges Ahead', in Archer, Simon and Karim, Rifaat Abdel (eds.) *Islamic Finance: Growth and Innovation*, London, UK: Euromoney Books.

Iqbal, Zamir (1997). 'Islamic Financial Systems', *Finance and Development (IMF)*, 34(2), June.

Iqbal, Z. (2001). 'Profit and Loss Sharing Ratios: A Holistic Approach to Corporate Finance', *International Journal of Islamic Financial Services*, 3(2), Jul–Sep.

Iqbal, Zubair and Abbas Mirakhor (1987). Islamic Banking, IMF Occasional Paper No.49, Washington: International Monetary Fund.

Iqbal, Munawar *et al.* (1999). Challenges Facing Islamic Banking, Jeddah, Saudi Arabia: IRTI, Occasional Paper #2.

Islamic Fiqh Academy of the Organization of Islamic Conference (1989). 'Islamic Fiqh Academy Resolutions and Recommendations', Jeddah, Saudi Arabia.

Kahf, Monzer (1998). 'Asset Ijara Bonds', in Ausaf, Ahmad and Khan, Tariqullah (eds), *Islamic Financial Instruments for Public Sector Resource Mobilization*, Jeddah, Saudi Arabia: IRTI.

Kahf, Monzer (1997). 'The Use of Assets Ijārah Bonds for Bridging the Budget Gap', in Ahmad, Ausaf and Khan, Tariqullah (eds.). *Islamic Financial Instruments for Public Sector Resource Mobilization*, Jeddah, Saudi Arabia: Islamic Research and Training Institute, pp. 265–316.

Kahf, Monzer (1996). 'Distribution of Profits in Islamic Banks', *Studies in Islamic Economics*, 4(1).

Kahf, Monzer (1994). 'Time Value of Money and Discounting in Islamic Perspectives Revisited', *Review of Islamic Economics*, 3(2).

Kahf, Monzer and Khan, Tariqullah (1992). Principles of Islamic Financing, Jeddah, Saudi Arabia: IRTI.

Karim, Rifaat Ahmed Abdel (2001). 'International Accounting Harmonization, Banking Regulation and Islamic Banks', *The International Journal of Accounting*, 36(2), 169–193.

Karsten, I. (1982). 'Islam and Financial Intermediation', *IMF Staff Papers*, March, 29(1), 108–142.

Khan, Mohsin and Abbas Mirakhor (1993). 'Monetary Management in an Islamic Economy', *Journal of Islamic Banking and Finance*, 10, Jul–Sep, 42–63.

Khan, Mohsin and Mirakhor, A. (1986). 'The Framework and Practice of Islamic Banking', *Finance and Development*, September.

Khan, Mohsin S. and Mirakhor, A. (1992). 'Islam and the Economic System', *Review of Islamic Economics*, 2(1): 1–29.

Khan, M. (1987). 'Islamic Interest-Free Banking: A Theoretical Analysis', in Khan, Mohsin S. and Mirakhor, Abbas (ed.). *Theoretical Studies in Islamic Banking and Finance*, Texas, USA: The Institute of Islamic Studies, pp. 15–36.

Khan, Mohsin S. (1986). 'Islamic Interest-Free Banking: A Theoretical Analysis', IMF Staff Papers, 33(1): 1–27, March.

Khan, M.Y. (2001) 'Banking Regulations and Islamic Banks in India: Status and Issues', *International Journal of Islamic Financial Services*, 2(4), Jan–Mar.

Khan, M.F. (1999). Financial Modernisation in the Twenty-First Century and Challenges for Islamic Banking', *International Journal of Islamic Financial Services*, 1(3), Oct–Dec.

Khan, M.F. (1991). Comparative Economics of Some Islamic Financing Techniques, Research Paper No.12, Islamic Research and Training Institute, Islamic Development Bank: Jeddah, Saudi Arabia.

Khan, Tariqullah and Ahmad, Habib (2001). Risk Management: An Analysis of Issues in the Islamic Financial Industry, Jeddah, Saudi Arabia: IRTI, Occasional Paper #5.

Khan, Tariqullah (1995). 'Demand for and Supply of PLS and Mark-up Funds of Islamic Banks – Some Alternative Explanations', *Islamic Economic Studies*, 3(1), Jeddah, Saudi Arabia: IRTI.

Khan, Tariqullah and Habib, Ahmad (2001). Risk Management: An Analysis of Issues in the Islamic Financial Industry, Jeddah, Saudi Arabia: IRTI Occasional Paper #5.

Maroun, Y. (2002). 'Liquidity Management and Trade Financing', in Karim, R. Abdel and Archer, S. (eds.). *Islamic Finance: Innovation and Growth* (pp. 163–175). Euromoney Books and AAOIFI.

Mirakhor, Abbas (1995). 'Theory of an Islamic Financial System' in *Encyclopaedia of Islamic Banking*, London, UK: Institute of Islamic Banking and Finance.

Mulajawan, D., Dar, H.A. and Hall, M.J.B. (2002). 'A Capital Adequacy Framework for Islamic Banks: The Need to Reconcile Depositors' Risk Aversion with Managers' Risk Taking', Economics Research Paper, 2–13, Loughborough University.

Naughton, S.A.J. and Tahir, M.A. (1988). 'Islamic Banking and Financial Development', *Journal of Islamic Banking and Finance*, 5(2).

Nienhaus, V. (1983). 'Profitability of Islamic PLS Banks Competing with Interest Banks: Problems and Prospects', *Journal of Research in Islamic Economics*, 1(1): 37–47.

Nienhaus, V. (1986). 'Islamic Economics, Finance and Banking – Theory and Practice', *Journal of Islamic Banking and Finance*, 3(2): 36–54.

Norman, A.A. (2002). 'Imperatives for Financial Innovation for Islamic Banks', *International Journal of Islamic Financial Services*, 4(2), Oct–Dec.

Obaidullah, Mohammad (1998). 'Capital Adequacy Norms for Islamic Financial Institutions', *Islamic Economic Studies*, 5(1–2).

Obaidullah, Mohammad (1998). 'Financial Engineering with Islamic Options', *Islamic Economic Studies*, 6(1), IRTI, IDB.

Obaidullah, Mohammad (1999). 'Islamic Financial Options: Potential Tools for Risk Management', *Journal of King Abdulaziz University (Islamic Economics)*. Saudi Arabia, 11, 3–28.

Obaidullah, Mohammad (2000). 'Regulation of Stock Markets in an Islamic Economy', Proceedings of the Third International Conference on Islamic Banking and Finance, August, Loughborough University, Leicester, UK.

Obaidullah, Mohammad (2001). 'Ethics and Efficiency in Islamic Stock Markets', *International Journal of Islamic Financial Services*, 3(2), Jul–Sep.

Obaidullah, Mohammad (2001). 'Financial Contracting in Currency Markets', *International Journal of Islamic Financial Services*, 3(3), Oct–Dec.

Obaidullah, Mohammad (2002). 'Islamic Risk Management', *International Journal of Islamic Financial Services*, 3(4), Jan–Mar.

Presley, John R. and Sessions, John, G. (1993). 'Islamic Economics: The Emergence of a New Paradigm', *Journal of Economic Theory*.

Qami, I.H. (1995). 'Regulatory Control of Islamic Banks by Central Banks', in Encyclopaedia of Islamic Banking and Insurance, Institute of Islamic Banking and Insurance: London, pp. 211–215.

Rahman, Y.A. (1999). 'Islamic Instruments for Managing Liquidity', *International Journal of Islamic Financial Services*, 1(1), Apr–Jun.

Rosly, A.R. and Sanussi, Mohammed M. (1999). 'The Application of Bay-al-Inah and Bai-al-Dayn in Malaysian Islamic Bonds: An Islamic Analysis', *International Journal of Islamic Financial Services*, 1(2), Jul–Sep.

Salehabadi, A. and Aram, M. (2002). 'Islamic Justification of Derivative Instruments', *International Journal of Islamic Financial Services*, 4(3), Oct–Dec.

Sarker, M.A.A. (1999). 'Islamic Business Contracts: Agency Problems and the Theory of Islamic Firms', *International Journal of Islamic Financial Services*, 1(2), Jul–Sep.

Sarwar, A.A. (1995). 'Islamic Financial Instruments: Definition and Types', *Review of Islamic Economics*, 4(1): 1–16.

Sundararajan, V., Marston, David and Shabsigh, Ghiath (1998). 'Monetary Operations and Government Debt Management under Islamic Banking', WP/98/144, Washington, DC: IMF, September.

Sundararajan, V. and Errico, L. (2002). 'Islamic Financial Institutions and Products in the Global Financial System: Key Issues in Risk Management and Challenges Ahead', IMF working paper, IMF/02/192, Washington: International Monetary Fund, November.

Udovitch, Abraham L. (1981). Bankers Without Banks: Commerce, Banking and Society in the Islamic World of the Middle Ages, Princeton Near East Paper No.30, Princeton, NJ: Princeton University Press.

Udovitch, Abraham (1970). Partnership and Profit in Early Islam, Princeton, NJ: Princeton University Press.

Uzair, Mohammad (1955). An Outline of 'Interestless Banking', Raihan Publications, Karachi.

Uzair, Mohammad (1982). 'Central Banking Operations in an Interest-Free Banking System', in Ariff, M. (ed.).

Zaher, T. and Hassan, K. (2001). 'A Comparative Literature Survey of Islamic Finance and Banking', *Financial Markets, Institutions and Instruments*, 10(4): 155–199, November.

ALSO PUBLISHED BY THE AUTHOR

Islamic Finance in a Nutshell: A Guide for Non-Specialists, 2010, John Wiley & Sons, Ltd, Chichester

Frequently Asked Questions in Islamic Finance, 2010, John Wiley & Sons, Ltd, Chichester

The Islamic Banking and Finance Workbook, 2011, John Wiley & Sons, Ltd, Chichester

Case Studies on Islamic Banking and Finance, 2011, John Wiley & Sons, Ltd, Chichester

Islamic Capital Markets, 2009, available from the author.

Sukuk: a Definitive Guide to Islamic Structured Finance, 2008, available from the author.

Islamic Banking and Finance in the Kingdom of Bahrain, 2002, Bahrain Monetary Agency.

Financial Economics, 2001, Financial Times-Prentice Hall (translated into Chinese).

Economics for Financial Markets, 2001, Butterworth's-Heinemann.

What Drives Financial Markets? 2001, Financial Times-Prentice Hall.

What Drives the Currency Markets? 2002, Financial Times-Prentice Hall.

Fed Watching: The Impact of the Fed on the World's Financial Markets, 1999, Financial Times-Prentice Hall.

The Valuation of Internet and Technology Stocks, 2002, Butterworth's-Heinemann.

The International Debt Game: a Study in International Bank Lending (co-author), 1985, Graham and Trotman.

A Businessman's Guide to the Foreign Exchange Market, 1985, Graham and Trotman.

Monetary Economics, 1985, Graham and Trotman.

Foreign Exchange Handbook, 1983, (co-author), Graham and Trotman.

Gold: An Analysis of its Role in the World Economy, 1982, Graham and Trotman.

The Finance of International Business, 1979, Graham and Trotman.

Index

ariyah (gratuitous transfer of the usufruct of property), 35
Abu Bakr, 18
Abu Hanifah, 21, 54
Accounting and Auditing Organisation for Islamic Financial Institutions (AAOIFI), 27–28, 43, 63, 77, 89, 103, 117
adhan (call to prayer), 3
agricultural partnership, 83
Ahadith, 2, 4, 14, 21, 38, 47, 78, 92, 118 *see also* Hadith
ajma'a (determine and agree), 20
al-aqd (contracts), 44, 129
Al-Maniya, Sheikh Abdullah Bin Suleiman, 29
Al Musleh, Sheikh Dr. Abdullah bin Abdulaziz, 29
alQaradaghi, Dr Ali, 27
Amanah (justice, faithfulness and trust), 27, 151
aqidah (Islamic creed), 39
Arbun (sale agreement), 151
asset-backed securities, 33, 247
Awqaf see *Waqf*
ayat (verses), 18

Bai' al-Dayn (sale of debt and receivables), 151
Bai' al-Muzayadah (sale and purchase transactions on auction and tender), 151
Bai' bil Wafa (sale of honour), 151
Bai' al-Istijrar, 151
Bai' Muajjal (credit sale), 44, 151
Bai al-'inah (double sale), 61, 151
Bai Bithaman Ajil (goods sale on deferred payment basis), 44–45, 114, 124, 151
Bakar, Dr Mohd. Daud, 28
Bank *Muamalat*, 148
bin Eid, Sheikh Dr. Muhammad Al-Ali Al Qari, 29

Council of Jurists (*Ulema* and *Fuqaha*), 13
counter value, 35, 60, 75, 87, 99, 112, 123
current accounts, 66, 243

Dhaman (guarantee), 134, 152
Dayn (debt), 152
Deposit, 16, 26, 35, 37, 66, 69
derivatives *see Maisir* (gambling)
Dhu al-Hijja, 3
Dubai Islamic Bank, 26, 51
Duyun (debts), 152

Elgari, Dr Mohamed, 27

Faith, 2, 9
family *Takaful*, 136, 152
Faqih/Fuqaha (Muslim jurist), 54
fasad (corruption), 41
fasting, 3
fatwa/fatawa (Islamic religious ruling), 24, 29
Fiqh (Islamic law), 25
Fiqh Academy, 28–29, 55
fuqaha (Muslim jurists), 54

gharar (uncertainty), 95, 106, 127
Al Ghunm bil Ghurm, 152

Hadith (sayings of Prophet), 4, 6 *see also* Ahadith
Hajj (pilgrimage), 1
Al Hajj Moulana Fazl Karim, 38
halal (permitted by *Sharia'a*), 152
haram (prohibited by *Sharia'a*), 152
Hassan, Dr Hussain Hamid, 27
Hawalah, 152
Hazrat Abu Hurairah, 38
Hazrat Al-Khudri, 39
Hazrat Jabir, 38
Hibah (gift and donation), 152
hoarding, of money, 33–34

'*id al-adha* (festival of sacrifice), 4
'*id al-fitr* (festival of breaking fast), 4
Ijara (leasing), 35, 60
Ijara Muntahia Bittamleek, 90
Ijma (consensus of opinion of learned
    men and jurists), 13, 15, 17, 20–22
Ijtihad (effort), 21
Iman, 4–5
imam (prayer leader), 3
'*inan*, 77–78
insurance, conventional *see* under *Takaful*
    (Islamic insurance)
International Association of Islamic Banks
    (IAIB), 24
International Islamic Financial Market (IIFM),
    28
International Islamic Insurance Company, 136
investment, 22–23
    accounts, unrestricted, 64–65
    Sharia'a compliant, 16
Islam *see individual entries*
Islamic banks
    gharar, prohibition of, 35
    key principle activities of, 33
    moral value system and, 35
    profit and loss sharing, 33–34
    riba, prohibition of, 39–40
    risk-sharing, 34
    sanctity of contracts, 35
Islamic banking
    definition, 31
    key principles, 33
Islamic creeds, 4–5
Islamic Development Bank (IDB), 27, 90
Istihsan (juristic preference and equity of a
    jurist), 153
Istisna'a, 103
Istisna'a sale, 50–60, 75

Jahala, 60, 74, 87, 99, 112, 123, 153
Jua'alah, 153
Justice, 10, 14

Kaaba (House of God), 2–4
Kafalah (suretyship), 92, 153

Liquidity Management Centre (LMC), 27
London inter-bank offered rate (LIBOR),
    52, 90

Madhab, 15, 59, 74, 87, 99, 112, 123
Maisir (gambling),1 27–128, 153
Majlis al-aqd, 44
makruh, 22
al-Masalih al Mursalah (public interest matters),
    17

Mecca, 2–4, 128–129
Mithli (fungible goods), 153
Mohammed, Prophet, 1–2
moral obligation, 3, 35, 49, 54
moral value system and Islamic banking, 35
mortgages, 50
Mudaraba (investment/trust financing), 31, 34,
    56, 63
Mudarib (managing partner), 51
muezzin (crier), 3
Mufawada partnership, 77–78
mujtahid (Scholar of Islamic law), 19, 153, 155
Murabaha, 31, 43
Musawama, 43–44, 154
Musharaka (joint venture financing), 154
mutawatir (authenticity proven by universally
    accepted testimony), 1, 17–18

pilgrimage, 1, 4
pillars of faith, 1
prayers *see Salat* (daily prayers)
products as *Sharia'a* compliant, 16
profit and loss sharing, in Islamic banks,
    32–33
    meaning of, 33
    Mudaraba Takaful model as, 155
    and risk-sharing, 34

Qard (loan of fungible objects), 154
qard al hassan (good loan), 33
qibla (direction), 2
Qimar see Maisir (gambling)
Qiyas (analogical deduction), 13, 21
Qualifications
    Sharia'a Board Scholar, 27–29
Qur'an, 1–4, 6, 8
    ayat, 18
    first revelation, 3, 17
    on *Kaaba* and rituals, 2–4
    on prohibition of interest, 3–32, 53
    and *Sunnah,* 13–14
    suras and, 18

Rab ul mall (investor of capital), 123
Al-Rahn (security), 92
rak'as (bowings), 2
Ramadan, 3–4, 17
religious duties of Muslims, essential, 1
riba (usury and interest), 37
    Al-Fadl, 154
    Al-Nasiah, 155
    corrupting the society, 41
    demeaning and diminishing human
        personality, 42
    Islamic rationale for banning, 39
    prohibition of, 39–40

as unjust, 40
as unlawful appropriation of other people's
    property, 41
Risk-sharing, 33–35

sadaqah (charitable giving), 3, 38, 155
Sahaba (Companions of the Prophet), 16, 19–20,
    93
Salaf (loan/debt), 155
Salam (contract of advance payment for goods),
    103, 106, 117–126
    sale, 50, 60, 75, 87, 99
    comparison with *Istisna'a*, 74, 113, 124
Salat (daily prayers), 1–2, 38
sarf (sale of price for price), 155
sawm (fasting), 1
Sayyidna Ali, 21
Shahada (profession and witness to faith), 1
Sharia'a
    banking with *Sharia'a* principles, 26
    definition, 13
    investment principles, 22
    objectives, 14
    products as *Sharia'a* compliant, 16
    sources, 16
Sharia'a Board Scholar qualifications, 27–29
Sharia'a Supervisory Board (SSB), 13, 23–26
Sheikh Abdullah Bin Suleiman Al-Maniya, 29
Sheikh Dr. Abdullah bin Abdulaziz Al Musleh,
    29
Sheikh Nizam M.S. Yaquby, 28
Sheikh Muhammed Taqi Usmani, 28–29
Sheikh Dr. Muhammad Al-Ali Al Qari bin Eid,
    29
Shirkah (partnership business), 77, 155
State Bank of Pakistan (SBP), 27, 29–30
Sukuk (Islamic bonds), 155
    Istisna'a, 60

Mudaraba, 63–64
Murabaha, 31, 43–44
Musharaka, 37
Salam, 106
Sunnah (way, practice and rule of life), 13–14,
    16, 156
suras (chapters), 18

Ta'awun (co-operative insurance),
    130
Tabarru' (donation), 128–130
Takaful (Islamic insurance)
    comparison with conventional insurance,
    127–128
    family, 136, 152
    as *Sharia'a* compliant, 132–133
    Wakala and, 134
    Waqf and, 156
Tapir, 156
tax, 65

Ujrah, 89
Ulema (religious scholars), 1, 13
Ummah (nation of Islam), 13–14
Umra, 4
Usmani, Sheikh Muhammed Taqi,
    28
Usufruct, 89
Uthman, 18

Wakala (agency), 134
Waqf (charitable trust), 156
Wasiyah (will, bequest), 134

Yaquby, Sheikh Nizam M.S., 28

zakat (almsgiving), 2, 28, 38,1 56
Zayd ibn Thabit, 18